HUNTING NAZIS
IN FRANCO'S SPAIN

subvention provided by
Jewish Federation of Greater Hartford

HUNTING NAZIS IN FRANCO'S SPAIN

DAVID A. MESSENGER

LOUISIANA STATE UNIVERSITY PRESS BATON ROUGE

Published by Louisiana State University Press
Copyright © 2014 by Louisiana State University Press
All rights reserved
Manufactured in the United States of America
First printing

DESIGNER: Michelle A. Neustrom
TYPEFACE: Chaparral Pro
PRINTER AND BINDER: Maple Press

LIBRARY OF CONGRESS CATALOGING-IN-PUBLICATION DATA
Messenger, David A.
 Hunting Nazis in Franco's Spain / David A. Messenger.
   pages cm
 Includes bibliographical references and index.
 ISBN 978-0-8071-5563-9 (hardcover : alkaline paper) — ISBN 978-0-
8071-5564-6 (pdf) — ISBN 978-0-8071-5565-3 (epub) — ISBN 978-0-8071-
5566-0 (mobi) 1. Denazification—Spain—History. 2. Nazis—Spain—
History. 3. Germans—Spain—History—20th century. 4. Fugitives from
justice—Spain—History—20th century. 5. Spain—History—1939–1975.
6. Spain—Relations—Germany. 7. Germany—Relations—Spain. 8. Allied Powers (1919–) 9. Repatriation—Europe—History—20th century.
10. National security—Europe—History—20th century. I. Title.
DP270.M47 2014
946.082—dc23

                                                   2013041712

For Maureena, William, and Jack,
with love

CONTENTS

ACKNOWLEDGMENTS   ix

ABBREVIATIONS   xi

Introduction   1

1. Denazification, Neutrality, and European Security
   after World War II   11

2. Intelligence Wars: *Nazi and Allied Spies in Neutral
   Spain during and after the War*   37

3. Neutrality, Postwar Politics, and the Diplomacy
   of Repatriation   70

4. Petitions to Franco: *German Activism and the Fight
   to Stay in Spain*   99

5. The Fate of Repatriation in Germany, Spain,
   and Beyond, 1947–1948   132

Conclusion   162

NOTES   171

BIBLIOGRAPHY   201

INDEX   211

ACKNOWLEDGMENTS

This project began as I completed my dissertation and first book and found myself in possession of a great deal of material on Allied intelligence in Spain that I had not used. A grant from the Center for Advanced Holocaust Studies at the United States Holocaust Memorial Museum (USHMM) in 2006 allowed me to participate in a seminar entitled "Intelligence and the Holocaust," which helped me to refine my ideas, to see how I could use material I had already collected, and to focus on what I needed to do to make a worthwhile project on the subject of Allied repatriation policy in Spain. I am grateful to Gerhard Weinberg, one of the seminar's leaders, as well as to the seminar participants, Steve Tyas, Kerstin von Lingen, and Michael Salter, for encouraging me in this work and providing support and feedback. Katrin Paehler, whom I first met at the seminar, has been incredibly supportive and incredibly willing to discuss writing, editing, and thinking on any and all issues concerning the fate of various Nazis after World War II; I am truly grateful. Hilary Earl, Carole Fink, Norman Goda, Sandie Holguín, and the welcoming community of the Association for Spanish and Portuguese Historical Studies encouraged this work, read pieces of it, and heard many papers that show up in bits and pieces throughout the book. At the University of Wyoming, Erin Abraham and Nevin Aiken read and discussed aspects of this project and, as nonspecialists, provided me with important insights. Chris Muscato and most especially Joanne Allen are thanked for their work on editing and copyediting the book. Finally, the comments of the readers assigned by LSU Press and the active encouragement over many years from Alisa Plant at the Press helped bring this project to its completion.

I thank Carroll College, in Helena, Montana; the Program of Cultural Collaboration between the government of Spain and U.S. universities; and the Center for Advanced Holocaust Studies at the USHMM for grants to start the archival work necessary to move forward. Funding for both writing and subsequent archival work came from the Mershon Center for International Security Studies at the Ohio State University and, at the University of Wyoming, the Faculty Grant-in-Aid Program, a College of Arts and Sciences Basic Research Grant, the Department of History, and the Global & Area Studies Program. The welcoming atmosphere created by faculty and staff in these programs encourages me every day. The staffs at the National Archives and Records Administration, in College Park, Maryland; the Archivo General del Ministerio de Asuntos Exteriores, in Madrid; and the National Archives of the United Kingdom, in Kew, were extremely helpful.

Parts of the text have previously appeared elsewhere. Large parts of chapter 1 appeared as "Beyond War Crimes: Denazification, 'Obnoxious' Germans and Allied Policy in Franco's Spain after the Second World War," *Contemporary European History* 20, no. 4 (2011), from Cambridge University Press, and parts of chapter 2 are from "Against the Grain: Special Operations Executive in Spain, 1941–1945," which appeared first in *Intelligence and National Security* 20, no. 1 (2005), from Taylor & Francis (www.tandfonline.com/doi/full /10.1080/02684520500059502), and then again in *The Politics and Strategy of Clandestine War: Special Operations Executive, 1940–1946,* edited by Neville Wylie (2006), published by Routledge. I thank these publishers for permission to include this material here.

My greatest debt is to my wife, Maureena, and my children, William and Jack, who encouraged and supported this work and accepted the long absences that came with it. This book is dedicated to them. Even when they could not see me at work, thoughts of them were never far away and kept me going. As this phase comes to an end, I remain just as stunned as Jack, who recently and quite loudly asked, "Dad, you're an author?!"

ABBREVIATIONS

ACC	Allied Control Council
FEA	Foreign Economic Administration (U.S.)
MEW	Ministry of Economic Warfare (British)
NSDAP	Nationalsozialistische Deutsche Arbeiterpartei (National Socialist Workers' Party of Germany)
OMGUS	Office of Military Government, United States
OSS	Office of Strategic Service (U.S.)
SD	Sicherheitsdienst
SHAEF	Supreme Headquarters Allied Expeditionary Force
SIS	Secret Intelligence Service (British)
SOE	Special Operations Executive (British)
SS	Schutzstaffel

HUNTING NAZIS
IN FRANCO'S SPAIN

INTRODUCTION

Walter Eugen Mosig was a businessman in 1930s Germany who dealt especially with firms in Spain and Argentina. When the National Socialists rose to power in Germany, Mosig joined the Criminal Police in Berlin. In 1936 he was sent to Spain as an observer of the Spanish Civil War, establishing contact with the Guardia Civil (Civil Guard, or national police) in the Nationalist zone, controlled by General Francisco Franco and his forces, who had risen up against the legitimate Republican government. He stayed until February 1938 and then returned to Berlin, continuing to work for the Criminal Police until 1942. At that point he transferred to Amt VI of the Reich Main Security Office (Reichssicherheitshauptamt, or RSHA), the foreign-intelligence arm of the Nazi Party's own intelligence unit, the Sicherhietsdienst (SD). Because of his experience in Spain, he was posted to Madrid in early 1943. His assignment was to gather political intelligence on Spain and on the German colony, as well as to secure German economic interests in the country, whose resources were crucial to Germany's war effort. Thus he was placed under cover as a representative of Sofindus, the para-state German company that managed all trade between Spain and Nazi Germany.[1] There he worked directly with the president of the organization, the leading Nazi within the German community of Spain, Johannes Bernhardt.[2] He also became intimately involved in the transfer of funds between Germany and Spain, especially through the Restaurant Horcher, established in Madrid in 1943.[3] Finally, his duties involved exchanging information with Spanish intelligence officials concerning Communist elements in Spain and across Europe.

Mosig was an intelligence agent on the periphery of World War II. His story has elements of an exciting adventure. But arguably for

Mosig, the adventure actually deepened once the war ended in May 1945. In occupied Germany being a member of the SD meant automatic arrest by the occupying powers France, the United Kingdom, the United States, and the Soviet Union. Mosig, however, stayed in Spain, where he continued to be protected by his Spanish associates. Soon enough he was offered a position within the Spanish intelligence community, with which he had worked so closely during the war. His supervisor was Colonel Anton Zea, in Spanish Military Intelligence (SIM), who assured him that remaining in the intelligence community would protect him from any Allied investigations into his work for the Nazi regime.[4] Nonetheless, both the United States and the United Kingdom asked for Mosig's arrest and repatriation to occupied Germany, where he would face denazification. Warned by his Spanish associates that he was in trouble, Mosig abandoned his post with SIM and went into hiding. He made inquiries in May 1946 about immigration to Argentina, an avenue reportedly opened up in part by the Spanish undersecretary of state, Tomas Suñer.[5] However, Mosig was arrested by Spanish officials in August 1946 and repatriated to occupied Germany, where he was placed in the U.S.-run Civilian Internment Enclosure No. 76, in Hohenasperg, Germany. From there he was transferred to the U.S. internment camp in Ludwigsburg. During a movement of prisoners from this camp in October 1947 Mosig escaped. Within a week he was back in Madrid. He remained in Spain for another year and then emigrated to Córdoba, Argentina, in 1948.[6]

In August 1972 Walter Mosig visited the American embassy in Buenos Aires and filed paperwork requesting immigration for him and his wife to Florida, where his son lived. On the application he listed his residence as Berlin from 1923 to 1943, Madrid from 1943 to 1948, and Córdoba thereafter, not mentioning his time in Spain during the Civil War or the more than a year that he was in U.S. internment in Germany. His immigration file was sent to the Central Intelligence Agency, which responded to his application with a detailed account of his time in the SD and the Gestapo, as well as his arrest and time in U.S. custody.[7] Although his FBI file holding the immigration paperwork contains no indication of what decision was made, presumably his application was denied on the basis of the CIA's response; however, this cannot be confirmed. Extensive searches on the Internet revealed no obituaries or other evidence about the last part of Mosig's life, and inquiries made to his family in the United States were not answered.

What led Mosig down all these paths following the war? He found himself, as an agent of the Nazi regime, in a fairly good place when the war ended, Madrid. General Francisco Franco had been part of a military coup against the Republican government in Spain in 1936, and with the assistance of Nazi Germany under Adolf Hitler and Fascist Italy under Benito Mussolini he had become the leading general of the rebellion and the ultimate victor of the Spanish Civil War in 1939. He had then established a dictatorship, which, as during the conflict, carried out military sentences and executed and imprisoned his former opponents within Spain, making the first priority of the new regime "an investment in terror," as Paul Preston has written.[8] Spain had declared its neutrality when World War II began but stayed close to Germany. Without officially declaring war, Franco's regime had nonetheless maintained close economic and political relations with the Axis states for most of the war.[9] Legally, Spain had altered its stance from neutrality to nonbelligerency in June 1940, returning to neutrality in October 1943. In practical terms, Spain's position had been clearly pro-Axis, a point underlined by the country's adherence to the German-Italian Pact of Steel, which had led to an increased Gestapo presence in Spain, closer military ties with Nazi Germany and Fascist Italy, and significant economic benefits for the Axis powers.[10] As Christian Leitz has pointed out, even Hitler and other leading Nazis had expected Spain to join the war, given that everything pointed in that direction.[11] While this had not happened, extensive German economic activity, close collaboration between Spanish and German intelligence agencies, including the use of Spain as a base for intelligence operations, and other linkages had soon formed. These circumstances had brought Mosig to Spain in 1943 and provided him with a relatively welcoming environment in May 1945, certainly compared with the rest of Europe, which was under the control of former

Nazi resisters, returned governments, and the military and political forces of the Allied victors.

In the late 1990s there was a great deal of sensational reporting about Nazis who had stayed on in Spain after the war, many of them remaining there for the rest of their lives. José Irujo, a journalist with the Spanish newspaper *El País,* wrote extensively about the network of Nazi spies in Madrid who regularly gathered at the Restaurant Horcher, where Mosig and others had spent time.[12] One of these was Reinhard Spitzy, a Nazi spy posted to Madrid in 1943, whom Irujo found in 1997 living in Santillana del Mar, a small village in the Cantabrian region of Spain, and who became the primary character in Irujo's book *La lista negra*.[13] In 2010 the *Guardian* newspaper published an article titled "Costa Blanca's Hidden Nazis," which examined, in part, best-selling novels in Spain based on hidden Nazis, revealing that behind the fiction was a strong element of truth.[14]

While these stories draw us in with the hook of "hidden Nazis," the present book seeks to give a fuller story of how the fate of Nazis in postwar Spain played out. As indicated, Mosig was pursued in Spain because of pressure from the Allied powers to return him to Germany. And he was returned, although only briefly in the context of his postwar life. I examine here the policies that impacted Mosig's postwar experiences in Madrid and occupied Germany. Why did the victorious Allies pursue individuals like Mosig after the war? How did they do this? What was the response of the Spanish regime, and how did this change over time and in different cases? How did these Germans themselves perceive the situation, and what actions did they take? Indeed, while it was difficult and largely unsuccessful, there was a sustained Allied effort to prevent Spain from becoming a Nazi haven. How did former Nazis come to live comfortably in Spain?

I start by examining the concept of denazification as it emerged at the end of the war. In late 1944 British officials began to consider the postwar fate of those "technical and specialized enemy personnel in neutral countries." Shortly before the war ended, the British Ministry of Economic Warfare (MEW) ordered its embassies in neutral states to consider for repatriation "Germans whose activity overseas will serve to maintain German commercial or national interests or influence after the war in the country in which they reside, whether or not they have worked directly against British interests hitherto."[15] In May 1945 U.S. intelligence agents with the Office of Strategic Services (OSS) in Spain were ordered to compile a list of all German nationals "engaged in any activities, be they espionage, political or commercial," that were "detrimental to Allied interests" in preparation for their deportation to occupied Germany. In response, the British and U.S. embassies agreed upon a list of more than sixteen hundred potential repatriates from Spain in July 1945.[16] Soon the Allied powers in Berlin began to coordinate policy, and for the first time the phrase *obnoxious Germans* appeared in documents identifying those who were not war criminals but nonetheless were sought for repatriation from neutral states to occupied Germany because of wartime activities.[17]

Who were these "obnoxious Germans"? Essentially they were Nazi intelligence agents, Schutzstaffel (SS) members, and other party officials who, had they been in occupied Germany, would have been subject to denazification measures such as automatic internment, interrogation, and hearings or trials. As defined by the Economic Warfare Department of the British Foreign Ministry, obnoxious Germans were those "who have been associated with the enemy's espionage, sabotage or similar activities; who have been openly engaged in anti-Allied or pro-Nazi activities such as propaganda or the organization of local German nationalist enterprises; or whose activity overseas served to maintain German commercial or national interests or influence, whether or not they worked directly against Allied interests."[18] This was the definition the British developed in September 1945.[19] It was later amended slightly by a U.S. proposal to allow investigators to consider "mitigating factors" in individual cases, but its essence remained.[20]

The removal of Nazi influence, real or perceived, across Europe was at the heart of these efforts. Despite the many criticisms that are rightly leveled against Allied denazification policy, it was a program designed to deal with the very real fear of revived Fascism and National Socialism in Europe. It is too easy to overlook the significance of denazification to early postwar conceptions of security in Europe; the extension of denazification to neutral states through the repatriation of so-called obnoxious Germans reminds us of the scope of the project. In the case of Nazis in Spain, the threat of Nazi activity was real, although it was largely insignificant by the late 1940s, as it ultimately was in Germany itself. Just as in occupied Germany, the repatriation program fell short of its goals in terms of the number of individuals deported and interned. Yet the story of how this came to be is important. The extent to which Allied policy considered Nazis acting as Nazis to be a security threat in the aftermath of the war is striking. The mechanisms and policies put into place in countries like Spain to deal with this threat underline its importance to concepts of national security that held sway in the period between World War II and the Cold War, a period aptly described by Tony Judt as one in which there remained "unfinished business."[21]

In the case of Walter Mosig, U.S. intelligence reports after his escape from custody in occupied Germany emphasize that he continued to contact former SD officers within and outside Allied internment camps, suggesting that Nazi networks continued to exist in Germany and formerly neutral states like Spain.[22] The United States did not view former Nazis staying on in Spain in an individual context; rather, like former Nazis in Germany itself, they were viewed as members of groups. There was an assumption that these people would continue to work with one another as Nazis and thus in some way continue Nazism. Even before the war ended, the British military attaché in Madrid, Brigadier William Wyndham Torr, wrote that "it has become increasingly obvious that the Germans, realizing that defeat was inevitable, would do all they could to prepare some disguised organization in Spain, so that whatever happened to their official representation and known commercial interests, as a result of the Allied peace terms, they would still have in place some secret means of fostering their interests, maintaining contacts, and generally preparing for the day when they could once more come into the open as a commercial and military power."[23] So the primary goal was the same as in occupied Germany: to eliminate all vestiges of Nazism.

While the continuation of Nazism was clearly a threat to the national security of the United Kingdom and the United States in the aftermath of the war, an equal threat to U.S. security was the potential for individual Nazis to continue to hold influence over the Franco regime and thus hinder the regime's transition to a post-Fascist Europe. Even though regime transition was not required in Spain, some form of policy change had to take place. The continued presence of Nazis under Spanish protection might suggest that they would influence policies and actions of Franco's regime and make them more anti-U.S. and antidemocratic.

A theory taken from transitional-justice literature, that of spoilers, can be useful in outlining what the United States wanted to occur in Spain. Defined broadly, spoiler literature looks "at agency and at the individuals and small groups that take advantage of structural failures within the political process."[24] While this definition is usually applied to rebel groups or factions in the aftermath of a civil conflict, it also works in the Spanish case. Those Nazis seeking to influence the Spanish regime and their Spanish allies within the regime were thought to reject the post-Fascist reality of the aftermath of war. Even though the regime itself did not need to change, the threat of spoilers who would maintain some form of Nazism within Francoist Spain was enough to motivate policy regarding the desired repatriation of such individuals into Allied custody. Spoilers themselves are from the previous era's national or local elite, and only removing them from positions of power and influence can eliminate them as a threat.[25] Nazis in neutral states after World War II fit the typology of "limited spoilers," defined by Stephen Stedman as those who have specific goals that fall far short of total power or rule; in their case, simply having continued influence suffices.[26]

Unlike in cases following civil war, the Nazi spoilers in Spain were in no position to actually wreck the peace settlement or change the course of the war's outcome. Their threat was more subtle and had to do with the direction of the Franco regime and the perpetuation of Nazi ideas in the broader Spanish sphere. Spoiler literature defines the actions of a patron, who may be slow to realize the illegitimacy of some spoiler action, as equally problematic to the peace settlement.[27] Thus the national-security interest of the United States was to remove obnoxious Germans from Spain and thus negate the actions of those in the Fascist-inspired Falange movement or elsewhere in the Spanish regime who were in effect perpetuating Fascism. A preliminary interrogation protocol designed by the State Department in May 1945 for obnoxious Germans outlined lines of investigation of interest to the U.S. government. The protocol was designed for use by embassies and the OSS in places like Madrid. Areas of inquiry included the use of German para-state organizations such as the German Ibero-American Institute in Spain and Latin America to continue Nazi influence in various states after the war; the role German schools might have in neutral states; the continuation of Nazi propaganda in the local press; and especially the role of German economic resources in the local economies.[28] In these lines of inquiry we can see clear linkages to the literature on spoilers and the belief that Nazi agents could continue to play that role. As the Western Department of the British Foreign Office acknowledged in December 1946, the threat represented by obnoxious Germans "may depend to some extent on the disposition of such Governments as hold power within Spain in future."[29] To what extent would Spanish patrons be willing to involve Germans who stayed in Spain?

I begin by examining Allied thinking about obnoxious Germans. Chapter 1 outlines the origins of the policy of Nazi repatriation developed by the governments of the United States and the United Kingdom in an attempt to return former Nazi agents and officials from neutral states such as Spain back to German territory. Once in Germany, the United States and the United Kingdom ruled as the occupying authority, along with France and the Soviet Union, in the form of the Allied Control Council (ACC). They could thus use the powers of government to assert authority over agents and officials of the previous German regime. Chapter 2 examines how Nazis wanted for repatriation in Spain were identified and makes important linkages between wartime intelligence gathering about German activities in Spain and the Allied intelligence work carried out following the war as repatriation lists were created.

Any account of the repatriation process, however, needs to include the Spanish government of Francisco Franco. Chapter 3 examines the diplomatic side of repatriation, focused on the talks between the United States and the United Kingdom, on the one hand, and Spain, on the other. Who was deemed necessary to repatriate? Who was deemed not worth repatriating or valuable enough to try to keep in Spain? Why? Finally, how did the actual process work, not only in the realm of diplomatic negotiation but on the ground in the towns and villages of Spain, where these Germans lived?

I turn in chapter 4 to the Germans themselves, examining the reaction within the German colony to the repatriation policy and the efforts of many to avoid such a fate. They too were actors in this drama, and an understanding of their activism is vital. Finally, chapter 5 looks at the different experiences of those repatriated to Germany, those who remained in Spain, and those who hid and escaped to other countries, especially Argentina. It also examines the gradual end of the repatriation policy from 1946 through 1948.

In terms of the number of people whose repatriation to Germany was sought compared with the number actually repatriated, the policy described here was a failure. When one considers how many of those who were repatriated actually stayed away from Spain for good, it was an even greater failure. However, what drives this study is not numbers. Rather, it seeks to illuminate Allied goals concerning Nazis abroad, especially in an undemocratic state like Franco's Spain. The scope of Allied ambitions was remarkable and deserves some reflection as we debate whether denazification in fact occurred in Europe following the war. Similarly, while a focus on Spain's reluctance to conform to Allied demands is indeed central to any analysis of this policy, the question of Nazi influence in Spain following World War II must be considered from the angle of those who were neutralized or fled Spain. Were some Allied ambitions for eliminating a Nazi presence within Franco's regime achieved despite the presence of former Nazis in Spain? Finally, the role of the German colony in this process is important and often overlooked. While much that follows focuses on intelligence gathering, foreign policy, and political calculations made by the governments of the United States, the United Kingdom, and Spain, the Germans at the center of this effort were not silent. They had an opportunity in Spain to play an active role in shaping their own future. When we consider how Germans so involved with the Nazi regime moved from war to peace, it is important to consider the role they themselves played. They were not passive. They, like many other Germans after the war, had to find ways to recast their experiences with the Nazi regime in order to pursue a new future.

What follows, then, is an account of the repatriation policy driven by the United States and, to a lesser extent, the United Kingdom. This was both a diplomatic effort and an intelligence operation. The release of hundreds of thousands of documents by both governments and their intelligence agencies since the U.S. Congress passed the Nazi War Crimes Disclosure Act in 1998 has been vital to this project; in fact the project as described above would have been impossible without such an action. Indeed, Walter Mosig's British Secret Service file was only released in August 2011, just two years before the completion of this book. This book also considers the response of the Spanish regime of General Francisco Franco, which was not monolithic but multifaceted and varied from ministry to ministry and even from region to region. Finally, it considers the activism of Germans with strong ties to the Nazi regime in making and re-making their past and their future within a different sort of Europe—not the liberated, occupied Europe of the Allies but the Europe of the neutrals, and the dictatorial neutrals like Spain at that.

Walter Eugen Mosig had an amazing postwar story, but he belonged to a small but important group of Germans who had a very different path from war to postwar than we might imagine. Questions about neutrality, justice, and international law can be seen to coexist with diplomatic maneuvers, political deal making, and personal interventions. The result is a story that is unique but also reveals much about the complexity of reconstruction in post–World War II Europe.

1

DENAZIFICATION, NEUTRALITY, AND EUROPEAN SECURITY AFTER WORLD WAR II

On September 10, 1945, in Berlin the occupying powers in Germany —France, the United Kingdom, the Soviet Union, and the United States—acting as the Allied Control Council (ACC), passed a resolution ordering all Germans who had been officials or intelligence agents of the previous Nazi regime and now found themselves in territories that had been neutral during the war to return to Germany. Furthermore, the ACC requested that the governments in states where such Germans were living deport them to territory under the control of the ACC.[1] By September 22 the ACC's Directorate of Prisoners of War and Displaced Persons had been given authority to implement this resolution, and it in turn created the Combined Repatriation Executive to act inside occupied Germany and through the embassies of the ACC states in the targeted countries: Afghanistan, Ireland, Portugal, Spain, Sweden, Switzerland, the international city of Tangiers, and Vatican City.[2]

Both the broader ACC policy on obnoxious Germans and its application to Spain had longer histories than a simple housekeeping of postwar issues. Concern about obnoxious Germans grew out of two distinct policies that developed as the war came to a close in Europe. The first of these was denazification, including how to deal with both Nazi war criminals and those who were not technically war criminals but of concern nonetheless. The second was a policy on how to deal with neutral states that, by their actions in a Nazi-dominated continent, had significantly challenged prewar ideas about neutrality and thus bore new responsibility for actions that, while technically neutral, had in practical ways benefited a genocidal regime.

Denazification, as defined by Perry Biddiscombe, refers to "the full range of Allied/Soviet reform and punishment measures in occupied Germany," but most often it is used with reference to "the specific liquidation of the National Socialist Party (NSDAP) and the elimination of its influence" in government and business.[3] That is the sense in which the term is used here. This more specific meaning grew out of Allied discussions of war crimes and the potential for trials of accused war criminals. The need to prosecute war crimes as an important part of the postwar settlement began in Moscow in October 1943, when three of the Allied powers, the United Kingdom, the Soviet Union, and the United States, met. The Moscow declaration that came out of this meeting stated that war criminals who had committed offenses that crossed national boundaries required some form of Allied trial, as opposed to a national trial.[4]

Before long this broad definition had to be made into policy that could be carried out inside occupied Germany. In Washington in 1944, as Frank M. Buscher has emphasized, the debate over the German occupation focused on the role punishment would play. The State Department linked punishment with broader democratization efforts and saw trials as essential; the War Department emphasized the practical need for a short occupation of Germany; and the Treasury Department, led by Henry Morgenthau Jr., proposed harsh terms, including deindustrialization, which eventually became the centerpiece of the Morgenthau Plan.[5] For Morgenthau, trials were not needed for the Nazi leadership, who simply should be shot.[6] A move to remake Germany as a pastoral, deindustrialized country would follow.

Morgenthau's ideas, however, were not entirely embraced. Many others argued for an extensive campaign of reeducation. The emphasis on war-crimes trials developed as part of the plan to reeducate Germans through the use of the justice system. In thinking about trials, however, it soon became clear that the mechanisms of justice also needed to take into account those Nazis who did not technically fit into the category of war criminals defined at Moscow but who nonetheless posed a significant threat to the security of occupying forces and could conceivably be charged with other criminal offenses based on their activities during the war.

An understanding of the situation of other Nazi criminals emerged simultaneously in a number of places. In January 1945 a registry of suspected war criminals, the Central Registry of War Criminals and Security Suspects (CROWCASS), was created. Based in Paris, this unit soon developed three lists, one for those detained on specific war crimes, one for those wanted for war crimes but not yet detained, and one for any other individuals deemed security threats because of their membership in suspect Nazi organizations.[7] As Tom Bower has written, what emerged, especially from this third category, was a kind of "personality black list."[8] At the same time the U.S. military developed a policy for occupation that proposed the internment of all members of the SS and the Gestapo, whether they would be sent to trial or not, purely for security reasons.[9]

The result was the policy of automatic arrest inside occupied Germany. The joint U.S.-British Germany Country Unit (GCU), created to plan the occupation for the Supreme Headquarters, Allied Expeditionary Force (SHAEF), emphasized the need to define Nazis as broadly as possible in order to determine their status concerning arrest, detention, and trial.[10] The preferred solution was automatic arrest and internment, with investigations to follow.

The GCU created SHAEF's *Handbook for Military Government in Germany*. Developed in June 1944 for SHAEF's commander, General Dwight D. Eisenhower, the handbook argued that the Germans who posed the greatest threat to security for an occupying force were the members of the police, the paramilitary, and intelligence units of the Nazi Party, namely, members of the Gestapo, the Sturmabteilung (SA), the SD, and the SS. Thus all such individuals should be detained and interned following the U.S. Army's entrance into Germany.[11] Despite the emphasis on war crimes and trials, then, it was clear that security and justice concerns meant that policy would have to be expanded to consider many who would not be subject to legal prosecution for crimes.

Drawing upon the work of its own GCU, CROWCASS, and similar documents produced by the OSS's Research and Analysis Branch, Central European Division (populated by leftist German exiles),

SHAEF's November 1944 "Directive for Military Government in Germany" again emphasized the significance of automatic arrest and internment in a wide variety of cases.[12] What emerged from the initial discussion of war crimes, then, was the first significant effort to consider denazification in its entirety, and to recognize that trials were only one part of the policy. Biddiscombe makes the point that traditional theory about military occupations operated on the assumption of the "welfare of the governed"; that is, occupiers assumed that the majority of the population was passive and that they could rely on the usual structures to administer territory under their control. This was not the basis for an occupation grounded in the broad definition of denazification, however. The concept of denazification manifest in the creation of extensive lists of individuals subject to automatic arrest, and a subsequent deconstruction of governing structures at all levels was a radical shift.[13]

What becomes evident in charting the various policies developed to deal with Nazis who were not technically war criminals but of concern nonetheless is that the Allied powers, especially the United States, were coming to view the occupation according to a thesis of collective guilt. Applied to Germany on a broad scale, this meant that the logical policy to be implemented was one of collective punishment.[14] The final year of the war, with its brutal fight to the finish across Europe and an unprecedented level of violence east and west only reinforced this line of thinking, creating a sense of anxiety and fear across the continent. One result was that soldiers, U.S., British, and especially Soviet, entered Germany with the intent to destroy, not liberate, the population.[15] The message emanating from SHAEF and other offices of the U.S. government in the fall of 1944 was no different: Germany was Nazified, and this had to end, with the implementation of Allied force and then Allied law. As William I. Hitchcock writes, soldiers entered German territory with the sense that "the occupation aimed to educate Germans about their moral and political failings and this required a distant, cold and firm demeanor."[16] This sense was articulated by General Eisenhower, who in stating that the German people were responsible for Nazism highlighted the roles of members of the Gestapo and the SS, whose membership alone, he argued, "should be taken as *prima facie* evidence of guilt."[17]

War-crimes trials and the International Military Tribunal (IMT) at Nuremberg were the most significant developments to result from these attitudes toward occupation. Previous considerations about individual and group responsibility inside Nazi Germany informed the writing of the London Charter of August 1945, which established the IMT and the Nuremberg war-crimes-trials process.[18] As with the SHAEF handbook and other directives, the practical need to associate individuals with groups rather than to investigate every individual case predominated. Most important here was the decision to try Nazi Party organizations, and not just individuals, at Nuremberg. This was carried over into Allied Control Council Law No. 10, which stated that membership in any organization tried at the IMT could lead to an individual's being tried within an occupying zone.[19] In the short term, this reinforced the military's earlier plan to intern members of suspect organizations in civilian internment camps. The U.S. Joint Chiefs of Staff (JCS) resolution 1067, adopted following Germany's collapse in May 1945, modified SHAEF's earlier 1944 directive, allowing zonal commanders in U.S.-occupied areas to make decisions about internment and arrest on a case-by-case basis, especially if the person in question could be useful in reconstruction.[20] This was a significant compromise, but it did not lessen the ambition of the program, for inside Germany ACC Directive 24, issued in January 1946, used JCS 1067 to outline ninety-nine categories of Nazis subject to automatic arrest and detention.[21] In the long term, this led to a series of subsequent trials, both at Nuremberg and within the U.S. zone, with a total of 1,885 prosecutions in the U.S. zone from 1945 to 1949.[22]

Denazification was officially defined at the Potsdam Conference, attended by the occupying powers, in July and August 1945, and again the need to eliminate Nazism, using punishment to do so, was emphasized. The official Potsdam goals were to destroy the National Socialist German Worker's Party (NSDAP) and its affiliated organizations; to dissolve any Nazi institutions; to prevent future Nazi activity; to repeal Nazi laws; to arrest and intern war criminals of the former regime; to remove Nazi officials from public and semipublic life; and to remove Nazi influence from the German education system.[23] Combining ideas on reeducation with those of punishment and viewing internees as a potential threat to order and stability, Potsdam, like the documents that came before it, sought to remove Nazism and totalitarianism from German life not just as political movements or ideas but also as a cultural force; similarly it sought to make Germany's economy and politics less militaristic.[24] The best way to do this, in the minds of Allied planners, was to remove those people and groups who had thought and acted differently.

Whatever the intent of denazification as broadly conceptualized in documents like JCS 1067, the reality was that its implementation fell far short of its ambitions. Clearly, those ambitions were separated from reality in many ways. On one level, contemplating a trial for each suspect based on his or her membership in certain organizations was simply too impractical given the nearly 2 million individuals in the U.S. zone who qualified. Therefore, both at the Nuremberg IMT and in subsequent trials the emphasis of the United States was on major war criminals, not everyone who may have qualified under earlier definitions of the term *war criminal*.[25] On another level, the inherent practicality of the "welfare of the governed" theory of occupation emerged on the ground in day-to-day operations. In the summer of 1945, amidst a food shortage, unemployment, and the need to simply have functioning municipal governments, U.S. soldiers and commanders could not, and did not, arrest local businessmen, government employees, and others who were seen as necessary just to keep things running.[26]

When U.S. troops entered German territory, they were the ones responsible for carrying out investigations, sometimes assisted by members of the OSS and the army's Counter Intelligence Corps (CIC), many times not. The Public Safety Branch teams of the military government, charged with primary responsibility for carrying out denazification investigations, were tremendously understaffed. One result of both the need for German assistance in administration and the need for manpower to help with investigations was the creation of denazification panels, *Spruchkammern*, run by Germans, which had far more limited sanctions than internment and very often used only a minimal legal standard, if any, in enforcing the law. Ultimately, the U.S. Military Governor of Germany, General Lucius D. Clay, moved toward amnesties based on age, income level, and disabilities.[27]

Broadly speaking, denazification in the U.S. zone of occupation resulted in some 2 million individuals' suffering some form of punishment, such as loss of employment, and 400,000 were interned for some time.[28] These are not insignificant numbers. Yet many others who could have been investigated were not, or they were dealt with only in a very limited way. Deciding what constituted a war crime took a long time, allowing many who could be considered war criminals to escape; once trials began, many were short and not exhaustive; and the impossibility of dismissing all public officials associated with Nazism led to more amenable measures, like the *Spruchkammern* civilian denazification process.[29] Historians have debated the reasons for this: John Gimbel argued that faced with the task of rebuilding, U.S. pragmatism won out; Lutz Niethammer stated that anti-Communism and U.S. opposition to a social revolution in German industry and society encouraged the United States to bring Nazis back; Tom Bower agreed, especially once denazification was back in German hands; others, such as James Tent, have argued that U.S. ambitions were for radical transformation but that on-the-ground decisions and practical obstacles resulted in something less than a complete transformation.[30] Hitchcock has suggested simply that American occupiers not only needed the Germans for reconstruction but in the process came to like them and became sympathetic to the idea that Germans, like others, had suffered in the war.[31] Nonetheless, the consensus is clear that the policy goals of arrest, internment, and removal of Nazis as representative of Nazism did not live up to their name.

That historical reality, however, should not deter investigation into the ambitious conceptualization of denazification that predominated early on. The initial identification of Nazis as a security threat, a definition applied to people who were not themselves war criminals, deserves closer examination. As John Gimbel has written, in the early days of U.S. occupation, denazification directives, from the initial SHAEF measures through military laws implemented in 1945, became more and more comprehensive as loopholes were closed. This resulted in a chaotic system that often meant arbitrary implementation, which led to a wholesale review of denazification conducted by the Denazification Policy Board in the last quarter of 1945. The conclusions of the board's report are useful in considering the aims and ambitions of denazification, which spilled over to neutral states in the repatriation program. What threat did groups of Nazis, or individuals associated with certain groups, represent in Germany? It was that the conditions that had led to Nazism in Germany might reappear and that there would be Nazis in place to take advantage. While German attitudes had to become more democratic, those who had ruled during the Nazi era had to be taken out of the system, at least for a time. Drawing on this report, Allied Control Council Law No. 24, of January 1946, maintained the principle of automatic arrest for a variety of categories of Nazis. According to Gimbel, "OMGUS [Office of Military Government, United States] was determined to remove the leadership group from German cultural, political and economic positions of importance."[32] Similarly, the decision by the United States to move forward with subsequent IMT trials in Nuremberg in 1946 under Telford Taylor, even without Soviet participation, can be seen in a similar light.[33] What is significant from the perspective of denazification and its definitions is the breadth of the concept and its adherence to ambitious aims even as in practice it was moderated.

The single-minded focus on a comprehensive and complete denazification program was most apparent in the conviction of its supporters. Among early occupation officials, writes Edward N. Peterson, "to be moderate was to be weak which was to be pro-Nazi." For these U.S. officials, mandatory arrest was a given. Serving time in a civilian internment camp was the logical next step, resulting in some 94,000 held without charge in the U.S. zone by October 1945. Eighty percent of those held were members of organizations on trial at Nuremberg, which explained their automatic-arrest status.[34]

Even in the British zone of occupied Germany, where there was less enthusiasm and less ambition than in the U.S. zone, and a genuine lack of enthusiasm "for radical action or retribution," denazification still was developed early on with a high level of commitment from officials. In October 1944 the War Office produced a policy directive for Allied commanders on denazification that echoed U.S. thinking in eliminating Nazi organizations and automatically dismissing members of these groups from their positions or interning them, with internment targeting approximately 90,000 in the British zone alone. Although in practice the British would implement measures in the field with a great degree of discretion on the part of commanders, in theory their positions were not too far from the those of the United States. In any event, since initial occupation covered both armies as part of SHAEF, the final SHAEF *Handbook for Military Government in Germany* applied to British commanders too. Once SHAEF turned the British zone over to the British element of the ACC, the Public Safety Branch oversaw denazification. In September 1945 the Public Safety Branch prepared its own directive on automatic arrest, which allowed investigation of those in the compulsory-arrest categories first and underlined a more "practical" British approach compared with the U.S. approach.[35] However, in January 1946, with the issuance of ACC Law No. 24, the British zone again was governed by denazification policies similar to those governing the U.S. zone.

How did these ideas come to be applied outside of Germany's borders? In places where Nazi occupation gave way to new regimes, similar processes became an important part of transition. Indeed, it is now clear that the use of trials against Nazis outside occupied Germany was far more extensive than once thought, with some 52,721 convicted in Eastern Europe and 2,890 in Western Europe in the 1940s and 1950s. The greatest issue for most of these countries were not German Nazis but rather local collaborators, and here the variety of investigations, internments, and punishments is striking, including the 10,000 to 15,000 French summarily executed in the aftermath of liberation. Many more were investigated or faced investigations and internment of some kind. Until sometime in the late

1940s—whether in 1949 or earlier is debatable—an intensive period of prosecution and investigation of Nazis across Europe was part of the transition from the war. The use of the law, in trials, investigations, people's tribunals, and other processes, was part of an important global phenomenon of institutionalizing human-rights norms as an alternative to Nazism's vision for Europe.[36] Investigations and policies that did not necessarily lead to trial were equally relevant.

The records of early postwar investigations into Nazis in Spain and other neutral states demonstrate that attitudes similar to those within the occupied zone and formerly occupied countries motivated the creation of ambitious policy in a similar way. As early as August 1944 the head of the OSS mission in Portugal, writing to his counterpart in Madrid, emphasized that the pursuit of enemy personnel and their resources in neutral states was a high priority that required the OSS to "stay on the job" even as the war wound down.[37] Once the war ended, agents began to interview personnel at the German embassy who might prove helpful, with the goal of finding Nazis in hiding, and these Germans were informed, in the words of one agent, that "it was my duty to exterminate Nazism in Spain."[38] In the original September 1945 directive and in a subsequent communication to neutral states, the obnoxious Germans were declared to be sought because "their presence abroad constitutes a danger in view of the possible future renewal of the German war effort."[39] In the U.S. State Department the official responsible for seeing this through came from the Special War Problems Division;[40] in the British zone the key player was the Joint Intelligence Committee of the British occupation.[41] The ACC's Combined Repatriation Executive was to coordinate the gathering of information for interrogations and investigations from occupiers in Germany, Allied missions in the neutral states, the State Department in Washington, and the Foreign Office in London.[42] Thus the policy on obnoxious Germans in neutral Europe was in fact developed as part of the Allied denazification policy in defeated Germany.

The task was far more challenging in formerly neutral states, where regimes did not change and the process of transition thus could not be institutionalized in the same manner. In nondemocratic states like Spain and Portugal, where liberal notions of rights and the rule of law did not exist, the challenge would be even greater. In these states, Allied ambitions were to eliminate Fascist elements on a global scale, remove the economic impact Nazi Germany had had around the world, and create conditions conducive to Western interests. The ACC deemed repatriation of particular groups of Nazis from neutral states the appropriate response on all counts. The way to do so was to send them back to occupied Germany, where they would face denazification procedures, as if they had been found there in the first place.

If repatriation stemmed in part from the conceptualization of denazification being developed in occupied Germany and elsewhere, it can also be linked to new and emerging ideas of neutrality that came with the end of the war. Spain, with its complex relationship with the Axis powers and the concept of neutrality during the war, is a good example. Spain had developed extremely close economic and political ties with Nazi Germany during the Spanish Civil War and in World War II despite never having joined the war. The only way the United States and the United Kingdom could counteract these ties during the war was with a series of "economic warfare" policies that sought to limit the impact of Spanish material support for the Axis, not by forcing Franco to choose sides but rather by offering a combination of economic and trade incentives and punishments meant to keep Franco neutral.[43] British actions involving the bribery of Spanish generals also contributed to the success of the Allies' strategy in Iberia.[44] Whether or not Franco actually intended to join the Axis, Allied policies provided enough incentives not to. These were desperate actions that became a complicated policy approach to the Franco regime, one whose postwar consequences were not foreseen at the time of implementation.

Since the Allies never forced Franco to choose sides, his close ties with Axis states and their various state and para-state entities remained even after the move from nonbelligerency back to official neutrality in 1943. Spain provided significant assistance to the Axis cause until the end of the war.[45] This assistance ranged from general trade of strategic materials to the use of the Spanish merchant marine to assist Germany, the supply of German submarines from Spanish ports, acceptance of the activity of Gestapo and German intelligence agents on Spanish soil, and a full range of pro-Nazi propaganda throughout Iberia, some of it from official German sources, some inspired by Spanish admirers of Nazi Germany.[46] While there clearly was a shift in Spanish policy once the Germans began to lose the war, the inconsistent actions taken by Spain, even after 1943, contributed to what William Slany, of the State Department Historical Office, has called the "complex phenomenon of neutrality during World War II."[47] How was Spain—officially neutral, in reality active in the war—to be treated in the immediate postwar period? Clearly, the United States and the United Kingdom had offered their support in order to keep Franco out of the war, and Franco had taken it. But he had not abandoned his ties with Nazi Germany, ties that were arguably closer than those he had with the Allies. He had not been neutral from a moral standpoint.

As early as 1944, knowing of Germany's economic and political involvement in places like Spain during the war, economic-warfare analysts in Washington and London began to consider the possibility that Nazi Germany might attempt to conceal gold and other assets in neutral states like Spain in order to prepare for the rebuilding of their movement after military defeat and that neutrals would permit this. In other words, the moral ambiguity with which neutrality had been handled during the war might very well continue. This was what led to the creation of Operation Safe Haven, a program formulated over the course of 1944 to uncover such hidden assets and make use of them for restitution and postwar reconstruction. As Slany has written,

The specific goals of Safe Haven, as they came to be formulated in spring 1944, were to restrict and prevent German economic penetration beyond Germany, to block Germany from transferring assets to neutral countries, to ensure that German wealth would be accessible for war reparations and for the rehabilitation of Europe, to make possible the return of legal owners of properties looted from countries once occupied by the Germans, and to prevent the escape of strategic German personnel to neutral havens. The overall purpose was to make it impossible for Germany to start another war.[48]

In 1944 the United Nations Monetary and Financial Conference at Bretton Woods, New Hampshire, known as the Bretton Woods Conference, tasked Commission III ("Other Measures for International Monetary and Financial Cooperation") with setting up an ad hoc subcommittee to deal with enemy assets. It was within this ad hoc group that the Polish and French delegates proposed creating a way to force the cooperation of neutral states in blocking any transfers of Axis assets to neutral territory, retrieve looted assets from neutral states, and ideally liquidate any Axis assets found in neutral states for use by the United Nations. The United States welcomed these ideas and soon drafted a proposal that became Bretton Woods Resolution VI, passed in August 1944. This document clearly blamed the Nazi regime and its entities for "transferring assets to and through neutral countries in order to conceal them and to perpetuate their influence, power, and ability to plan future aggrandizement and world domination."[49] Yet the need for neutrals to account for allowing this to happen was also present. When the U.S. Executive Committee on Economic Foreign Policy approved a document that formed the basis of Safe Haven in December 1944, it emphasized that the actions of neutral and nonbelligerent states "contributed in greater or less degree to German purposes" and that their decision not to associate with the Allies demonstrated that these states were "not committed to United Nations decisions regarding the control of Germany and Japan and long-term measures for political and economic security."[50]

Much of this policy was grounded in the experience of pursuing economic-warfare objectives during the European conflict and the difficulty experienced in places like Spain, which had actively traded military materials with Germany. It was also designed to secure significant reconstruction materials following Germany's surrender, particularly given the situation in the Pacific, where the war with Japan continued.[51] Yet the moral element was equally present, as was the need for neutrals to answer for their actions.

Before World War II there was no emphasis on either economic issues or morality as components of neutrality. The Hague Neutrality Convention of 1907 dealt only with military neutrality. Profiting from warfare and refusing to submit to any sort of moral test were acceptable.[52] During World War II, definitions were tested when first Italy and then Spain adopted a position of nonbelligerency instead of neutrality. While Italy used this only as a preface to eventually joining the war on the Axis side, in Spain General Franco maintained his position from 1940 to 1943, when he returned to official neutrality. The relatively unusual state of nonbelligerency adopted by Spain (and by Italy for part of 1940, before joining the war) implied some movement away from having no moral position to a position that favored the Axis, at least on some intellectual or emotional level.

As a result, neutrality in the aftermath of World War II could not be considered parallel to ideas of neutrality from before the war. Because Spain, for example, dealt with the Nazi state in ways that assisted the German war and German occupation across Europe, Antonio Marquina has argued that Spain carried out policies "directly related to the suffering of the Jews and other people opposing the Nazi and Fascist dictatorship in Europe."[53] Thus there was a need in the immediate postwar period to come to terms with moral implications of what previously had been simply a legalistic measure within international law.

Often overlooked, Safe Haven represented an early effort to recognize the complex relationship between European neutrals and Nazi Germany. Bretton Woods was therefore a parallel, in some sense, to the international legal precedents that came out of the International Military Tribunal at Nuremberg. It is in this light that one can suggest, as Carlos Collado Seidel has done, that Breton Woods Resolution VI implied a "revolution" in international relations with regard to the responsibilities of neutral states in war.[54] It altered the legal ramifications of neutrality. Bretton Woods stated, in essence, that the horrors of Nazism across the continent made it legal for the Allied powers to intervene in the economic and political affairs of neutral states who had ties to Germany; thus neutrality as an international concept was no longer a complete safeguard against the reparation and other accounting efforts that inevitably follow war.

Before long the same logic was applied not just to the transfer of funds but to the activities of Nazis and their organizations in neutral Europe. As the war in Europe expanded in 1941 to encompass the entire continent, primarily through German occupation of conquered states and territory, some 7,500 Germans were residing in Spain. One historian estimates that by the last year of the war that number had grown to 20,000.[55] When the war ended, the American embassy believed the German colony to number in the neighborhood of 9,000, some 3,500 of whom had been engaged in activities of the German government, in German espionage, or in German wartime economic activities.[56] These Germans comprised a small group involved in business and other activities since the 1920s or earlier, a significant number who came during the Spanish Civil War for either military or business purposes, and a large number sent during World War II in order to play a role in military intelligence, diplomatic and cultural relations, and economic activities. Of this last group, most were linked to the German government and/or the NSDAP in some way. When the ACC took up the issue of numbers in 1946, a British report concluded that repatriation criteria were met by some 2,000 Germans in Spain, of whom 1,400 had worked directly for the German government and 600 had had ties with the German government if they had not held official positions. By contrast, Portugal had 600 such Germans; Sweden, 220; Argentina, 116; and Switzerland, potentially 9,000 such Germans, the only country with numbers exceeding Spain's. The Swiss government refused to cooperate with the Allied powers and conducted their own repatriation program, independent of the ACC.[57]

Of course the more aggressive economic and espionage activities of the Nazi government in Spain attracted the attention of the Allies during the war. Concern about German acquisition of wolfram (tungsten) and other military supplies formed the basis of what the Allies called their economic-warfare policy in Iberia, and intelligence gathering in the sphere of economic smuggling provided Allied intelligence with a great deal of wartime work. Wolfram is a tungsten metal of great strength, and over the course of the war it became extremely valuable for the production of gun barrels and shell casings, as well as for aircraft parts, and it was especially important for the German arms industry. By 1940 it was the product Nazi Germany most wanted to receive from Spain, and indeed Spanish wolfram went from accounting for 10 percent of Spanish foreign-currency receipts in 1942 to accounting for 20 percent in 1943.[58]

Early on, Allied efforts were confined to preemptive purchases of wolfram from Spain through agencies such as the United Kingdom Commercial Corporation (UKCC), in competition with the German governmental companies ROWAK (Rohstoff-Waren-Kompensation Handelsgesellschaft) and Sofindus (Sociedad Financiera e Industrial). Allied officials assumed that trade with the Franco regime could keep Spain constantly on the edge of a decision to join Germany at war by providing necessary material goods to Spain. At the same time, such trade similarly denied important strategic supplies to the Nazis. This required an assertive Allied policy of offering Spain important goods at low prices and purchasing Spanish strategic minerals at high prices. The U.S. and British governments had other sources to meet their own wartime needs for wolfram and other minerals; the motivation in Spain was preemption, not necessity.[59] By 1943 the United Kingdom and the United States were benefiting from such trade with Spain through the acquisition of strategic minerals such as iron ore, pyrites, and wolfram, but it was a constant struggle to obtain such goods and limit Germany's purchase of them. Economic warfare in Spain was also an area in which subtle differences between the policies pursued by Churchill and by Roosevelt appeared. Whereas the United Kingdom wished to entice Spain with Anglo-U.S. products and by paying higher prices than the Germans paid for strategic minerals, the United States, as Denis Smyth explains, saw economic warfare as "an occasion for coercion rather than an opportunity for courtship."[60]

U.S. fears that Spain's economic relationship with Nazi Germany would have larger consequences were motivated in large part from the belief that smugglers and pro-Nazi elements within Spain would attempt to get more materials to Germany through unofficial channels. As a result, Allied economic warfare was accompanied by extensive intelligence tracking German smuggling and illicit purchases of wolfram and other materials.[61] This was especially apparent as 1943 turned into 1944. Not content simply to continue making preemptive purchases of wolfram, the Allies began to press Spain to impose an embargo on its wolfram trade with Nazi Germany. The effort was largely a U.S. initiative; at its center was the State Department, supported by Congress and especially by the Board of Economic Warfare and Vice President Henry Wallace.[62] The ultimate result was the May 2, 1944, agreement by which Spain would limit its wolfram trade with Germany in return for Allied oil.

In conjunction with that agreement, the Allies presented the Spanish government with a list of 222 German espionage agents, including 42 from the Protectorate of Morocco, requesting that Spain deport them.[63] This demonstrated again the linkage between concerns about Nazi economic activities in Spain and the broader question of Nazi influence. In December 1944 the Franco government reported that it had confined 750 individuals of German citizenship in camps in Sobrón and Molinar de Carranza; however, most of these people had been rounded up since the liberation of France in August 1944 and included many German border guards and customs officials who had been posted on the Franco-Spanish border during the German occupation of France. Internees accused by the Allies of espionage conducted within Spain were held at a separate camp at Caldas de Malavella, in the province of Girona; they included some of the individuals on the list of German agents the Allies had provided to the Spanish government.[64] Yet not all the agents on the Allied list were interned, nor did the Spanish intend to proceed with returning these individuals to Germany. By January 1946, following a new Allied list of 255 names, the Spanish government concluded that only 100 of these individuals should in fact be deported.[65]

After the war, Spain, with Franco's history of noncompliance concerning the deportation of Germans and a new list of 1,600 wanted

for repatriation, was the country where the conditions for implementing repatriation were the most challenging, and it had the largest group of obnoxious Germans desired by the Allied powers. Of
these, most were state and para-state employees, including individuals linked to Nazi intelligence operations, but 15 percent were business owners and employees wanted purely for Safe Haven reasons.
Following Spain was Portugal, which, like Spain, remained under an
authoritarian dictatorship, that of Antonio Salazar. Five hundred
German officials were wanted for repatriation to occupied Germany
there, with another 100 desired for Safe Haven reasons. Seventy officials and 150 Safe Haven candidates were in Sweden, and 116 names
had been passed on to the Argentine government, although because
of its declaration of war in the spring of 1945, technically Argentina
was no longer a neutral state subject to the obnoxious German policy
of the Allied powers.[66] Switzerland, as noted earlier, carried out its
own program.[67] While the Swiss did not officially share information
with the United Kingdom and the United States, by mid-1946 an
estimated 9,000 Germans had been expelled from the country.[68]

Portugal proved to be as problematic as Spain in terms of implementing a clear and decisive policy that conformed to Allied demands. In response to initial lists provided by the British and U.S.
embassies of some 500 Germans that they wanted repatriated, Portugal had only agreed to the deportation of 25 by January 1946.[69]
Four were repatriated by air in November 1945, and then 111 were
sent by ship in March 1946.[70] The result, according to one British
official, was to leave the most wanted Germans "to continue their
undoubtedly dangerous activities," which included an assault against
an anti-Nazi pastor of the German Protestant Church in Lisbon.[71]
Despite being an ally of the British and ceding military bases in the
Azores to the Allies in 1943, Salazar's regime had a history of close
economic and other ties with Nazi Germany. During the Spanish
Civil War, Salazar's government had helped facilitate Nazi Germany's
supply of Franco.[72] During World War II, Salazar's military, police,
and intelligence were generally pro-Nazi, and economic relations,
especially in wolfram trade, were significant.[73]

The Spanish and Portuguese failure to deport German agents during the last year of the war suggested that in addition to the policies connected with Safe Haven a new, postwar policy to accomplish earlier goals was also needed. The main fear was not that Spain would become Nazi but rather than the presence of former Nazis would mean that Nazi ideas could be infused into the Spanish regime. As the Western Department of the British Foreign Office acknowledged in December 1946, the threat represented by obnoxious Germans "may depend to some extent on the disposition of such Governments as hold power within Spain in future."[74] This fear was reinforced by the developments concerning automatic-arrest categories and denazification inside occupied Germany and a general desire to remove certain elements from the future politics of postwar Europe. Together these factors led to the beginning of a program of forced repatriation, the program that became identified with the term *obnoxious Germans,* which was officially enacted by the ACC in September 1945.

If denazification and new conceptions of neutrality helped shape plans concerning repatriation, broader foreign-policy debates over Franco's dictatorship strengthened the U.S. commitment to the policy. In his instructions to the new U.S. ambassador to Madrid, Norman Armour, in March 1945 President Franklin D. Roosevelt underlined that Spain's relations with Nazi Germany could not be forgotten and that international ostracism of the Franco regime would be the preferred policy of his administration unless Spain made significant internal changes and reoriented its foreign policy. He went as far as to equate the Allied victory with "the extermination of Nazi and similar ideologies."[75] Mark Byrnes argues that Roosevelt's appointment of Armour as ambassador to Madrid represented a return to idealism in U.S. foreign policy in general after the necessities of wartime made dealing with Franco the realistic choice. The emerging U.S. opposition to Franco was on ideological grounds, and it was shared by many in the State Department, the OSS, and other governmental departments.[76]

The emergence of an increasingly anti-Franco position within the Roosevelt administration did not mean, however, that Spain had to change its regime. Andrew N. Buchanan argues that while Roosevelt was definitely "swinging onto an anti-Franco tack," the United States never sought to openly support the Spanish Republican movement or Republicans in exile; the fear of a renewed civil war in Spain, or at least violence and chaos in some form, constantly informed U.S. policymakers; and U.S. capitalism's need to find markets and help secure Spain against Communist impulses motivated policy more often than not.[77] Rejection of the Franco regime's place in the new world order was accompanied by a belief in nonintervention in internal affairs and a fear of renewed civil war, and these views were shared by the British. As Enrique Moradiellos has put it, what was desired was public rejection of Franco but only occasional "pin-pricks" in terms of policy.[78] As Byrnes underlines, it is essential to understand that Roosevelt's new aggressiveness toward Franco was popular but not unanimous; FDR was at the center of this effort, but the effort was not fully developed at the time of his death in April 1945.[79]

A complicating factor was the increasing interest of the Soviet Union in Spanish affairs as World War II came to a close. This became most obvious at the Potsdam Conference in July 1945, when the Soviet delegation presented the U.S. and British delegations with a memorandum on Spain calling for support for forces wishing to remove Franco, since the Soviets argued that Franco had been forced on Spain by Hitler and Mussolini. The statement of the three powers at the conclusion of the conference clearly marked Franco's Spain for international ostracism, banning it from the United Nations and other international organizations. In the long term, as Enrique Moradiellos has made clear, as tensions between the West and the Soviet Union increased into 1946, the Potsdam statement came to represent the most criticism the West was going to voice about Franco.[80] However, in the short term, this was not apparent, and the general sentiment in the West was that while the Soviet position was too extreme, certainly Franco needed to show that he would change aspects of his government, even if it was clear that complete regime change was out of the question.

In 1945 and 1946 there was no tension between "idealist" and "realist" approaches in U.S. foreign policy toward Spain. Rather what was occurring was a kind of balancing act, led by Roosevelt, between those two poles, incorporating aspects of each.[81] If regime change was out of the question, how could some of the ideal goals to remake the world for democracy be seen in Spain? How could the United States measure change while being pragmatic about Spain's disorganized and divided opposition, the need for trade, and the desire to keep communism out of the region? The elimination of Nazi influence in neutral states was an ideal test of change without upheaval in Spain, Portugal, and other formerly neutral states.

The British Foreign Office was very much in agreement with this sentiment, and the British Labour government that came to power in July 1945 was content with a policy of rhetorical condemnation and political nonintervention interspersed with symbolic anti-Franco actions. Nonintervention had the support of Foreign Secretary Ernest Bevin, who in August 1945 spoke in the House of Commons about his dislike of the Franco regime, while reaffirming his and his government's desire to avoid renewed civil war in Spain. British policy rejected any sort of military, political, or economic sanctions.[82] Despite agitation by Harold Laski and others on the Labour Left, and despite Prime Minister Clement Attlee's own anti-Francoist views during the Civil War and after, the cabinet supported the position of Bevin and his Foreign Office advisers.[83] For example, in October 1945 the cabinet agreed to support Bevin's recommendation that the United Kingdom ban only the trade of weapons and semimilitary equipment with Spain and not enforce a broader ban on all equipment that might later be converted to military use.[84] Douglas Howard, of the British embassy in Madrid, approached the French representative Bernard Hardion and stated that the issue was not one of replacing Franco but rather one of altering the regime and its political system to conform more closely to Western ideas.[85]

The fear of renewed civil war in Spain and the potential for a Communist victory and thus Soviet influence over the western Mediterranean dominated British thinking. Ambassador Sir Victor Mallet wrote on December 3, 1945, that while it was "idiotic to attempt to prophesy exactly how and when Franco will disappear," it was clear that "no new regime wants to be born of a fresh insurrection and blood bath." He continued, "There has been enough killing for one generation, even in bloodthirsty Spain; and thus it is that fear of this operates so strongly in favor of not disturbing the dreary status quo."[86] Thus, as in the United States, what was desired from Franco was a sign of willingness to adapt to new realities, something far short of regime change. The policy of repatriating former Nazis in Spain provided a perfect way to measure whether Franco would conform with the Allies' desire to achieve the balance between accepting Francoist reality and seeking some sign of pro-Western change after the war.

The treatment of obnoxious Germans, then, was not only about removing the threat they posed but also a way to measure Spain's compliance with the consequences of Allied victory. As Secretary of State James Byrnes wrote, if the Spanish thought that rounding up Germans was a "favor" to the Allies, then "they should be disabused of this notion; we believe that it is one easy way for them to start improving their international position if they want to do so," and if not, then "international criticism will inevitably become more severe if the Spanish Government fails to take advantage of the opportunity offered to cooperate in the removing of these obnoxious Germans."[87] Derrick Hoyer-Millar, of the British Foreign Office's Western Department, bluntly stated, "From the general point of view of future Anglo-Spanish relations, it was highly desirable that it should be brought home to the Spaniards that Germany really had lost the war and that it had made a mistake in backing the wrong side."[88]

The multiple motives behind this policy, to eliminate Nazism and to test the Spanish government, are made clear in a letter of the British ambassador to Madrid, Sir Victor Mallet, to his consuls general in Spain on April 1, 1946:

The purpose of making the lists so long is to combat the extensive degree of penetration into Spanish official and commercial life achieved by the

Germans during the civil and world wars, and to prevent the formation or continued existence of a nucleus of Germans among whom strongly Nazi and anti-British ideas might be conserved, as it were in cold storage, until such time as they could be brought into the open against the interests of His Majesty's Government and possibly in reinforcement of similar ideas harbored by a section of the Spanish people.[89]

In mid-1946, following up on the initial policy decision of September 1945, the ACC revisited the question of obnoxious Germans and requested from the Prisoners of War and Displaced Persons Directorate a census of obnoxious Germans in each neutral state and a clear description of who was being targeted.[90] The Economic Warfare Division of the British Foreign Ministry emphasized the spoiler role of ex-German officials: "Obnoxious Germans are those who have been associated with the enemy's espionage, sabotage, or similar activities; who have been openly engaged in anti-Allied or pro-Nazi activities such as propaganda or the organization of local German nationalist enterprises."[91] The linkage of "German nationalist" activity after the war with revived Nazism was not new. Indeed, it was crucial in defining spoiler activities and was quite apparent within occupied Germany. The first mission, then, was to find these Nazis where they continued to proclaim Nazism after the war was over. This was done, in the first instance, by tracking what were called "werewolf" groups. The term *werewolf* first was used in occupied Germany and came to represent groups carrying out "a string of guerrilla attacks aimed at both the enemy powers and the German 'collaborators' who worked with the occupiers in maintaining civil government."[92]

In the end, the real threat posed by violent groups was largely overblown, despite some notable attacks, such as the assassination of the mayor of Aachen. More widespread, and more representative of nonviolent spoiler activity, was consistent and growing opposition to denazification measures inside Germany, expressed by a wide variety of groups.[93] Often this opposition expressed itself as nationalistic sentiment and resentment toward the outside imposition of reeducation and a purge of local and national officials.[94] Beyond criticizing denazification, many former elites and Nazi party members desired to shape denazification to their own ends. As Donald Bloxham has argued, they "sought to undermine its [Allied policy] foundations to the end of creating a 'usable past' on which German national identity could be reconstructed."[95] The effort of Germans to continue to find a way to express national sentiment, often driven by former Nazis, was in many respects a nonviolent way of spoiling the peace process, at least as it was conceived by the victor states through their denazification programs.

The Economic Warfare Division introduced an additional reason for repatriation, namely, economic security. An obnoxious German was also someone "whose activity overseas served to maintain German commercial or national interests or influence, whether or not they worked directly against Allied interests."[96] The postwar aim here was simply to replace German economic power with that of the Allies. While the spoiler issue and fear of continued Nazi political influence over neutral states drove the repatriation policy, other considerations were not absent. National security in a time of transition meant securing the interests of the victors. This was especially so in Spain, the neutral state with the most ingrained and developed economic relationship with Nazi Germany. Removing Germans would allow the United States and the United Kingdom to become valuable trading partners for the future. Such sentiment was apparent not only in the development of the repatriation policy but in Safe Haven generally. Given that Nazi economic activities in Spain had lasted longer than its intelligence operations, economic targets were more likely to have support in official Spanish circles.[97] By August 1946 the British preferred that the repatriation issue be handled by the Economic Warfare Department of the Foreign Office instead of by the political officials who dealt with Spain.[98]

The United States consistently defined the issue in more political terms. In October 1946 the United States proposed a more precise definition of *obnoxious Germans* to the ACC. This definition returned to documents of the occupation in order to clarify the category of those engaged in pro-Nazi and anti-Allied activity, listing in particular any member of the Nazis Party and its subsidiaries; any other "schools or agencies dedicated to the systematic dissemination of propaganda" that was pro-Nazi; and, in economic terms, "any enterprise which, under the guise of a commercial concern and simultaneously with its specific purposes, has in fact been an organization promoting the Axis plans for politico-economic penetration."[99]

CONCLUSION

Spain, along with other neutral states, posed a significant challenge to U.S. and other Allied policymakers in the immediate aftermath of World War II. For most, neutrality in Europe during the war had meant important and often beneficial relations with Nazi Germany. Although these states could not be treated as belligerents in the conflict, traditional ideas of neutrality that reflected an arm's-length relationship with war did not apply in 1945. The realization that neutrality had been redefined by the experience of Nazi domination in Europe demanded a set of innovative policies on the part of the Allies in order to recognize the change that had occurred and to lay some blame at the feet of neutral states that had rewritten international norms on their own.

More than punishing neutral states, though, the repatriation policy of the Allied victors had significant postwar goals as well. Much can be learned from reflecting on the postwar goals that the Nazi repatriation policy sought to accomplish. The fear that Nazis who stayed in Spain would continue to influence Franco's authoritarian regime and thus provide a base for a potential reemergence of Nazism was certainly overblown. Yet it was a real fear at the time. While Franco or his regime posed no threat to peace in Europe, the fear that Nazi "spoilers" would continue to disrupt the postwar settlement was a serious one. As a result, neutral states had to account for their past in a manner that paralleled, in some ways, what defeated states had to go through. Denazification was not limited to occupied Germany.

Of course, before they could be in a position to force neutral states to conform to denazification goals through repatriation, the

U.S. and British governments needed to understand the extent of Nazi involvement in Spain. As we shall see in the next chapter, an examination of the Allied intelligence apparatus and its anti-Nazi work in Spain during the war set the stage for repatriation operations that followed World War II.

2

INTELLIGENCE WARS

*Nazi and Allied Spies in Neutral Spain
during and after the War*

A state with ties to local as well as German and Italian Fascism, but one still recovering from three years of civil war, Spain by the end of 1940 was in the middle of an internal debate about whether to remain neutral or join the Axis.[1] Eventually it chose a status of "non-belligerency," which did not reassure the British, since Benito Mussolini had declared the same status before entering the war alongside Nazi Germany in April 1940. Indeed, an offer of Spanish belligerency was made to Nazi Germany in the summer of 1940, when Hitler met Franco at Hendaye, France, albeit with a number of territorial and material conditions attached.[2] While the offer was not accepted by Hitler, Spain's participation in the Anti-Comintern Pact, its willingness to discuss war at Hendaye, and its statement of nonbelligerency were all gestures that made clear its allegiance to the Axis.[3] Thus throughout the war the Franco regime was "repeatedly on the verge" of a decision to join the Axis in war.[4] This situation drew both Nazi and Allied elements to Spain in order to try to influence the regime's decision whether to enter the war. Intelligence agencies, monitoring each other as much as the Spaniards, proved to be vital actors in pursuit of political, economic, and strategic goals of the Allies in wartime Spain.

Germany sought to exploit Spain's economic resources and to monitor Allied activities in the Mediterranean and the Atlantic from Spain even if Spain did not enter the war. In response, the United States and the United Kingdom made an effort to encourage, cajole, and force Spain to remain as true as possible to the obligations of neutrality, which meant limiting German influence on the Iberian Peninsula. The same policy was pursued in other neutral states, such as Portugal. The neutral states of wartime Europe were crucial to the military strategy of the Allied nations in many respects. The United Kingdom, fighting alone after the French defeat in June 1940, faced years of recovery from the initial successes of the German attacks in central and western Europe and was in no position to launch an offensive campaign on the Continent. Even the arrival of the United States on the Allied side in December 1941 did not bring instant relief—U.S. forces too had to prepare for engagement on the Continent. Thus Allied strategy in Europe from 1940 to 1942 focused largely on the "containment" of Nazi advances. Keeping neutral states out of the war was a significant part of this, and nowhere were the challenges greater than in General Francisco Franco's Spain.

Without this wartime history, the resources needed to pursue the repatriation policy after the war would not have been present. While inspired by denazification measures being developed in occupied Germany, the repatriation campaign was built on a history of Allied intelligence against the Nazi presence in Spain going back to the war. As in many other neutral states, in Spain Allied intelligence activities not only tracked Nazi agents but also uncovered detailed financial and economic arrangements made by the German government, its various entities, and individual agents and other Nazis. This wartime knowledge and experience directly translated into the continued gathering of economic intelligence and the tracking of specific Nazis in Spain once the war ended. As the Allies moved to consider the fate of "obnoxious" Germans and their potential threat across the neutral states of Europe, the realization that intelligence similar to that gathered during the war was still needed defined the intelligence mandate through 1945 and into 1946.

GERMAN INTELLIGENCE ACTIVITIES IN SPAIN

In the years 1933–39 a major transformation occurred within the German colony in Spain, masterminded by operatives of the National Socialist Party, that resulted in a situation in which, in the words of Ronald Newton in reference to the German colony in Argentina in 1943–47, "with few exceptions the communal organizations—religious, educational, welfare, musical, sport, social—had declared their formal adhesion to Hitler's New Order . . . teaching cadres in the larger schools came to be dominated by recently arrived apostles of the New Germany, most of them party members, the children of leftist and Jewish parents were driven off . . . [and the] German Labor Front organized the employees of many German firms."[5] This pattern was repeated in many countries. In Spain, these developments built on a history of commercial relations that dated from the turn of the century, when Deutsches Bank helped create the Banco Hispano-Alemán and the Banco Alemán Transatlántico.[6] Following World War I, when French and U.S. cultural and economic elements were active in the Iberian Peninsula, many Spaniards as well as Germans sought to reinvigorate cultural, scientific, and economic ties between their countries.[7]

In Spain, the Nazis were already exerting influence over the German colony when civil war broke out in July 1936. One of the most prominent members of the German colony in Spain, Johannes Bernhardt, managed to persuade Hitler to provide air support to aid Franco's movement of troops from Spanish Morocco to the mainland. This eventually led to Hitler's dispatch of the Condor Legion, a unit of the Luftwaffe, to fight in Spain and to a rapid expansion of German economic interests in Spain.

The Condor Legion's twenty-nine months of service in Spain was significant for the development of German activities in Spain that followed. Nearly 19,000 Germans volunteered to serve in the legion over the course of the civil war.[8] Many had ties to Spain or had had a relationship with the German colony in Spain before the war. By 1939 the ties between Germans in Spain, Nazism, and the Spanish regime of General Franco were even closer. The respective air ministries established exchange programs for officers; the Spanish Fascist movement, the Falange, had formal ties to the Nazi Party; and the Gestapo established relations with the Civil Guard.[9]

Although Italy's Benito Mussolini provided the majority of the Axis military support to Franco, Germany's attempt to economically colonize Spain had longer-term effects.[10] In October 1936 the German plenipotentiary for the Four-Year Plan, Hermann Göring, created the company ROWAK to manage German trade with Franco's zone in Civil War Spain. In 1938 Sofindus was created, and it became a holding company for all German government-owned mines, companies, and properties in Franco's Spain. Johannes Bernhardt, the instigator of German support for Franco, led this enterprise throughout World War II.[11] The economic power of Sofindus expanded the German presence and built upon the foundation established during the Civil War by the Condor Legion.

Germany's expanded economic presence in Spain was equaled by the massive expansion of German intelligence operations, which, as with economic matters, was generally carried out with the acquiescence of Francoist officials.[12] Intelligence officers were first posted with the Condor Legion, and in 1937 a broader German military operation began when Abwehr agents were sent to monitor British Gibraltar. By 1939 the Abwehr detachment in Spain, KO-Spanien, had become one of the largest foreign operations of the Abwehr, with two hundred personnel and more than one thousand subagents. It had a close relationship with Franco's intelligence services, first in Burgos and then, after the Civil War ended, in Madrid through the Spanish General Staff. The organization was led from 1939 to 1944 by Gustav Leissner, alias Gustavo Lenz, and then, after 1944, by Arno Kleyenstuber. It included sections on intelligence gathering about Allied activities in the region; sabotage in the vicinity of Gibraltar, Morocco, and Algiers; counterespionage against Allied agents in Spain; and specific intelligence-gathering operations related to French Morocco, Allied aviation, the Atlantic coast, and the Canary Islands, as well as to Gibraltar and the Straits (Operation Bodden).[13] Leissner exerted a strong influence throughout the organization, making sure that even in locales far from Madrid the organization was discrete and competent and on good terms with Spanish authorities.[14]

The Abwehr in Spain was organized into three departments, Espionage, Sabotage, and Counter-Espionage; the Espionage unit was further divided into army, navy, and air force units. Naval intelligence was the largest unit, with agents based in Cueta, Tangier, La Línea, Cadiz, Seville, Valencia, Barcelona, San Sebastian, Bilbao, Vigo, and Santander. Walther Giese, the Abwehr agent responsible for intelligence activities in Galicia, recalled that intelligence gathering about Allied-related shipping, especially concerning wolfram, was a primary focus. Much of the work also included identifying Allied agents in the area, who had been sent to uncover information about German shipping of wolfram from Spain. Giese concluded that the gathering of shipping information and the identification of Allied agents were the Abwehr's two most successful operations in Spain.[15] Both underlined the significance of naval intelligence to German operations in Spain.

It was quite common for German intelligence in Spain to use Germans familiar with the country, those who had been members of the colony before 1936 or who had come to Spain with the Condor Legion or German business during the Civil War. The Abwehr agent Richard Molenhauer first went to Spain in 1932 to work for the Spanish affiliate of IG Farben, Única Química y Bluch SA of Barcelona. Evacuated at the start of the Spanish Civil War, he returned at the end of 1936 to serve as the IG Farben representative in Nationalist territory. He worked in Spain until he was called back to Germany for military service in 1942. In February 1944 he was transferred to the Abwehr and sent back to Spain to work on translating reports from agents in Madrid.[16] Josef Boogen arrived in Spain in 1929 and joined the Condor Legion in 1936, and by 1941 he had established himself in Bilbao as a representative for several German machinery firms. His office there served as a cover for numerous German agents who passed through the area, and by 1943 he was suspected of being the primary Gestapo agent in Bilbao and working with the leading Abwehr agent in the city, Otto Hinrichsen. Hinrichsen himself had also come to Spain in 1936, although he had worked in Spain in the 1920s, when he married a Spanish woman and had two children born in Spain. During the war he served both the Abwehr and the Nazi Party as a party leader in Bilbao. His son served in the German army during World War II.[17]

Military intelligence was not the only game in town, for the SD, the security and intelligence service of the SS, was also heavily engaged in Spain. Formal German intelligence operations in Spain began with a police treaty signed between Germany and Franco's Burgos-based government on July 31, 1938. The first official police attaché sent to Spain from Berlin was a representative of the Gestapo, part of the SD.[18] This was Paul Winzer, who remained in Madrid until the end of the war. There was close collaboration between the SD and the Spanish Dirección General de Seguridad (DGS) on issues such as the internment of Spanish Republican activists in occupied France. SD agents were dispatched to all the German consulates across Spain to monitor the German colony, and after 1941 SD agents were sent by the SD's head of foreign intelligence, Walter Schellenberg, to gather intelligence on Spain and the Allies that had more than just military value.[19] SD agents were placed not only in German consulates but also in a number of German firms, many with ties to the SS.[20] At war's end the SD and Gestapo had fourteen agents under diplomatic cover in the German embassy and consulates and many more with no official cover, mostly placed in Spanish communities as commercial agents or salespeople for German-affiliated companies.[21] Ernst Hammes was head of the Gestapo in Spain at the end of the war, with Heinz Singer and Karl Arnold representing Amt VI, the SD's foreign-intelligence service.[22] Another prominent leader was Walter Eugen Mosig, introduced in the introduction, who had been active in Spain since the Civil War and during World War II was part of Amt VI alongside Singer and Arnold.[23]

Over time the SD expanded its operations in Spain and came into increasing conflict with the Abwehr. This was not unexpected; the SD had long sought to surpass the Abwehr in its activities and responsibilities.[24] In the aftermath of the plot to assassinate Adolf Hitler on July 20, 1944, which involved the head of the Abwehr, Admiral Wilhelm Canaris, the Abwehr was taken over by Schellenberg, the Amt VI head. Because Canaris had been closely linked with Spain and with the conservative authoritarianism of Franco, not ideological Nazism,[25] the change was felt in Spain rather quickly. Former chargé d'affaires of the German embassy Sigismund von Bibra described the new SD agents flooding into Spain as "arrogant" and said they "insinuated the immediate removal of those members of the Embassy staff not willing to help."[26]

The impact of Germany's war effort in Europe was clearly felt in neutral states like Spain. In 1941 some 7,500 Germans were resident in Spain; by 1945 that number had grown to some 20,000.[27] By September 26, 1946, U.S. intelligence was able to compile a list of known German agents who had served in Spain during the war. Although incomplete, the list created from German embassy records and interrogations of Germans in Spain and Germany was nonetheless impressive, with 650 names.[28]

ALLIED COUNTERESPIONAGE

Even as Franco began to shift toward the Allies and speak of true "neutrality" in the autumn of 1943, Spain provided significant assistance to the Axis cause until the end of the war. Documents released in the last few years in the United States and the United Kingdom have allowed historians to expand their knowledge of intelligence work across many neutral states, beyond what was already known from cases like that of Allen Dulles in Switzerland. The final wartime phase of Allied intelligence gathering in Spain, from 1943 on, focused on how Germany used private enterprise to smuggle goods, especially wolfram, out of Spain in violation of Hispano-German and Hispano-Allied agreements.[29]

It was the British, the first involved in a full-scale war on the Continent against Germany, who initially developed Allied strategy in Spain. As early as 1940 it was clear that a German invasion of Iberia or Spain's entering the war on the side of the Axis threatened the United Kingdom's Mediterranean position and might delay a planned U.S. landing in North Africa. The United Kingdom's policy became to do everything possible to prevent Spain from entering the war and/or encourage Spanish opposition in the event of a German move into the peninsula. The primary means for pursuing such a policy was diplomatic. Ambassador "on Special Mission" Sir Samuel Hoare sought to affirm British acceptance of the Franco government, often using a variety of economic and other incentives.[30]

Beginning in May 1942 and increasingly after the success of Operation Torch, the U.S. invasion of French North Africa on November 8, 1942, Hoare and his U.S. allies also pressured the Franco government to eliminate or limit Nazi influence by taking actions such as expelling German agents operating in Spanish territory.[31] For such pressure to be effective, the resources of British intelligence were necessary. What information could be gathered about Spanish contacts with Nazi Germany, about Franco's assistance to the enemy's armed forces, particularly its U-boats operating in the Atlantic and the Mediterranean, or about economic ties that furthered the German war economy? Both covert and overt sources provided details about Hispano-German trade and smuggling and about the presence of Axis agents in Spain. All British intelligence operations in Spain were managed by the naval attaché Alan Hillgarth, who worked closely with Hoare.[32] When information was uncovered, Hoare and his staff used it to demand that Spain conform to a position of strict neutrality or else risk losing British aid. Intelligence in Spain thus served in a complementary role to the Foreign Office's campaign to preserve Spanish neutrality and dampen pro-German sentiments within the Franco government while developing a workable Anglo-Spanish relationship.

The primacy of diplomacy seemed to bear fruit. The Secret Intelligence Service (SIS) activities in Spain became focused on uncovering German intelligence operations, most famously unearthing Germany's infrared surveillance system located in the Western Mediterranean, code-named Bodden. Information about Bodden obtained by the SIS and naval intelligence was used by British embassy officials from May to December 1942 to shame the Spanish government into reigning in German covert activities in the Iberian Peninsula.[33] The embassy's actions eventually led to the dismantling of Bodden, if not an end to German activity in the region.[34] Most significantly, the use of intelligence in the pursuit of diplomacy appeared to work well in the context of Spain and thus cemented the relationship between the SIS and Hoare's staff. Kim Philby, a SIS operative in Iberia during the war who later was revealed to be a prominent Soviet spy, reflected on the unusual fact that the Foreign Office and Hoare "had less than [the] usual crop of inhibitions" when it came to using intelligence in a diplomatic protest against the Franco government.[35]

Given the predominance of this diplomatic strategy, it is surprising that the Special Operations Executive (SOE) came to play a significant role in the pursuit of British goals in Spain. The purpose of the SOE, as envisaged by Prime Minister Winston Churchill, was to "organize, arm and control the European underground movements on a large-enough scale" that they could assist the British military.[36] This seemed to fly in the face of the diplomatic emphasis desired by the British in Spain. Thus H Section, the SOE division responsible for Spain, Portugal, and Spanish Morocco, was created in 1941 only to assist the movement of SOE agents and French Resistance members across the Pyrenees into occupied France.[37] Previous writers have emphasized that this was a secondary role: when intelligence came to matter in Spain, it was intelligence gathering done by the SIS, and not the sabotage and resistance work of the SOE, that emerged as predominant.[38]

While the SOE made contacts with potential saboteurs and Spanish opposition figures,[39] by 1943 H Section had taken on more responsibility and was dedicated to counterespionage activities and the potential "sabotage of Axis politico-military and economic interests."[40] A variety of activities were considered to fall within the realm of economic sabotage. Of course, actual sabotage or destruction of Axis economic stocks was included, in line with the SOE's mandate. Indeed, Basque operatives on both the Spanish and French sides of the border were considered for sabotage operations to be carried out on French territory in 1944. The potential targets were trains carrying illegal German shipments of wolfram. In this instance, because of opposition from Hoare and the SOE's French section, planning did not lead to action.[41] Other, subtler forms of sabotage were considered. These included persuading exporters to slow down shipments, pressuring neutral traders to stop trading with the Axis, suborning shipmasters in order to intercept ships transporting goods to the enemy, and fomenting strikes among dockworkers loading ships engaged in Axis trade—"in general attacking or interfering with Axis interests by 'unknowledgeable' methods."[42]

Beyond sabotage of Axis economic activities, intelligence gathered about such activities also could be used. In September 1943 H Section's new directive to engage in economic-intelligence gathering was approved by the Foreign Office and the Ministry of Economic Warfare.[43] The MEW representative at the Madrid embassy, Hugh Ellis-Rees, was informed that the new directive was part of "a full scale economic offensive against Axis commercial and economic activities in the Peninsula" and that the "Foreign Office have now agreed that the stage has been reached where more drastic methods may be resorted to, and for this purpose S.O.E. are permitted to enter the field to assist and reinforce the overt activities of M.E.W." The SOE was authorized to expand its activities in Spain, but in a way that was "complementary" to the activities of Ellis-Rees and carried out with the full knowledge of the ambassador.[44] The appointment of Harry Morris as head of mission and the increase in SOE personnel in Spain followed approval of the new directive.

In July 1943 a SOE agent was sent to Iberia in order to determine what role intelligence agencies could have in limiting or stopping German smuggling of wolfram.[45] The SOE's Major P. Mandestan indicated that wolfram was primarily being smuggled from Portuguese and Spanish mines to France via the railway line running through the Spanish border town of Irun. Moreover, Irun contained a major German storage facility (capable of holding 800–1,000 tons of wolfram) and was effectively the primary conduit of German smuggling in wolfram, accounting for deliveries to Germany that exceeded official German purchases by five hundred tons annually. What emerged from this early intelligence was a SOE-run network of agents who provided Ellis-Rees with information concerning German efforts to trade and smuggle wolfram out of Spain and into occupied France.[46] Ellis-Rees then used that information in confronting the Spanish government. In short, "all he has to do is to report the facts to the [Spanish] authorities who will take necessary action; no action by us is required."[47] The use of British intelligence in a *note verbale* to draw Spain's attention to Hispano-German violations of neutrality was well established by Hoare, who had used SIS information about German espionage activity, most notably in the Bodden case.[48]

A number of SOE agents and subagents were involved in tracking German wolfram smuggling throughout northern Spain. In the summer of 1944 regular reports of German smuggling were sent to London by Morris and his agents in Spain. One report from an SOE agent in Irun identified only as "VS" was typical. Dated June 18, the report stated that forty tons of wolfram had been clandestinely shipped across the border from Irun the previous evening.[49] This information was passed on to Ellis-Rees, in Madrid, who reported it to the Spanish Ministry of Foreign Affairs and forced the Spanish Customs Service to admit that the incident had indeed occurred. The result was that official shipments of wolfram to Germany stopped for the month, and the German wolfram quota for June was not met.[50] Such direct connection between intelligence gathering and diplomatic action demonstrated the value of economic-intelligence operations in Spain.

Just as British operations expanded to include economic intelligence, so too did the work of the wartime U.S. intelligence organization, the Office for Strategic Services, or OSS. By the end of 1943 there were forty-four OSS agents in Spain, Portugal, the Azores, and Madeira, many with networks of local subagents working for them.[51] These agents were under the direction of H. Gregory Thomas, economic attaché at the U.S. embassy in Lisbon. OSS activity in Spain primarily concerned intelligence collection across the border in southern France and information on Spanish factory output and Spanish military forces. However, intelligence on Hispano-German wolfram smuggling and other Spanish violations of neutrality was also important. Economic intelligence, in fact, gave the OSS the ability to expand operations in Spain, for it was the arrival of U.S. governmental "oil observers" in the spring of 1942, charged with making sure German oil exports did not exceed agreed-upon amounts, that provided the OSS an ideal opportunity to add a significant number of agents in Spain.[52] By the summer of 1944 OSS agents, working with OSS contacts in Spain and in Switzerland, had uncovered a plan to move wolfram stocks from Spain through France with the assistance of a number of leading Spanish military figures.[53] As with the British, economic intelligence did more than just sustain U.S. intelligence operations in neutral Spain; it allowed them to grow significantly.

In many places, OSS and SOE agents were able to collaborate and share work in the pursuit of wolfram smugglers. The SOE and the OSS had signed an agreement in June 1942 that limited OSS activity to French North Africa and Spanish Morocco. Operations in Spain were to be led by the British Foreign Office, according to the terms described earlier, using intelligence only in the service of diplomacy.[54] Yet the OSS was not banned from Spain, and it doubled the size of its Iberian operation in 1943; these agents were involved in breaking up a number of smuggling rings, in cooperation with "British counterparts," presumably the SIS and the SOE.[55] The records of H Section suggest that there was some degree of coordination between the SOE and the OSS in the field, although it is impossible to assess how extensive or organized this was. U.S. wolfram observers were involved in most Irun operations, and SOE chief Morris expected to receive reports from "the US observer" at Irun, presumably an OSS agent, in addition to receiving reports from its own agents.[56] The SOE's own agent in Irun implied that field coordination was common, describing in one report how he had gone out alone at one o'clock in the morning to track a smuggler, since "at this hour it might be difficult to advise the US."[57]

Intelligence was by no means the only aspect of Allied wolfram policy in 1943–44, nor was it the most significant. Preemptive purchasing of wolfram by the United States and the United Kingdom remained the most significant way, over the course of 1943, for the Allies to limit German supplies.[58] In 1944 the Allies, especially the United States, began to pressure Spain to impose an embargo on its wolfram trade with Germany. In early 1944, negotiations with the

Franco government to limit Germany's ability to purchase wolfram were pursued by both Allies, despite some significant disagreements between them on how firm to be with the Spanish government.[59] A deal that limited German purchases of wolfram to very small levels was finally achieved on May 2, 1944, but fears of German smuggling above such limits, already realized by evidence of smuggling in 1943 and 1944, spurred Allied intelligence.[60] The official British history of economic warfare notes that Allied negotiators in Spain made full use of the "good information from their secret sources."[61] Later, the intelligence gathered was used openly, in meetings between British and Spanish officials, to enforce the wolfram agreement.

NAZI AGENTS AND DENAZIFICATION

In conjunction with the May 1944 wolfram agreement, the Allies presented the Spanish government with a list of 222 German espionage agents their intelligence gathering had identified, including 42 from the Protectorate of Morocco, with the request that they be deported.[62] While economic intelligence had been the main focus of SOE and OSS work before May 1944, after that it was clear that Allied intelligence was to be used to monitor Spanish compliance with both the wolfram aspects of the deal and the tracking of Nazi agents.

By December 1944, while individuals had been arrested and held, in general little action had been taken by the Spaniards. As the war came to a close, the U.S. and British embassies again submitted lists of names of those identified as German agents in May 1944 who had not been rounded up or deported from Spain. An April 30, 1945, document listed 69 such names.[63] These lists formed the basis of a future Allied policy against so-called obnoxious Germans.

The lack of Spanish compliance, even as Germany was losing the war, led to a more concerted effort in 1944 and into 1945 to track the movements and activities of known German agents. One of these was Alfred Genserowsky, the head of Abwehr operations in San Sebastian. Genserowsky's activities included everything from monitoring Allied shipping to running agents into France and collecting French identity cards for agents to use in hiding at the end of the war.[64] As with the wolfram campaign, U.S. and British diplomats used the intelligence gathered on people like Genserowsky to press the Spanish government to act. The first record of Allied demands for Genserowsky's expulsion from Spain came in March 1944, when a British protest, the second made to the Spanish, listed a series of agents identified by British intelligence.[65] The U.S. ambassador to Spain mentioned Genserowsky and six other agents in conversation with Foreign Minister Martín Artajo on May 7, 1945; on May 26 he followed up with a list of 134 agents whom the United States wanted arrested, including Genserowsky. The U.S. pressure followed similar demands from the British.[66] Genserowsky was known to be one of the key Germans in contact with Spanish intelligence agents in northern Spain and coordinated his activities with theirs. In the aftermath of the war, to demonstrate their commitment to ending Nazism, Spain arrested one of its own military intelligence agents, José Jiménez y Mora, for his ties to Genserowsky.[67] Spain reported on May 31, 1945, that Genserowsky had been ordered interned.[68] Spanish documents indeed indicate that Genserowsky was informed about his internment on May 21, and in response he solicited the right to move to Segovia for health reasons and report weekly to the police there; this was granted on July 11, 1945.[69] As a result he was never held in prison or in an internment camp.

In conjunction with the monitoring of existing agents, Allied intelligence was also beginning to focus on the possibility of a rush of Germans to Spain as the war turned against the Nazi regime. While reports of such movement began to increase dramatically beginning in May 1944, it was the influx of intelligence agents that most concerned the Allies, even if many of the German intelligence groups were deemed "inefficient" by that point in time.[70] The fear was that Spain was a perfect place for the Nazis to go underground, a state "where the regime is favorable to Germany and similar in its nationalist ideals."[71] The possibility of hunkering down in Spain was increased by the fact that German intelligence had extensively used German commercial firms as cover for wartime activities, so that many Germans who should be removed from Spain were not serving in any official capacity, which made it easier to stay once the war ended. In a June 1944 communication from Ambassador Hoare to Foreign Minister Anthony Eden, shared with U.S. consular officials in Spain and North Africa, Hoare was already arguing for the need to examine all German companies once the war ended, as well as the need to take immediate control of official German buildings that housed embassy and consular officials and German records.[72]

On September 29, 1944, OSS analysts began to assess information from a variety of sources suggesting that the Nazis planned "stay-behind" networks in neutral countries like Spain.[73] These networks would serve the dual purpose of hiding Nazi assets sought in the Safe Haven program and protecting Nazi agents and others from repatriation to occupied Germany, as well as protecting Nazis who might arrive in Spain as the war ended. They would also keep the Nazi ideology alive within the German colony. The fact that the SS under Hitler, working through the SD, had taken over the Abwehr in the aftermath of the assassination attempt on Hitler in July 1944 also contributed to the potential for stay-behind activity in neutral countries, because the SD members, being so integral to the Nazi Party and the SS, were, in the words on one U.S. intelligence report, "more compromised than any other section of the German nation" and thus would resist the party's dissolution to the end.[74]

On the British side, SOE officials in London and Madrid saw a unique opportunity to build on the experience of tracking wolfram and agents, which would result, they hoped, in a definition of a post-hostilities role for the SOE, namely, continuing to track the Germans agents with whom they were already familiar. In a memorandum to his superior, Major R. G. Head, chief of the H Section, wrote that as war slowly ended in various theaters "the neutral countries from an S.O.E. point of view are, I think, becoming of increasing significance. Speaking for Spain and Portugal, I am more that ever convinced . . . that the Germans are going to ground now in the neutral countries and that by the time hostilities cease we shall find that many of the birds have flown to well-timed and well-hidden nests."[75] Head went on to articulate a role for the SOE. While he acknowledged that the United Kingdom's primary foreign-intelligence agency, the SIS, would of course take a leading role in gathering intelligence regarding hidden German officials and assets, he believed that "there is probably a considerable amount of action called for on the evidence they should be able to produce. This action would be an ideal task for S.O.E. in Iberia: our present work, in the financial world of Lisbon and Tangier, and with wolfram in Spain, has given us invaluable contacts and, moreover, a considerable experience of black-markets and general under-handed dealing."[76]

The idea of involving the SOE in the diverse work associated with the question of enemy assets was simultaneously occurring to Hugh Ellis-Rees. Writing to London only a few days after Head, he described the tracing of German assets (individual, corporate, and state) in Spain as work "outside the scope of ordinary trading programmes and economic relations with Spain." While he acknowledged the necessary leadership of the MEW and its Enemy Branch, responsible for economic intelligence, in the work of asset discovery, he suggested that in the field SOE agents led by Morris would be naturals for the actual tasks involved, especially in the pursuit of specific German agents. Morris, wrote Ellis-Rees, had "useful contacts," "good knowledge," and the "confidence of all the staff," including Ambassador Hoare, whose approval for such a proposal Ellis-Rees had obtained prior to writing to propose SOE involvement in the upcoming project.[77]

Based on these initiatives, the SOE directed Morris in Madrid and his counterpart in Lisbon to consider the possibility of SOE action with regard to economic and financial intelligence aimed at uncovering German assets and agents inside Spain.[78] Throughout 1944 and into 1945, discussions in the United States and then in the United Kingdom sought to establish the necessary requirements for managing Safe Haven.[79] In Spain, the project initially was built, for the most part, on economic intelligence already being gathered by officials such as the MEW's Ellis-Rees. The goal was to turn his wolfram intelligence operation (i.e., the SOE) in Madrid into an economic-intelligence branch, which would gather information and give it to diplomatic officials, just as had been done with wolfram intelligence. In other words, intelligence gathered would be presented to Spanish officials as a way to prompt Spanish policing of German behavior. Morris concluded that, as with wolfram, the question of enemy assets in Spain required such economic intelligence "because no matter what the diplomats may be able to achieve, much will undoubtedly have to be done by other and less open means . . . in order to deny to the enemy the use of his assets."[80] Back in Madrid, Morris approached his U.S. and French counterparts to coordinate the intelligence aspects of Safe Haven, and he requested to be appointed the British embassy official responsible for Safe Haven in Spain, which would allow him a public role as well as a clandestine one in the upcoming campaign.[81]

Within the U.S. administration there was a great deal of infighting over whether the State Department or the Treasury Department would oversee the Foreign Economic Administration's (FEA) management of Safe Haven,[82] and the consequences were felt in Madrid as well. In the days following V-E Day—May 8, 1945—the entire OSS staff in Madrid resigned owing to the belief fostered within the U.S. embassy that intelligence against the Germans would no longer be needed. In June 1945 Gregory Thomas, head of the OSS in Iberia, was instructed by the OSS director, William Donovan, to ignore the State Department and carry on with anti-Nazi intelligence activities; later in June the OSS became the agency responsible for processing all paperwork emerging from German embassies and consulates, putting it in an ideal position to continue intelligence operations against Nazis in Spain. Nonetheless, Ambassador Carlton Hayes worked from the middle of 1944 on to reduce the OSS contingent within the embassy, and Hayes's aide Walton Butterworth persuaded Norman Armour, who succeeded Hayes in March 1945, to do the same.[83]

Yet the OSS did have supporters in Madrid, chiefly Byron Blankinship, who became head of Safe Haven in Spain when the war ended. Before long a Joint Intelligence Office was created within the embassy to coordinate intelligence gathering and diplomatic activities associated with Safe Haven. After V-E Day this meant that the OSS went through the contents of what was found in the German embassy and then processed these materials alongside information gathered from interrogations of Germans willing to "talk in exchange for a notation on their records which might operate in their favor on 'judgement day.'" One example of this can be seen in the U.S. investigation of the Officina Technic Francisco Liesau, which was largely funded by German money. Counterintelligence information regarding a contact who knew the owner, Liesau, was passed on to Thomas, who shared it with Blankinship and other embassy officials. Then a diplomatic request to add the company to the black list used to freeze assets was passed on to the Spanish government.[84]

Ultimately Morris, Ellis-Rees, and others would find SOE operations in Spain shut down by their rival agency, the SIS. Indeed, after the dispatch of the joint SIS-SOE head to Madrid in January 1945, the files on German assets dried up. Despite the creation of a joint SIS-SOE command, most of the information on the covert side came from the SIS and its agents. In general, the SIS, as it had throughout the war, begrudged the existence of a rival organization, and at the end of 1944 the desire to return covert and sabotage operations, as well as intelligence gathering, to the SIS was shared by Anthony Eden in the Foreign Office.[85] On July 19, 1945, the order came to shut down the SOE in Iberia.[86] Yet despite the loss of the SOE, the importance of linking economic intelligence gathering and agent tracking in wartime with intelligence requirements for Safe Haven and repatriation was well established in both the British and U.S. cases. Moreover, the connection between the two postwar operations, Safe Haven and the pursuit of so-called obnoxious Germans, was also made. In a meeting between SIS and OSS agents in Madrid in March 1945, the representatives of the two agencies highlighted the postwar significance of Safe Haven and "keeping check on enemy nationals during the period immediately following the war."[87]

Outside Spain, the OSS played a vital role in gathering evidence and making policy for war-crimes trials, as well as other policies associated with denazification. They were joined in this endeavor by the army's Counter Intelligence Corps. The motives for OSS involvement were many. Like the SOE leaders, OSS director Donovan wanted to carve out a postwar role for his agency, and he saw war-crimes work as an important part of this. By October 1943 Donovan was able to inform President Roosevelt that the OSS already had lists of potential criminals. Donovan not only modeled his efforts on the similar initiative of the British SOE but saw the two agencies as potential partners. The key planning office within the OSS was the Central European Division of the Research and Analysis Branch, populated by German exiles who also were involved in developing general denazification policy (see chapter 1). Donovan was also one of the first to see the need for denazification policy to operate outside of occupied Germany, outlining to Roosevelt the potential for the extradition of suspected criminals back to Germany from other parts of the continent.[88] In Spain, the OSS contingent introduced itself to the new ambassador, Armour, by underlining that its wartime experience in penetrating Spanish and Nazi agencies, its connections to a variety of sources, and its experience in tailing and surveilling agents "all apply" to Safe Haven and its linked policies.[89] After the OSS officially was disbanded in October 1945, its successor, the Strategic Services Unit (SSU) of the U.S. War Department continued this work, with many of the same agents, until the Central Intelligence Agency was created in 1947.

AFTER THE WAR

After the war, both British and U.S. intelligence units were charged with the dual mission of tracking German agents and diplomats as individuals and attempting to uncover hidden assets that could be linked to the German state and/or the NSDAP. Because they had extensive knowledge of German economic penetration in the region since the Civil War, Allied agents first focused on the German leadership in Spain, which included not only staff of the German embassy in Madrid but also leaders of German economic firms, especially those linked to the German state. As noted in chapter 1, the international sanctioning of Operation Safe Haven through the passage of Resolution VI of the Bretton Woods Agreement was matched by the Franco government's decree of May 5, 1945, to allow the blocking of Nazi state and para-state assets. Second, the Allies moved on to consider the hiding of private assets by German individuals many of whom had had links to the state or its intelligence agencies.[90] Third, policy directives specifically targeted agents and Nazi officials and raised the question whether they would be allowed to stay in Spain. In May 1945 the FBI liaison in the U.S. embassy, Frank Siscoe, was informed by contacts that German agents had no intention of ending their activities when the war ended.[91] As a result, the OSS was ordered to prepare a census of German nationals engaged in espionage and other activities of concern to the Allies in preparation for deporting them to occupied Germany. As one agent wrote, "The whole question of expulsion in connection with current events in Europe has been transformed into a question of repatriation."[92]

Even before the war ended, a Joint Intelligence Committee was created within the U.S. embassy, made up of Donn Paul Medalie, the head of counterespionage for the OSS in Spain, Frank Siscoe, of the FBI, the military and naval attachés, and LaVerne Baldwin and Earle Titus, of the OSS counterespionage unit, under cover as secretaries in the embassy.[93] This group examined documents taken from the German embassy after V-E Day and sought out German officials who were willing to talk about the intelligence and financial arrangements made by the German government, the Nazi Party, and other entities as the war ended. Leonard Horwin, the official U.S. representative for Axis affairs, who worked closely with the committee as did Bryon Blankinship, was sent to Madrid by the FEA to coordinate Safe Haven matters.[94] As the war ended, U.S. Ambassador Armour and the British chargé d'affaires, James Bowker, met with Foreign Minister Artajo to press the point about German agents. Armour expressed his dissatisfaction that as the war ended only twenty-five German agents were being held in custody by Spain and said that Spain needed to be ready to meet greater U.S. demands regarding German agents.[95] Within the U.S. embassy in Madrid, there was a real fear that the German colony in Spain might develop into a source for the maintenance of Nazi ideology, intelligence operations, and potential sabotage.[96] Similarly there was a belief that elements in Spain, especially the Falange, would seek to incorporate Nazi elements into the Spanish regime.[97] As noted in chapter 1, these thoughts merged with developments within occupied Germany concerning the internment of Nazi officials and agents, specifically the decision to create categories of individuals subject to automatic arrest. Together, the work of Allied policymakers in Germany concerning denazification and the concerns of U.S. personnel in Madrid and other neutral states resulted in the program of forced repatriation enacted by the ACC in September 1945.

Indeed, plans to expand the Madrid program of deportation of select agents to one of mass repatriation of German officials were already under way before the war ended. A list of potential repatriates had already been prepared by the British for U.S. comment in March 1945. The British put forward an extensive list, leaving only a minimal number of German officials solely to perform consular functions for the German colony. As to the others, "their presence in Spain raises the question of German plans for penetration and possible attempts to use Spain as a basis for winning the peace. From this point of view every German in Spain is potentially undesirable, and special consideration should be given to the devising of some method of denuding the country of as many German residents as possible."[98]

For those working in Madrid there was no break between the war effort and the ACC policy that emerged in the autumn of 1945, for the transition from pressing the Spaniards on German agents in 1944 and 1945 and preparing for their repatriation after V-E Day was seamless. Indeed, one of the last wartime meetings between the British embassy and representatives from the Spanish Foreign Ministry, on April 9, 1945, involved going through the May 1944 Allied list of agents and highlighting some sixty-nine cases in which no action whatsoever had been taken by Spain.[99] As noted earlier, OSS agents were asked to prepare lists of German agents on May 8, 1945; on May

26 the U.S. embassy presented the Spanish government with a list of the names of 135 agents the United States wanted expelled, building on wartime requests; and in July the U.S. embassy instructed all consulates general to prepare lists of German officials and agents in their regions for deportation purposes.[100] LaVerne Baldwin, the U.S. embassy official responsible for repatriation, articulated the expansive nature of this program best in a June 1945 memo to his superior, Chargé d'Affaires Walton Butterworth:

As many Germans as possible of all classes [should] be removed promptly from Spain and forcibly questioned under Allied control. The degree of assistance granted to Germans now and in the past by the Falange, the continued pro-German attitude of many Spaniards who have failed to realize that Germany has lost the war, persistent activities by Spaniards to extend aid to Germans in matters of concealing official German property, to the delusion of the Allies by the Spaniards, the activity of Germans in travelling freely within Spain, their gay and happy public appearances, activities in meeting together clandestinely, the large amounts of money they possess in currency free from blocking provisions, and the active transferal of German assets from person to person, which is still continuing, are all augmented by the continued presence of Germans in Spain. There are constant signs of German efforts to prepare for the collapse by sending to Spain persons charged with organizing post-war espionage, and presumably heretofore unknown to our counter-espionage services. There is definite proof of German intentions to continue espionage; they are training radio agents here; they have large funds of liquid capital which they propose to put into Spanish or Western Hemisphere investment; and they continue plans for economic and espionage penetration of the Western Hemisphere, including the United States. All of these are based on Spain and on the German residents here, and would be circumvented and discovered in large part should their participants be returned to Allied hands.[101]

All this was done before the formal repatriation policy had been approved by the ACC in Berlin. As a result, by September 1945 the

U.S. and British embassies in Madrid compiled a list of some 1,600 Germans desired for repatriation, including all military and diplomatic personnel, espionage agents, and Germans linked to businesses that had strong ties to the Nazi regime. This list was created from existing intelligence, the input of consuls general, German embassy records, and transcripts of interrogations and interviews of Germans in Spain and Germany carried out since the end of the war. Of the 1,600 individuals named, some 650 were identified as intelligence agents.[102]

As Baldwin's memo indicates, the multiple motivations gained from dealing with Franco's Spain during the war continued to hold value for many in the U.S. embassy. The need to be as comprehensive as possible dominated the thinking of these officials. Such enthusiasm for this policy spread from the embassy to consular and intelligence officials on the ground in Spain. This can be seen in detail in regions where Allied intelligence had long been active tracking Germans, not only in Madrid but in Bilbao, Vigo, and Barcelona as well. Bilbao, along with Madrid and Barcelona, was a significant site of Nazi operations during World War II. Germans had settled in the industrial city in the eras before and after World War I and established a prominent business community there, led by Friedrich Lipperheide Henke, founder of the plastics firm Lipperheide y Guzman. Other leading businessmen from the 1920s and early 1930s included Josef Boogen, Otto Hinrichsen, and Eugene Erhardt. From 1933, and especially with the start of the Civil War in 1936, these individuals became active in the Nazi Party. Hinrichsen, for example, served with the Condor Legion. Josef Boogen had come to Spain when his father established a business there in the 1920s.[103]

The situation in Bilbao was typical of Nazi actions across Spain. Intelligence agents were sent, but a large number were in fact recruited from the existing German colony, especially as those individuals joined the Nazi Party. In Bilbao, Santander, San Sebastian, and Pamplona, British and U.S. intelligence identified forty-eight individuals for repatriation in 1945, all linked to German consulates, the Nazi Party, and/or German intelligence agencies.[104] As one member of the U.S. consulate put it, the main issue for postwar policy was which Germans to investigate "in view of the fact that there are so many Germans in this vicinity."[105]

In the Basque and Galician regions Nazi wartime operations led by the Abwehr were dominated by naval intelligence gathering during the war, especially through contacts with Spanish seamen who might have observed Allied shipping in the Atlantic and the provisioning of U-boats off the coast.[106] By 1944 the shipping of wolfram had surpassed naval intelligence as the primary purpose of Nazi operations, where German contacts with Spanish shipping and transport businesses became very useful.[107] Indeed, the firm Minerales Españoles, with German financing, not only shipped wolfram to occupied France but also served as the center of German propaganda publishing in La Coruña.[108] While these operations continued until the end of 1944, when France was liberated, the region at that point became a place of clandestine and open crossings of the border for fleeing Germans, and the Nazi structure in the area took care of these newcomers as well.[109] Bilbao also was a center of activity for German agents who were supplying German troops holding out on the Atlantic coast of France into the spring of 1945.[110]

As a result, Allied intelligence in pursuit of Nazis in the Bilbao area moved seamlessly from wartime tracking to peacetime monitoring of known agents. This involved both an identification of German businesses and Safe Haven targets, outlined by the U.S. consulate in Bilbao in June 1945,[111] and a list of Gestapo, Abwehr, and SD agents desired for repatriation to Germany, prepared by the OSS in September. This list not only included the remaining two consular officials but also a number of prominent Germans considered agents, people like Hinrichsen, Boogen, Lipperheide, and others. Similar lists were prepared for Santander, San Sebastian, and Pamplona, for the Nazi network operated as a unit throughout the Basque region.[112]

Contacts within the German colony were also important for U.S. and British officials in developing and broadening their extensive first list of potential repatriates. The man responsible for the German embassy at the end of the war, former chargé d'affaires von

Bibra, was interviewed on numerous occasions and provided extensive information on the German intelligence setup in wartime Spain.[113] Others on the repatriation lists actively sought to speak with U.S. and British officials once the war ended. The former German consul in Bilbao, Friedhelm Burbach, spent a lot of time in meetings with U.S. Consul Harry Hawley, stating that he had not been part of the Nazi Party after 1937 and that during the war he had mostly performed "humanitarian work," rescuing Germans and others, including French Gaullists, and finding them passage on ships leaving Bilbao.[114] Burbach later went into hiding because he feared repatriation, only returning to live openly in Bilbao in May 1947.[115] Friedrich Lipperheide, the Bilbao businessman, traveled to Madrid twice in 1946 to plead his case in meetings with U.S. embassy interrogators.[116] In Vigo, Donald Marelius met with most of the German colony to obtain information and to take statements, which he forwarded to the U.S. embassy. Hermann Kuhne argued that for forty of his sixty-one years he had resided in Vigo and as a businessman had traded with all sorts of companies, not just German ones.[117]

In addition to providing information on German activities, many in these meetings tried to improve their position so as to avoid repatriation. The SD agent and financier Hans-David Ziegra constantly offered to work for the United States. Ziegra visited the U.S. consulate in Seville with the former German consul general there, Gustav Draeger, on June 11, 1945. The discussion ranged from the involvement of German ships in Spain in supplying the German garrisons on the west coast of France in early 1945 to postwar Nazi activities, which Draeger stated did not exist in Seville, to individuals in Seville who had been involved in Sofindus business activities during the war. Ziegra offered to compile a list of all German companies operating in Spain.[118] Almost all the wartime German consuls general were interviewed by U.S. Consular officials, as were many other Germans. In Vigo, Vice Consul Marelius tracked down the former German consul, Richard Kindling; the propaganda chief, Gustav Kruckenberg; and the former director of the German school, Otto Habnicht, who despite being a long-time resident of Spain had returned to Germany to be trained by the Nazis in advance of taking charge of the school.[119] One of the more prominent SD agents in Spain, Walter Eugen Mosig, sent by Walter Schellenberg to Spain in 1943 under cover for Sofindus to gather political intelligence on Spain,[120] paid two visits to the U.S. embassy, in August and September 1945. There he acknowledged his activities as gathering intelligence from Spain by paying off Spanish contacts but denied any other activities, despite U.S. evidence that part of his role for the SD had been to monitor and suppress anti-Nazi behavior within the German colony during the war, or, as his interrogator in September 1945 put it, that he was "a 100% Nazi and a bloody assassin."[121]

In other instances, the U.S. consulates and the U.S. embassy relied on information provided by prominent anti-Nazis within the German colony, some of whom had nonetheless worked for the German government in Spain during the war. One such person was W. O. Frohberg, assigned to the Abwehr in Spain in 1943, who was interviewed by U.S. embassy officials in October 1945, when he provided information on the use of Abwehr and Nazi funds invested in Spanish businesses in the Barcelona area.[122] In these instances, discretion was used by U.S. authorities. The Abwehr agent Karl Schwarz von Berg was investigated and interviewed in Spain before it was determined that his role had not been significant and therefore he could stay in Spain.[123]

Those desired for repatriation were categorized in two ways, first based on their wartime activities and second based on their attitudes and actions in the immediate postwar era. In the case of Federico Lipperheide, the leading German businessman in Bilbao, evidence gathered during the war was augmented by Allied intelligence interviews with members of the German community. One of these sources interviewed by British agents indicated that in addition to smuggling iron ore to France using his company's ships, Lipperheide had been responsible for the distribution of Nazi propaganda to France and South America from his Bilbao base. The extensiveness of Lipperheide's wartime activities sealed the case against him in the eyes of the OSS, guaranteeing him a place on repatriation lists.[124] For the Gestapo representative in the Bilbao consulate, Rolf Konnecke, his wartime activities were enough to make him a repatriation target. A member of the Hitler Youth from 1926 and the SS from 1936, Konnecke went to Spain with the Condor Legion in 1938 and was placed in the Madrid embassy in 1942, then moved to Bilbao. This history alone was sufficient for repatriation, according to OSS agents, who stated quite bluntly that they were positive he would "play a prominent part in the new set-up somewhere else in Spain, using another name."[125]

Equally important to Allied intelligence was how these Nazis acted once the war ended. In addition to evidence gathered by Allied intelligence concerning their wartime activities, what evidence about Nazi agents existed after the war that raised concerns about werewolf or other types of activities that might be interpreted as a desire to continue Nazism in Bilbao? On May 8, 1945, after local officials closed the German consulate in Bilbao, a meeting of Nazi Party leaders in the community took place in the office of Otto Hinrichsen, who owned a typewriter company in town. There monies from a German tanker in port were distributed among the leading Nazis.[126] Suspicions of the creation of a Nazi "stay-behind," or "werewolf," group led to all those at the meeting being identified for repatriation. The use of wartime funds from German state or other enterprises was a clear sign to the Allies of continued Nazism. In Bilbao, many prominent Germans began living together to consolidate resources. Chief among these was Edward Bunge, who consistently withdrew funds from a variety of banks in the city and then, along with Lipperheide, began arranging hiding places for Burbach and other Germans.[127]

One of the most important Bilbao agents was Georg Demel, owner of the Bar Germania. German agents and Spaniards working with them met at the bar to coordinate activities during the war. Demel was identified as a SD agent with contacts not only in Spain but also in Argentina. The Bar Germania remained open, and after the war Demel obtained Spanish citizenship to protect him from repatriation. The continued existence of this enterprise naturally raised the suspicion of the OSS. Lipperheide too continued to operate in the open.[128]

Not every agent could operate as freely in the open as Demel and Lipperheide. Spanish authorities were very conscious of their own support for German military espionage in the Basque country, near the Atlantic Ocean and the French border. Allied intelligence reported that the Spanish High Command (AEM) was concerned that the most prominent and publicly most well known agents not be seen to be too active once the war ended. Friedhelm Burbach had resided in Iberia since the 1920s and had become the first Nazi Party representative for Spain and Portugal in 1933. His wife was Portuguese, and after the war he sent his daughters to Portugal to claim citizenship there while he stayed on in Bilbao. However, being the public face of the Nazi regime in Bilbao, he was shunned by most other members of the German colony after the war, and he purportedly paid off the Bilbao chief of police to avoid arrest. Yet that was not enough, and after being interviewed by U.S. officials in January 1946, he went into hiding in a rural part of the Basque country.[129]

A similar process of investigation and monitoring of German agents occurred in Barcelona, which, along with Madrid and Bilbao, had long been a center of the German colony in Spain. Here the significance of maintaining ties with Spanish officials or even working with Spanish officials to some extent was seen as an indication of Nazi spoiler activity. In the summer of 1945 leaders of the Francoist trade union in Barcelona recommended the former agent Karl Thie for a job at Radio Barcelona, which was seen by British intelligence as a clear attempt to continue to spread Nazi propaganda and thus a violation of neutrality by Spain.[130] In the case of Karl Moser Andress, an employee of the German firm Merck, which was believed to have been used as a cover for numerous Nazi agents during the war, relationships with prominent Spaniards paid off more directly. Because of his close ties to the Spanish police, Andress was able, in Barcelona after the war, to employ a police agent to track him and prevent his arrest, which was requested by Allied officials in September 1945.[131]

More official ties to the Franco regime were found in the case of Hans Heinemann, a German agent in France who arrived in Barcelona in 1943, where he took part in wolfram smuggling. His close wartime ties with the Spanish government led to postwar work with the Spanish military. The liberation of France in 1944 revived the desire of Republican exiles based in France to free Spain from Franco's control, and thousands of the more politically active Spanish Republicans who had participated in the French Resistance remained armed in the hope that an assault on Spain would develop. Outside of the largest attempted incursion, in the Val d'Aran in October 1944, led by the Spanish Communist guerrilla group Unión Nacional Española (UNE), most armed activity took the form of smaller border skirmishes between small groups of Republicans and border guards.[132] The Spanish response was to fortify the border by moving additional troops under the direction of General José Moscardó e Ituarte to the region. Heinemann, a close associate of Moscardó's, left his day job as a bar owner in Barcelona to work along the border two or three days a week, especially putting Moscardó in touch with his contacts in the French region of Pyrenées-Orientales.[133] Although the United States had no interest in supporting Spanish *maquis* or disturbing the peace along the Franco-Spanish frontier, the use of a former Nazi agent in the region was of concern.[134]

In Vigo, Nazi Party and Gestapo personnel were often one and the same; one German resident claimed that Conrad Meyer was head of both the party and the intelligence office there until he fled at the end of the war.[135] During the war, Galicia had been the center of wolfram smuggling, as well as a crucial base for espionage activity concerning the French border and shipping. Bilbao and Vigo were the centers of operation in the north, and the region was one where close cooperation existed between consular officials, Nazi Party members, local Spanish police, and intelligence agents. Both the Abwehr and the Luftwaffe intelligence services were active in the region.[136] The postwar transfer of intelligence materials and personnel from the German military to the Spanish government concerned U.S. investigators greatly. Thus, news of Abwehr weather stations in Galicia being taken over by the Spanish Air Ministry, but employing the same German personnel, raised alarms among U.S. officials dealing with the Franco regime in the era of denazification.[137]

More overt activities in which Nazis were seen as continuing to act as Nazis after the war also drew the attention of the U.S. and

British intelligence services. Continuing their activities and not conforming to Allied expectations as defeated opponents was possible in
the relative security of Franco's Spain. Many U.S. and British officials
feared that such activities would gradually develop in a more nefari-
ous form than simply resentment toward the Allies. Within British
intelligence, one agent, agent 23793, began tracking such activities as
the war ended with a weekly report called "23793's Gossip Column."[138]
In June 1945 the British military attaché in Madrid, Brigadier William Wyndham Torr, prepared a report in response to two concerns
raised by the War Department: continued German influence over
the Spanish military and the Falange and the role of Germans in
Spanish industry, especially industries linked to military production.
Torr reported that special temporary passports, protection from the
Dirección General de Seguridad, and access to the Falange's social
services group were granted to prominent German agents and officials beginning in May 1945, which raised the specter of continued
Nazi activity, which Torr viewed as far more likely than the Nazifi-
cation of the Falange or the Franco regime.[139] Nazis acting as Nazis,
the fear of the Nazi "stay-behind" networks that began to consume
Allied intelligence in 1944, could not be permitted following the war.

Eventually, *stay-behind* was replaced by *werewolf*, often written
as *werwolf*. The term *werewolf* came to refer to resistance against
Allied occupation and a continuation of Nazi ideology in some organized form. What was most relevant for those outside Germany
was evidence that the regime itself, in its last days, had set in place
structures for such movements, often linked to the SS.[140] On May 7,
1945, the U.S. embassy's LaVerne Baldwin reported that a number
of employees of the German government had abandoned the embassy in order to set themselves up as just such a werewolf group.
Included were the head of the German foreign-intelligence service,
Hans Thomsen, and Johannes Bernhardt. This group was closely
tied with so-called left-wing Falangists, who were angry with Franco
for letting the Germans down; they were also linked to the head of
Spain's Dirección General de Seguridad, Francisco Rodríguez Martinez. Another Nazi Party leader, Herman Heydt, was prepared to

finance the group with NSDAP money through a series of sports clubs he planned to establish across Spain.[141]

While Allied intelligence was of course focused on the leadership that had been attached to the German embassy in Madrid, it was also concerned with late arrivals to Spain who seemed to come with a specific werewolf mission in mind. One of these individuals was Teodoro Schade, alias Shubert, who arrived on a flight from Berlin with others on May 4, 1945. Once in Spain, Schade attempted to contact leading SD members and recover radio sets and other telecommunications devices. In conversations with other Germans and employees of the Heinkel firm in Spain, he reportedly stated that his mission was to "cultivate and keep high the German idea."[142] This was exactly the sort of spoiler activity that Allied authorities feared from stay-behind networks.

Other, more prominent exiles fleeing to Spain as the war ended came under the same suspicion. The most infamous of these was Léon Degrelle, the former leader of the Fascist Belgian Rexist Party and leader of the Belgian Waffen-SS in combat, whose plane had crash-landed on May 8, 1945, in northern Spain carrying Belgian Fascists with German documents.[143] Degrelle spent much of the next year in a hospital in Bilbao. Spanish authorities were not inclined to deport Degrelle, given that the 1870 Spanish-Belgian convention forbade extradition for political reasons and that many Falangists argued for his protection; indeed, the Spanish press hardly acknowledged that Degrelle was in Spain.[144] Nonetheless, with Belgium pressing and the issue subject for debate at the United Nations, Degrelle disappeared from a San Sebastian hospital in August 1946. Spain claimed he had left the country, but in actual fact he was hidden by friends within the Falange until the mid-1950s, when he obtained Spanish citizenship.[145]

Other Germans in Madrid who were connected with the German embassy and/or the Nazi Party came under immediate suspicion by Allied intelligence for continued activity once the war ended. The British shared information with the OSS about Dr. Herbert Hahn, treasurer of the Nazi Party in Spain. Briefly arrested by Spanish authorities in May 1945, he was released in June on the condition that he regularly check in with local police. From then on he was monitored by Spanish intelligence and reportedly spent his time spreading money, often counterfeit, among the Nazi community in Madrid.[146] The most notorious Madrid agent of concern to the OSS in the aftermath of the war was Hans Lazar, the former head of the press section of the German embassy in Madrid and thus the key propagandist of the Nazi regime in Spain. An Austrian who transferred from the Austrian Foreign Ministry to the German one after the 1938 *Anschluss,* Lazar served in Madrid from September 1939 until the collapse of the Nazi regime in May 1945, making him one of the longest-serving members, if not *the* longest serving, of the embassy staff. He was linked to a network of journalists and propagandists sent to Spain by the regime who remained as the war ended, nine of whom were identified to U.S. authorities by one member of the German colony as potentially troublesome.[147] One of these associates, Anneliese Muendler, a former Spanish correspondent for the Nazi paper *Voelkischer Beobachter,* parlayed her experience into a position with the *Arriba,* the official newspaper of the Falange.[148]

After the war Lazar himself set about compiling information on the German colony with the intent of gaining the protection of the Vatican for their return to Germany without the involvement of Allied occupation authorities. The Allies' belief that these individuals continued to represent Nazi views in Spain sparked Allied demands for their repatriation. Similar fears of influence over policy in Spain were expressed in the case of Herbert Vollhardt, the technical assistant to Air Attaché Eckhard Krahmer at the German embassy. Although there was nothing to suggest espionage in Vollhardt's work, and he himself willingly sat down with Allied interrogators in Madrid in March 1946, his skill as an electrical engineer and air force expert led to the OSS view that he "undoubtedly would play an important part in any plans which the Germans may have had or may later conceive for the preservation of technical 'know-how' and the continuation of scientific research outside Germany during the post-war period."[149]

At a meeting of British and U.S. officials responsible for repatriation in Madrid in August 1945 the connection to broader denazification efforts in occupied Germany was made explicit. The repatriation campaign would be implemented by the use of short lists given to the Spanish, to be followed by new lists once arrests and deportations had been carried out. In this way, the targeting of Germans for arrest would conform with denazification and interrogation priorities in the occupied zones.[150] Such a policy emphasized intelligence agents, especially SD officials who were part of the SS, who were subject to automatic arrest in Germany.[151] In this way, wrote LaVerne Baldwin, not only would the most useful figures from Spain be sent to Germany for interrogation and satisfy denazification needs but it would "have the effect of breaking up the Nazi organization within Spain by taking the ring leaders and possibly thus preventing the disappearance of too many important figures."[152] The ambitious goal of repatriation, growing out of wartime knowledge of the Nazi presence in Spain, was thus set.

CONCLUSION

Postwar Allied intelligence operations in Spain drew upon the experience of wartime intelligence gathering, where the similar goal of weakening German influence on Spain was pursued. New documents and materials allow us to have a much more detailed view of the range of intelligence operations in neutral Europe during the Second World War, and the linkages with postwar operations that these initiatives had. As the brief section on the Spanish werewolf indicates, even if Allied fears were misplaced and exaggerated, they nonetheless drove intelligence-gathering and were built on a solid history of understanding the myriad ways in which the Nazi regime, the German colony in Spain and the Franco Government had interacted with one another during the wartime years. This formed the basis of intelligence required to implement the repatriation program that followed the end of the conflict in Europe.

3

NEUTRALITY, POSTWAR POLITICS, AND
THE DIPLOMACY OF REPATRIATION

Whatever the considerations for transitional justice in Europe, punishment of criminals, investigations of spoilers, and so on, at the end of the day neutrals were very different from the defeated or even collaborationist states. They were not occupied by the Allies; they did not have new or restored governments. The practical implementation of these legal changes thus required the cooperation of neutral states like Spain. Repatriation, if carried out, was not going to be imposed, but negotiated.

As the U.S. and British governments used intelligence to put together a detailed diplomatic press, Spain inevitably was forced to play along and carry out some of the policies the Allies demanded regardless of Spain's own legal view of the responsibilities (or lack thereof) concerning wartime neutrality. However, in acknowledging the precarious position of Spain in postwar Europe, the Franco regime did not simply fall down in the face of Allied demands. The ongoing negotiations concerning the repatriation of obnoxious Germans reveals as much about Spain's fairly aggressive foreign policy as it does about the Allied desire to extend denazification beyond Germany's borders. While the Allied embassies and consulates developed on-the-ground policy based on broad ideas of denazification and their knowledge of Nazi Germany's extensive networks in Spain, the Spanish government responded with its own ideas about neutrality and about what, if anything, it owed the international community.

THE SPANISH RESPONSE

The Spanish government took very limited action in 1944 to respond to Allied concerns about wolfram smuggling and about German agents with the May 1944 agreement, internment, and some expulsions. This action was expanded upon as the war came to a close. Knowledge of the repatriation policy being developed in occupied Germany coincided with Spanish efforts to demonstrate their commitment to carry out their 1944 promises to deport Nazi agents. Spain dramatically increased the number of suspect Germans interned, with some 200 internees at the high-profile civilian internment camp in Caldas de Malavella, by June 1945;[1] by November Spain had interned a total of 1,150 Germans, which the Spanish government deemed an appropriate response to Allied demands.[2] Indeed, many of the most prominent Nazi agents and diplomatic officials were held in the camp in Caldas de Malavella for most of the second half of 1945. These individuals were joined throughout the initial postwar period by many other Nazis who had entered Spain clandestinely, including those who feared prosecution for war crimes.

It would be incorrect to compare Caldas de Malavella to prisoner-of-war or other internment camps established across Europe during World War II or even to camps in Spain meant to hold refugees, most notably the one at Miranda del Ebro. Caldas de Malavella was (and is) a spa town not far from the city of Girona in Catalonia. German internees were sent there to live in the hotels and resorts and were not permitted to leave. These hotels, working through the civil governor of Gerona, billed the Spanish government for the room and board provided.[3] Given their living arrangements and freedom of movement within the town, it can hardly be called a camp. Indeed, the British embassy protested the "laxity of the conditions" there, writing that there was "no effective restriction whatever" on contact with the outside world, which, given the individuals being held there on suspicion of espionage, made no sense.[4] A similar protest from the U.S. embassy in late 1944 elicited a response from officials at the Interior Ministry, which was responsible for the camp, that measures had been taken to prevent those present from "carrying out all activities which led to their internment" in the first place.[5] Many within the Foreign Ministry argued that since these individuals were separated from their families, many of whom were Spanish-born, and prohibited from making a living, they were actually victims at Caldas and that Spanish internment was a "moral and humanitarian problem" as much as it was a judicial one.[6]

Spain's aggressive internment policy was short-lived. The number of agents held at the camp, all from the top-priority lists provided by the Allies, went from 32 in November 1944 to 53 in August 1945 and 70 that November but had fallen to 26 by February 1, 1946.[7] Allied intelligence had information that Spanish authorities had sent word out to any Germans not interned by November 1945 that they were safe.[8] Indeed, Spain had released all but four from the Caldas camp by June 1946.[9] A typical case was that of Wilhelm Pasch, purported to be a SD agent in Bilbao and listed by the United States as involved in espionage from 1944 on. Pasch was arrested and interned at Caldas in April 1945, just before the war ended, as Spain made its most significant effort to intern those agents on Allied lists. However, Pasch was released in June 1945, returned to Bilbao, and quickly found work as a salesman for U.S.-made machinery in northern Spain.[10] Another agent, Alfred Genserowsky, head of the Abwehr in San Sebastian during the war, received orders to report to Caldas in the summer of 1945 but had not done so by September.[11] Meanwhile, Herbert Hahn, the financial manager of the NSDAP in Spain, was arrested by Spanish officials as the war ended in 1945 but never sent to Caldas; instead, as noted in chapter 2, he was released into *libertad vigilante*, which meant that he had to check in monthly with police near his home in Cuenca.[12]

While changes in international law and the apparently weak position of Franco's Spain in the early postwar period suggest that there was very limited room for Spanish assertiveness, in reality the Spanish Foreign Ministry repeatedly attempted to oppose Allied demands concerning the economic and physical presence of Germans within Spain once the war ended. The short-lived internment policy is but one example of this. Another is the conversation that took place between foreign minister Martín Artajo and the former chargé d'affaires at the German embassy, Sigismund von Bibra, on November 14, 1945. Artajo made it clear to von Bibra, whom he assumed was the primary representative of the German colony after the collapse of the German government, that seven months of inaction on the part of Spain was too long; since the Allies had created occupation zones and were changing the political order in Europe, Spain had to respond. However, he emphasized that if von Bibra encouraged voluntary repatriation of prominent Germans, Spain would be in a position to argue on behalf of the majority of the German colony.[13]

By contrast, the moral rationale behind repatriation, Safe Haven, and the subsequent Resolution VI of the Bretton Woods Agreement was apparent to various officials in the U.S. government and rein- forced their commitment to pressuring Spain to act. While repre- sentatives of the Foreign Economic Administration did not play as big a role as State Department or Treasury officials in implement- ing denazification policy, they did set the terms of engagement in a series of reports drawn up in 1944 and 1945. Here one can see the connection between the need for moral action and changing inter- national legal definitions of neutrality. The FEA argued that in effect Spain had not been neutral during the war. In terms of economic intelligence, the FEA indicated that heavy industry and the mining, banking, and transportation industries were dominated by German governmental or private firms during the war and that German law allowed the government certain rights to manage even private in- vestment; this was in addition to the government-run firms ROWAK and Sofindus, established in Spain during the Civil War. That Franco allowed this was, in the words of one FEA report, equal to giving up sovereignty over part of the Spanish economy. Indeed, it used the word *denazification* in describing the U.S. goal in Spain. Given that the Spanish government, unchanged despite the outcome of the war, could not be trusted, the logical policy to be adopted was not "a devi- ation from international law but rather a step in the development of international law which is required by an unprecedented situation."[14] The assumption here was that Spain had to conform and could not negotiate its way out of the circumstances in which it found itself.

Of course, given existing definitions of neutrality and well aware of the extraterritoriality implied in legal acts like Bretton Woods

Resolution VI, the FEA emphasized that the United States could not force Spain to comply using international law alone; while the goals might be about international law, the means were to be negotiated as a "political action." Neutrals like Spain would be technically correct in objecting to Safe Haven and repatriation under established international legal norms.[15] Similarly, officials in the State Department were reluctant to impose wartime economic controls on neutral states after the war ended and sought to create a policy that would avoid the use of navicerts, blockades, and trade controls.[16] And as late as September 1945 Ambassador Armour noted that while he constantly stressed the U.S. opposition to the dictatorial nature of Franco's regime, "I feel we must, however, not lose sight of the fact that so long as the regime remains in power it is the one we have to deal with and on whose cooperation we must rely in such matters as repatriation of Germans, Safe Haven, aviation and other questions."[17] So the extent to which neutrality was to be reinterpreted in practice was undecided and unclear. This allowed room for Spain to make its own claims.

The result was that Spain both responded to Allied demands and negotiated space for its own interpretation of the postwar situation. From 1945 on, the Foreign Ministry consistently refused to accept a broader interpretation of neutrality and postwar obligation under international law. Especially objectionable to Spain was the idea that in the aftermath of Nazism's period of dominance neutrals that had done business with Germany now bore certain responsibilities to the Allies and the broader international community. Spain's agreements with the processes of Safe Haven and repatriation were purely political, necessary given Spain's precarious international position following the war. This did not mean that Spain simply buried its legal objections to the effort to change the implications of neutrality. Indeed, in accepting a more traditional definition of neutrality, absent any concept of moral judgment, and in responding to claims that some Germans had effectively become Spanish, Spain assertively pressed the Allies to recognize that it had no legal obligation to turn over assets or to deport individuals back to Germany on the insistence of Germany's occupiers. Thus the objections made by Spain can be interpreted as a strong assertion of Spanish sovereignty in the face of the Allied states, the Allied Control Council, and international agreements that sought to limit it. These legal objections had practical implications in assuring that no negotiation over the repatriation of Germans was going to go smoothly.

The Spanish government accepted the right to seize German assets under Bretton Woods Resolution VI in May 1945 not because it agreed with new international legal norms but rather for "political" reasons, to improve its position with the victorious Allies in the aftermath of the war.[18] Nonetheless, the Spanish law created in response to the Bretton Woods resolution froze all German assets in Spain and set up a separate division within the Economic Department of the Spanish Foreign Ministry, the Servicio de Bloqueo de Bienes Extrangeros, to implement and review the freezing of assets. This group was overseen by Emilio de Navasques, director general of the ministry's Political Economy Department. In September 1945 the U.S. government suggested that these assets be placed under the authority of the ACC, which now governed Germany. This was proposed because the United States did not want neutrals to seize German assets on their own. The initiative came from the Treasury Department, which argued that given the outcome of the war, "the rights of the Allies far outweighed those of the neutrals."[19] On October 22, 1945, this proposal became Law No. 5 of the Allied Control Council.[20] Spain, however, did not accept the law.

In a December 14, 1945, document the International Legal Office of the Spanish Foreign Ministry sent a twenty-page memo to the Servicio de Bloqueo outlining its objections to the entire process that was unfolding, including the Bretton Woods Agreement and the more recent actions of the ACC. It began by asserting that international treaties such as the Hispano-German convention of May 7, 1926, and the Hispano-Italian convention of 1867 regarding property rights of non-Spanish nationals in Spain trumped anything that came after. Moreover, by forcing Spain to accept Bretton Woods Resolution VI, the Allies had effectively forced it to violate its own neutrality and side with one of the "belligerents" of the war. But having done so, the Allies could not convince the Spaniards that international law had to change, for all the actions taken by Spain concerning German assets had been "unilateral acts of the Spanish state" motivated by "high politics." While Spain had acted in such a way to placate the Allies, it could not accept the ACC as the government of Germany because Germany was occupied by the Allies and the German state had signed no treaty ceding its sovereignty. Therefore, any Allied arguments about changes in international law would not be accepted by Spain, which had frozen German assets through a "national law" and would enforce it as such—which meant not handing any assets over to the ACC. The Foreign Ministry concluded in February 1946 that its interests were not those of the international community in the aftermath of war; rather, Spanish law simply sought to balance accounts and continue to allow businesses run by nationals of various countries, including Germany, to engage in "normal economic activity."[21]

When it came to German assets, Spain did eventually turn these over to the Allies and the ACC, but only after taking monies itself. In this regard, Spain took a position earlier held by Switzerland and eventually held by all the major neutral states involved with the ACC in negotiations concerning Safe Haven.[22] Despite repeated Allied complaints that this violated the terms of Bretton Woods, Spain insisted that it had complied with the terms of the international agreement in "good faith and with a spirit of cooperation."[23] Ultimately the Allies did not press Spain on this point, and the result was a May 1948 agreement on the liquidation of private German assets that allowed Spain to keep approximately 24 percent of the first $36 million worth of assets liquidated (approximately 75% of the total assets estimated eligible for liquidation). By July 1951 Spain had ended all liquidation of private German assets, having primarily shut down larger companies or subsidiaries and without making any real effort to dispose of securities, real estate, or patents.[24]

A similar perception guided the Spanish response to repatriation. During the war, even as part of the May 1944 agreement whereby

Spain promised to expel German agents, the Spanish government had insisted on its right to investigate specific Germans based on U.S. and British lists of names but stated that any decision on expulsion was Spain's, and Spain's alone.[25] Given that Spain was working from a list of some 220 agents provided by the Allies, this process would take time. This was a source of frustration to the British and U.S. governments throughout 1944 and early 1945; in September 1944 they pointed out that 57 had been expelled and almost nothing had been done in other cases.[26] Once the war ended, it was clear that the Spanish approach would not change. As with Bretton Woods, Spain insisted on its right to conduct any investigations and make its own decisions on expulsions. The Spanish Foreign Ministry prepared information on how other neutral states were addressing Allied repatriation policy. Ireland and Switzerland retained their rights to investigate and deport individuals; like Spain, Sweden and Portugal agreed to investigate individuals based on Allied reports, but the final decision on repatriation would be theirs alone.[27] Clearly, Spain was not prepared to adhere to Allied demands if they were not being enforced elsewhere. In a crucial memorandum prepared for the minister of foreign affairs in October 1945, the European Department laid out some basic principles for Spanish policy in response to Allied demands. While acknowledging that espionage had occurred on its soil during the war and that some agents should indeed be removed from Spain, the Ministry of Foreign Affairs also was committed to doing so on its own terms; it was not prepared to enforce lengthy internments of most Germans and adopted a core position that most of the Germans named by the Allies would not be repatriated.[28]

Beyond policy, the Spanish government, as it had with regard to Bretton Woods, developed a legal response meant to limit their obligations concerning the repatriation of German officials and agents to occupied Germany. Developed in mid-1946 by the European Department, this legal argument, like the one made with regard to assets, rejected the legitimacy of the ACC's being the government of Germany. The Foreign Ministry argued that on May 8, 1945, Germany's diplomats disappeared along with Germany itself. As a result, while they lost their right to diplomatic immunity, they gained the right of individual asylum in Spain. They therefore could only be deported if Spain determined them to be active security risks or if they violated the right of asylum given to them. Since the Spanish government did not recognize the ACC as the legitimate government of Germany, any decision to expel an individual at the request of the Allies was not a legal decision but rather one made "purely from a political point of view."[29]

Legal principle and practical politics came together in the Spanish government's decision to insist on conducting its own investigations into the cases of individuals raised by the Allies, and to do so using "incorporation into Spanish life" as the most significant factor in determining whether an individual should be repatriated to Germany. This phrase was first used by the political director of the Foreign Ministry, Roberto de Satorres, in a December 1945 discussion with LaVerne Baldwin and Christopher Bramwell, of the U.S. and British embassies, respectively. Germans who had resided in Spain for many years and those with a Spanish spouse and/or children of Spanish nationality would generally be exempt from repatriation.[30] Although Satorres claimed that he would be willing to deport all Gestapo and Abwehr personnel, Bramwell underlined that many of these recruits met Spain's definition for "incorporated into Spanish life"; Satorres simply responded that his experts would give their opinion on each individual case.[31] The concept of a German "incorporated into Spanish life" was shared by others within the European Department of the Foreign Ministry, which came to oppose Spain's internment of Germans following the end of the war on the grounds that that many of the internees were long-time residents of Spain, had been separated from their families, and had no means in Caldas to earn money and support their families.[32] After May 1945 Spanish officials used funds confiscated from the German embassy to support these individuals and their families, but the funds were insufficient and those within the ministry expressed their belief that the situation of these Germans was a "moral and humanitarian" one, because they had been interned simply based on their service to their country and only a small number were real spies.[33]

What did Spanish officials mean when they conflated the concepts of "incorporation into Spanish life" and "moral and humanitarian concerns" in assessing individual cases of Germans resident in Spain? Although not in the legal sense, incorporation was something akin to citizenship. Nancy Green has written of citizenship in such a way, not to refer to legal status but rather to refer more broadly to "the included" rather than the excluded; she emphasizes the use of citizenship as "the mark of the privileged . . . as a resource." And one of the benefits of citizenship is protection by the state. The emphasis here is, first, on how individuals—and officials—seek to use ideas of citizenship and community and belonging, not on how the state defines legal citizenship. As Green writes, "This means looking at citizenship as a personal tie," as "practiced identity."[34] Second, Green emphasizes how citizenship can be instrumentalized or used for various ends, in this case to request the protection of the Spanish state and avoid repatriation. Germans seeking such protections were in a state of liminality; in providing criteria such as those linked to the phrase *incorporated into Spanish life,* the Spanish state demonstrated its willingness to apply its protection to such individuals even if it could not provide them with legal status as citizens. The meaning of citizenship here suggests the classic concept of a nation as a political or contractual community as opposed to a cultural or ethnic one.[35] Of course, as Brian Singer points out, there are no purely contractual nations, and most nationalisms include both cultural and contractual aspects.[36] Given the authoritarian basis of Franco's Spain, the term *citizenship* is used here in a way that separates it from democracy. As Singer and others have argued, citizenship is usually, and quite properly, used in democratic and constitutional contexts, where the nation is created by the constitution, to which the citizen swears loyalty.[37] But as Immanuel Wallerstein has argued, it is incorrect to assume that all definitions of citizens refer to citizens of democracies, for "the story of the nineteenth century (and indeed of the twentieth) has been that some (those with privilege and advantage) have been attempting to define citizenship narrowly and that all the others have been seeking to validate a broader definition."[38] Such ideas were definitely in play here.

How did these concepts, principles, and perspectives work out in the actual implementation of repatriation as defined by the Allies and in Spain's assertion of its own ideas in relation to the concept of being "incorporated" into Spanish life? Spain's response to the repatriation program must be examined at three levels. Foreign Minister Artajo generally desired to respond to Allied concerns, although not in a way that constituted complete capitulation. He, like other Spanish officials, wished to preserve Spain's sovereign right to make decisions on its own, but he also recognized that "the political circumstances of the moment" compelled Spain to satisfy Allied demands, at least to some extent.[39]

At a second level, among Artajo's colleagues in the upper sphere of government and the military there was much hesitation concerning repatriation, especially in cases of Germans with whom they had developed close ties during the Civil War and World War II. To give one example, on February 7, 1946, Eduardo Merrello, an undersecretary of state in the Ministry of Industry and Commerce, forwarded a note to his colleague Tomas Suñer y Ferrer, undersecretary of state at the Ministry of Foreign Affairs, noting the achievements of four businessmen the Allies wished to repatriate, underlining their "absolute friendship for Spain" and especially their support for the "commercial interests of Spain," and thus demanding that they be exempted from repatriation.[40]

Finally, at the local level, compliance with Madrid's orders, when given, was even rarer. Francisco Rodríguez Martínez, head of the Dirección General de Seguridad, reported to the interior minister, Blas Perez Gonzalez, in November 1946 that an October decree issued to all civil governors and all police chiefs across Spain authorizing the arrest of some eighty Germans had resulted in only four arrests. Rodríguez went on to state that in places with a history of large German or foreign populations, such as Galicia, he had no authority to enforce measures emanating from Madrid.[41] Occasionally bizarre comments like that of Satorres to Christopher Bramwell of the British embassy that many of those the Spanish interned were not Nazis but actually half-Jewish refugees did not help matters.[42]

REVISING REPATRIATION LISTS

Implementation on the Allied side meant constant revision. One of the first tasks assigned to U.S. consular officials, often working in conjunction with their British counterparts, was to definitively locate residents of their regions who were already on the Allied deportation lists and confirm their addresses and history. Included on the list were those well known by U.S. officials to be agents of the Gestapo, the SD, and the Abwehr. Finding those individuals involved additional intelligence gathering on the part of consular officials and U.S. intelligence agents posted within the consulates. In Vigo, U.S. vice consul Donald Marelius was provided intelligence from interrogations of other Spanish-based Nazi agents and then directed to act upon this new information. Walther Giese, a prominent Abwehr agent in Spain and South America interrogated in Berlin in the autumn of 1945,provided significant information to the United States about the structure of Nazi intelligence in Iberia.[43] Based on this information Marelius in Vigo was able to chase down and interview Karl Bock, the purported head of the Abwehr in Vigo and surrounding areas.[44]

While the U.S. embassy in Madrid, working with the British, had fairly extensive lists of German agents by the time the war ended, the process of investigation did not end with the war. German sources such as Karl Zimmer were still providing lists of Abwehr and SD agents to the U.S. consulate in Barcelona as late as November 1945.[45] From Vigo, Marelius set out in December 1945 to interview the ten most prominent members of the Nazi regime still resident in the neighboring Galician port of La Coruña. Those Germans on the U.S. embassy's list of the most sought after had largely left the region, led by the Nazi Party head, Conrad Meyer. Nonetheless, after meeting with many members of the German colony, Marelius urged the embassy to broaden its list, noting that he had met with Alois Mailly, the head of the NSDAP in La Coruña, and he recommended that Mailly and six others also be deported, for "with these Germans out of the way, any nucleus which might become a future focus of Pan Germania at La Coruña, the capital of Galicia, would be destroyed."[46] Marelius performed the same sort of operation in Vigo and argued that Hermann Kuhne, the owner of a Vigo-based medical-supply company with offices and salesmen across Spain, was undoubtedly the Abwehr's paymaster and deserved to be included on repatriation lists because he "outranks in undesirability several Vigo Germans who already figure on the list."[47]

Yet given both the Spanish response to the idea of repatriation and the difficulty of completing lists and finding all the Germans desired for repatriation, the likelihood of moving some sixteen hundred Germans from Spain was nil. The enthusiasm for the program, as evidenced among many in the early days after the war ended, quickly diminished in light of the impossibility of carrying out the task. J. M. K. Vyvyan, of the German Department in the Foreign Office, concluded in late December 1945 that "we should now concentrate on dealing with the Germans whom the Spanish are willing to repatriate" rather than moving forward with a comprehensive list.[48] Vyvyan's colleague Peter Garran disagreed, writing that as long as the Soviet Union continued to bring up the presence of Germans in Spain in places like the United Nations it was necessary to pursue the policy wholeheartedly and at least see how much the Franco regime could be pressed to act.[49] The British embassy in Madrid split the difference, arguing for a small list of desired Germans but vigorous pursuit of those cases. As one embassy official put it, the Spaniards would do their best to delay any progress, and the war had shown that "the Spanish authorities are past masters of snatching any excuse we give them for taking their eye off the ball!"[50]

Another motivation for reducing the number of Germans listed for repatriation was the practical matter of transportation. How would these Germans be moved from Spain to occupied Germany? Spain insisted on the Allies' arranging the means of transport and paying for it.[51] While this was accepted by the United States and the United Kingdom, given all the other postwar activities in Europe, it was easier said than done. When the United States raised the possibility of repatriating non-German collaborators from Spain back to their home nations—France, Belgium, and elsewhere—the British rejected the proposition, "seeing that under the much more important repatriation scheme of official and obnoxious Germans, the transport question has so far prevented an effective execution of this plan."[52] Moreover, within occupied Germany the British representative in the ACC Political Division reported that Allied officials in occupied Germany would not be able to deal with repatriates until the demobilization of the Wehrmacht was complete, in April or May 1946, and then to a maximum of one thousand people. The German Department of the British Foreign Office thus underlined that in real terms what was possible was the repatriation of a "smaller numbers of Germans such as officials and agents, whose evacuation may only be obtained at short notice, as a result of argument with the host governments."[53]

Finally, there was genuine debate among the Allied embassies regarding what constituted a clear case for repatriation, and over time that changed to reflect the reality that not everyone on the initial list of some sixteen hundred Germans was going to leave Spain. For instance, one of the agents arrested by the Spanish in October 1945 based on U.S. information was Helmut Waldemar Karl Riesterer, a businessman in Palma de Mallorca, where the Abwehr had been quite active during the war. On November 3, 1945, Riesterer was transported to Madrid to be interrogated by Earle Titus at the U.S. embassy, where he argued against his repatriation based on his expulsion from the Nazi Party in 1943 and stated that he had not worked for the Abwehr, but for the Todt Organization, which recruited laborers in Spain for German factories in wartime. Nonetheless, he had been involved in Abwehr radio-network operations across Spain and thus he was listed as an agent. By March 1946, however, Titus had begun to argue that Riesterer be removed from Allied expulsion lists because he had been resident in Spain since 1932 and had been forthcoming in his November 1945 interrogation about his Abwehr and Todt activities and because the Germans who really mattered to U.S. authorities in Germany were those attached to the SS and other groups.[54] Titus's colleague LaVerne Baldwin replied that what mattered was intelligence activity and that the Abwehr counted, so Riesterer should be repatriated.[55] In the end Riesterer was not repatriated and he returned to the embassy to meet with Titus in February 1947 in order to officially remove his name from the list of agents to be repatriated. By that time Titus had Nazi Party records from Germany confirming Riesterer's expulsion from the party in 1943. However, the British embassy still believed him to have been an important Abwehr member in Palma de Mallorca, and while he remained in Spain he was denied travel visas that would allow him to visit family in his native Switzerland until the end of 1948.[56]

A repatriation case in which there was more unanimous support for suspension was that of Harold Weinzetl. Weinzetl had been prominent in the NSDAP organization in Madrid and had worked for the Gestapo within the German colony. However, he had ties to the British; in fact his uncle was the postwar consul general for the United Kingdom in Paris. In a petition to the U.S. embassy protesting his repatriation to Germany his mother, also British, argued that her son had occasionally supplied information to British intelligence in Spain during the war. While the U.S. embassy confirmed that Weinzetl had made contact with the British military attaché, Wyndham Torr, in Madrid, it had no evidence that his information had been useful. Nonetheless, his planned repatriation to Germany, scheduled for March 4, 1946, was suspended on the advice of the U.S. embassy.[57] There is no record of Weinzetl's subsequently being repatriated to Germany. Similarly, eighty-two-year-old Eduardo Schafer y Reichert, who had been the head of Germany naval intelligence in Barcelona before and during the Spanish Civil War and an active participant in naval intelligence during World War II, was removed from repatriation lists for "humanitarian reasons."[58]

The end result was a trimming of repatriation lists because of Spanish objections, the transportation dilemma, and further debate concerning just who should be repatriated. Working from the original list of some 1,600 German officials and agents whose repatriation was desired, the British and U.S. embassies launched a diplomatic effort to force Spain to agree to repatriation on a significant, if not complete, scale. The Germans desired for repatriation were organized into different priority categories, and the top two priority lists, comprising 255 names, were presented to the Spanish government on November 12, 1945.[59] Spain responded with a list of 100 Germans it was willing to deport, although Satorres did not rule out the compilation of other lists.[60] On March 15, 1946, the two embassies presented a list of 401 names divided into three priority categories to the Ministry of Foreign Affairs in Madrid.[61] In addition, the Spanish had interned 1,237 "para-militaries"—German soldiers, border guards, and deserters who had fled to Spain from France as France was liberated in the summer of 1944 and whom the Allies agreed to move back to Germany in 1946 even though none of them met the criteria of obnoxious status or would face any investigations once back in Germany.[62]

Meanwhile, the issue became more politicized internationally. Within the ACC, January 1946 saw a debate over how forcefully to pressure neutral states like Spain to act and whether the ACC should pressure these states itself or let negotiations at the embassy level take their course.[63] Speaking in the United Nations on January 18, the Soviet Belorussian delegate Kuz'ma Venediktovich Kiselev named Germans wanted for war crimes in the Soviet Union who he claimed were present in Spain.[64] Within the British Foreign Office, Derrick Hoyer-Millar, of the Western Department, grew concerned that the Soviet Union would further exploit the situation and create complications within the ACC in occupied Germany. While Hoyer-Millar emphasized the principle of the policy—that "it should be brought home to the Spaniards that Germany had really lost the war"—he also saw the increased pressure as offering a chance to simply cut a deal with Spain and do something rather than nothing, then wrap up the policy.[65] Very quickly, then, by January 1946 Spanish reluctance and the practical issues of implementing policy, combined with a growing sense of the Cold War and Soviet meddling in Spain, had led the British to favor any action but full implementation of repatriation as conceived in the ACC statement of September 1945. In a pattern similar to the one that developed with regard to hidden German assets, then, repatriation moved from a policy connected to denazification in its broadest sense to a diplomatic sticking point with Franco whose resolution required a deal of some kind. While such a resolution would not be easy or come quickly, the dynamic on the Allied side did change, dividing those who pursued the policy in its fullest form and those who came to see it as an item in the Anglo-Spanish and U.S.-Spanish relationships that needed some action in order to be moved off the agenda completely.

That did not mean that the British, or the Americans for that matter, were willing to make a deal at any cost. In February 1946 the British ambassador to Madrid, Sir Victor Mallet, met with Spanish Foreign Minister Artajo. When Artajo complained that he was fed up with Allied pressure, Mallet replied that it was Spain that had "made the atmosphere for getting these questions settled . . . seriously disturbed."[66] Walton Butterworth, the chargé d'affaires at the U.S. embassy (and the first in charge, since in protest against Franco's authoritarian rule the United States had not replaced Norman Armour with an ambassador), also pressed Spain in early 1946, but with more optimism. He argued that despite Spain's insistence on investigating cases involving Germans with ties to Spanish life, the Foreign Ministry's acceptance of U.S. and British lists and its willingness to intern potential deportees represented "an immediate concrete basis on which to begin," although he still was concerned about Spain's use of "many ambiguous terms," which would require the Allied powers to make "persistent efforts."[67] As R. Sloan in the Foreign Office put it, while the Spanish to some extent "hold the whip hand over the repatriation of Germans," there still was merit to the arguments that the Allies could do more than simply complain and that any Spaniard who aligned himself with Nazis was "surely making himself liable to be arraigned by the Spanish people when Franco goes."[68]

The U.S. government agreed to provide air transport between Spain and Germany to extradite those candidates who were on the top-priority lists and upon whose repatriation the Allies and Spain were in agreement. This operation commenced in December 1945, with four flights planned and 80 seats secured. On December 29 two flights carried 11 and 12 Germans from Spain to Germany.[69] In January two flights were organized to carry a total of 45 individuals, but the Spanish reported that they had arrested only 33, for which the Foreign Ministry official Satorres was harshly criticized upon a visit to London at the end of January 1946.[70] On January 29 the next air transport, carrying 23 Germans, left Madrid for the U.S.-occupied zone of Germany. Although the number of Germans transported was smaller than even the number of those arrested by the Spanish, British intelligence officials considered the actual start of operations over a period of two months "a useful beginning and [it] will certainly have a sobering effect on other Germans in Spain."[71]

Air operations were extensive in February and March 1946, followed by two final flights in May and August 1946, respectively. Those on the January 29 flight included former German embassy chargé d'affaires Sigismund von Bibra; the head of the SD in Spain, Arno Kleyenstuber; and the head of the NSDAP in Spain, Hans Thomsen. These were followed by former Abwehr head Gustav Lenz on February 6; by one of the leading Abwehr agents in Spanish Morocco, Herbert Langenheim, on February 12; by the financier Hans-David Ziegra on February 25; and by the key SD agents Karl Arnold and Walter Eugen Mosig on August 23.[72] From January to March 1946, the most active period of the air operation, 65 Germans were repatriated from Spain.[73] The aircraft sent by the United States to Spain in this period could carry 128 men, but none of the flights were full. Of the 65 sent by March only 49 were from the top two priority lists of 255 Germans wanted for repatriation. Many who were supposed to be on these flights fell sick at the last moment, which only added to Allied suspicions that arrest warrants were not being issued by the Spanish Dirección General de Seguridad in these cases.[74]

Meanwhile, the border guards and other Germans were successfully transported by U.S. trains from Spain to Germany in February
1946.[75] Transport of larger numbers of Germans by boat to Germany
began in March 1945. The British ship *Highland Monarch* left Argentina and Uruguay in February 1946 with some 900 Germans, most
of them naval personnel from the German ship *Graf Spree* who had
ended up in Argentina. Arrangements were made to stop in Portugal
and Bilbao to remove other "obnoxious Germans" from Iberia, with
the aim of taking some 150 additional Germans from Spain and 60
from Portugal.[76] On February 9 the British embassy gave German
Baraibar, at the Spanish Foreign Ministry, a list of 252 Germans desired for transport via ship. These constituted the third priority list
of names of Germans compiled by the U.S. and British governments.
The Germans on this list were not sought for immediate internment
but were to check in voluntarily at the British-American Repatriation
Centre for Germans in Madrid or else be arrested by Spanish police
and be taken there to be processed for transport on the *Highland
Monarch*.[77] The creation of this list meant that by February 1946 the
names of 507 Germans had been given to the Spanish government
by the Allied powers.[78]

While the Spanish welcomed this initiative and the use of Allied
resources for physical repatriation, their compliance with the Allied
effort fell far short. Twice before the arrival of the British ship in
Bilbao, Ambassador Sir Victor Mallet met with Foreign Minister Artajo to impress upon him the need for Spain to arrest and bring to
Bilbao primarily Germans from the priority lists. By February 20,
1946, consular reports from both British and U.S. consulates general
suggested that arrests were not taking place and only 8 of the 252
designated Germans had checked in with the Repatriation Centre.
Artajo responded that he had been thinking primarily of the women
and children who would be left behind, which Mallet considered a
poor excuse.[79] Officially, the Spanish government stated that the "al-
leged slowness" of the Spanish response was "unfounded," since any
delay was only a result of the Spanish conducting their own inves-

tigations into cases because "most of the names contained in Priority Lists Nos. 1 and 2 were nevertheless entirely unknown" and thus Spain could not justify immediate detention of these individuals.[80] By March 5 the situation had improved, as 160 Germans had checked in voluntarily at the Repatriation Centre and the Spanish government promised to bring another 100 who had been arrested to Bilbao.[81] On March 7 the *Highland Monarch* left Bilbao with 206 Germans; however, although the Spanish had promised 100 individuals from the three priority lists, only 18 of the 206 passengers were named on those lists.[82]

The promised arrests did not occur, the official reason being a problem of communication between the Ministry of Foreign Affairs and the police, which Douglas Howard, of the British embassy in Madrid, dismissed owing to "the constantly Germanophile record of leading officials at Police Headquarters."[83] The majority of the repatriates were other Germans, generally not former government officials or agents, who were voluntarily leaving Spain. By the end of March, of the 507 names given to the Spanish from the three priority lists, 111 had left Spain; 105 were living in Spain under *libertad vigilante*, which meant that they had to check in monthly or weekly with police; about 100 were in hiding, and 191 had had no actions taken against them and were living openly.[84] The Spanish government had removed 80 names from this final group of 191 because of their ties to Spaniards, usually through marriage but often at the request of ministers, military officials, or other advocates.[85]

In summarizing the situation in early April 1946, Peter Garran, of the Foreign Office's Western Department, stated that despite these numbers, the Allies still held to the ultimate goal of repatriating an additional 950 officials and 450 agents.[86] It is striking that even after all the difficulty of arranging transportation and dealing with Spanish intransigence, the official number of 1,600 wanted for repatriation remained, at least in Garran's mind, and he argued that the use of priority lists was simply a tactic to get Spanish compliance, a "practical" step only.[87] Ambassador Mallet also advocated the continued use of lengthy lists because removing every Nazi influence in Spain remained his goal. He reminded the British consuls general in Spain that

Great importance is attached to the early removal of undesirable Germans from Spain by His Majesty's Government and other governments of the United Nations. . . . in many cases it is the members of the old German colony who were able to serve the Nazi best, and who by being virtually unaffected in many respects by the German defeat have retained most deeply engrained their Nazi principles.[88]

Mallet went on to outline the difficulties of transport, the efforts of Germans to avoid repatriation, and the issues of Spanish noncompliance, but he argued that with the use of ships a new effort was being made and that the Spanish had demonstrated a commitment to work harder to get individuals to the British-American Repatriation Centre. In continuing to express hope that the entire list would be dealt with he was likely in the minority in April 1946. As shown above, others had already accepted that the "practical" would likely be the best-case scenario. Nonetheless, both Mallet's and Garran's statements underline the importance that certain elements within the Allied governments would continue to attach to the repatriation policy as a test of Spanish goodwill and Spanish acknowledgment of the geopolitical situation in Western Europe after the war. Similarly, U.S. Secretary of State James Byrnes contacted the U.S. embassies in Madrid and the embassy in London on April 20 to urge that the repatriation program be forcefully pursued "to the maximum extent possible now." He said that Spaniards needed to "contradict the widespread impression regarding their complacency in giving refuge to Germans considered obnoxious by us . . . it is one easy way for them to start improving their international position if they want to do so."[89]

In the midst of these calls for more action, a new repatriation list was presented to the Spanish government on March 23, 1946. This list combined names from three previous lists given to the Spanish Government by the U.S. and British embassies—the two lists totaling 255 names in November 1945 and the list of 252 names in February 1946—minus those who had been removed from Spain. It was supplemented on April 4, 1946, by a list of 76 Germans resident outside the Spanish metropole in Spanish territories, mostly in North Africa.[90] This composite list comprised 401 names, reflecting the removal from Spain of 106 persons from the original three lists.

Even though Spanish officials were not very helpful in gathering Germans for the voyage of the *Highland Monarch,* the two Allied governments continued with more plans for maritime repatriation based on the composite list and the reduced number of aircraft for air repatriation provided by authorities in occupied Germany.[91] As a result, the British-American Centre for Repatriation in Madrid renewed its efforts to contact Germans and persuade them to voluntarily agree to repatriation, relying on U.S. and British consulates for information and to gather names.[92] The Spanish government for the first time performed its role of letting Germans in Spain know of the Allied policy and requesting their compliance. Notices appeared in Spanish newspapers in May 1946 inviting Germans to voluntarily repatriate to Germany via maritime transport.[93] This was the first time the Spanish government communicated directly with the German colony concerning repatriation; previously it had only informed the former German embassy official Sigismund von Bibra and relied on him to communicate with German citizens.[94]

Crucial for these developments in the spring of 1946 was the debate over Franco's Spain held at the United Nations. On February 26, 1946, France proposed to the United Kingdom and the United States that the question of Spain as a threat to international peace and security be placed before the United Nations. The British and the Americans were opposed to this, fearing that the forum of the Security Council would allow the Soviet Union to exploit the case, and thus they, together with France, issued the Tripartite Statement on Spain on March 4, 1946.[95] This statement outlined Franco's direct ties to Nazi Germany and Fascist Italy, suggesting Spain's inappropriateness for integration into the world community, but nonetheless called for nonintervention in Spanish affairs and asked the Spanish people to decide their own future.[96] While it is generally accepted that the Tripartite Statement was "weak,"[97] and while it did lead to France's abandoning its position to debate Spain in the United Nations, the die was cast. Poland took up the Spanish question in the U.N. Security Council, and the debate played out in April 1946, leading to the creation of a special subcommittee on Spain to investigate whether Franco's regime posed a an international threat.[98] While the British and U.S. governments did not want the United Nations to impose sanctions on Spain or to make the Spanish question a "major world issue," they nonetheless took advantage of the opportunity to emphasize that they did not view Franco favorably and that the repatriation issue was a major reason.[99] The British delegate, Sir Alexander Cadogan, speaking in the United Nations on April 9, noted that although former German military attaché General Eckhard Krahmer was supposed to have been arrested and given to the Allies for the repatriation flight in January, he was still unaccounted for.[100]

British officials referred to Cadogan's speech afterwards in a meeting with Spanish officials.[101] In the context of the U.N. debate, the British embassy in Madrid reported to London on April 26, 1946, that it had "not wasted the opportunity to strike while the iron is hot" and had pressured Spain on the question of repatriation. According to the embassy, the Ministry of Foreign Affairs in Spain "are beginning to appreciate the urgency of the position at least as regards the more important Germans on our lists."[102] Artajo admitted to Mallet on April 25 that the Spaniards had previously given German diplomats too much say in their own fate and that many had abused their freedom and now were harder to track down.[103] The actions taken in May, especially the public notices regarding repatriation, can be directly attributable to the impact of these events in April. The impact of this new geopolitical situation was also apparent to the State Department, which informed the military government in Germany to redouble its efforts in using German documents to support repatriation demands for those in Spain who had not served as officials in the German embassy positions but as agents, party representatives, and in other positions.[104]

It should not be assumed, however, that the Spanish were capitulating. In an internal memo prepared for the minister by the European Department of the Foreign Ministry in early April, it was noted that many of the eighty names Spain had insisted be removed from the Allied lists had been removed at the insistence of prominent governmental and military officials and that many of the persons named were people the United States and the United Kingdom wanted to repatriate because they had served in prominent positions during the war. Forcing the remaining Germans on the priority lists who had worked in the German embassy or consulates to leave Spain as requested by the Allied powers would help Spain "to more effectively defend the Germans actually linked to our country." In the minds of the department, these individuals were not those being protected by Spanish patrons, were on the Allied lists, and probably would voluntarily repatriate if given a small push by the government.[105] While the U.N. situation certainly played a role in forcing Spain to respond on the repatriation issue, Spanish officials did not capitulate; rather, they developed a clear and clever strategy that can only be interpreted as a Spanish belief in the strength of their position.

This was the situation in June 1946, when the United States arranged for the SS *Marine Perch* to depart Bilbao with repatriation candidates bound for Germany. The ship had berths for 947 people. Disappointment with the Spanish response was apparent even before the ship arrived in Bilbao on June 6, for by May 21 the Spanish had only registered some 235 people for transport despite having access to repatriation lists of many more names.[106] On June 8 British Ambassador Mallet held a final meeting with Foreign Minister Artajo to push for action, emphasizing the need to register individuals from the repatriation lists and not fill quotas with other Germans voluntarily repatriating, who were of no interest to the United States or the United Kingdom. Artajo replied that forcible repatriation was unpopular in the government and throughout the country and that he had been "bombarded" with requests for leniency. He added that Spain continued to "be kept in the dock" by the United Nations and the Allied powers.[107] This set the scene for disappointment. Despite

Spanish promises of 500 passengers, on June 9 the *Marine Perch* left Bilbao with 342 repatriates, including only 15 from the lists of desired repatriates and, in the words of U.S. chargé Phillip Bonsal, "no passenger of primary importance."[108] One of those who did not sail on the ship was perhaps the most prominent German in Bilbao, Friedhelm Burbach, the former German consul general there and a top-priority candidate. He was in hiding, reportedly in a secret room inside a home, which many Spaniards had built just for the purpose of hiding during the Civil War.[109]

The U.S. and British chargés d'affaires, Bonsal and Douglas Howard, confronted Artajo, asking him to explain the Spanish government's position. Artajo said that the public and most elements of the government opposed carrying out a policy "at the behest of a third party for political motives."[110] At the same time that the Allies were expressing their disappointment with the Spaniards over the *Marine Perch,* the Spanish government quietly began to cease operations at the German internment facility in Caldas de Malavella. By mid-June there remained only four internees, all of whom had been residents of Spain for more than twenty years, making it unlikely that the Franco regime would ever deport them.[111]

Meanwhile, rumors circulated that many Germans were being enrolled in the Spanish Foreign Legion as a way to avoid repatriation. Both the U.S. and British embassies raised the issue with the Spanish Foreign Ministry numerous times in the spring and summer of 1946, but few specific cases actually emerged.[112] Artajo prepared the ground for a change in policy by raising the idea of a final list of no more than some 150 Germans with the U.S. and British chargés d'affaires in August.[113] It appeared that the impetus the U.N. Security Council debate had given Spain to act in the spring was fading by the summer.

The last of the major maritime efforts at repatriation came in August, when the United States arranged for the SS *Marine Marlin* to travel to Bilbao. Following the Allies' issuance in July of a new combined priority list highlighting the remaining candidates for repatriation and revising the March 23 merger of the three priority lists, the Spanish Council of Ministers agreed in early August on the prioritization of repatriation for ninety individuals and published their names in the Spanish press, ordering them to depart on the U.S. ship at the end of the month.[114] This list was printed in a number of Spanish newspapers, such as the Falangist *Arriba*, on August 21, ten days before the departure.[115] The U.S. and British consulates and intelligence services actively monitored Spanish police activity and demanded more assertive action to correspond with Spain's public announcements that Germans should board the ship in order to be repatriated. Just days before the departure the U.S. embassy in Madrid sent the Spanish Foreign Ministry a list of names of those Germans on the priority lists resident in Bilbao who should be arrested.[116] Similarly, Phillip Crosthwaite, of the British embassy wrote directly to José Sebastian de Erice, the political director of the Spanish Foreign Ministry, demanding the arrest and transport to the *Marine Marlin* of Father Clemens Lange, a Catholic priest and "fanatical and dangerous Nazi" who was still involved in keeping Nazi ideals alive within the German colony; Crosthwaite emphasized that Lange's status as a priest made his subversive activities "all the more heinous."[117]

On August 31 the *Marine Marlin* left Bilbao with 252 Germans, including 164 brought to the vessel by Spanish police, 39 of whom were under direct arrest.[118] The involvement of the police, who were far more active than in previous repatriations, was remarked upon by Crosthwaite, who attributed this effort to Allied pressure, which had forced the Spanish Ministry of Foreign Affairs to see "the need for making a good showing this time."[119] Despite the show on the docks, however, the actual results were disappointing. A total of only 17 top-priority candidates left on either the *Marine Marlin* voyage or the final repatriation flight of top-priority candidates on August 23, and the *Marine Marlin* carried only another 25 from all other priority lists. Thus the majority of Germans removed from Spain were not on any Allied repatriation lists; they were Germans who either left voluntarily or were arrested by Spanish police and sent away. The priest Lange, in whom Crosthwaite had taken a personal interest in pursuing, remained in Spain until October 1946, when the pope ordered him to Rome in response to U.S. and British pressure.[120]

By the first of September 104 of the 255 individuals from the first two priority lists and 66 of the 252 on list 3, or 170 of the 507 whose names had been given to the Spanish by the Allies, and not even a majority of the 90 the Spanish themselves had named for repatriation, had left Spain.[121] By then even previously strong supporters of the policy, such as Ambassador Mallet, were calling repatriation a "well-worn theme" in Anglo-Spanish relations about which no one retained any enthusiasm.[122] When Mallet met with Artajo on September 16, 1946, to reproach him for the poor results of the *Marine Marlin* effort, Artajo repeated his argument that repatriation was unpopular in Spain and suggested that the time had come to end the whole policy.[123] The Foreign Office told Mallet that the debates about Spain in the United Nations and in Parliament should prove to Artajo that this was still a British priority, and Mallett reiterated to Satorres, of the Foreign Ministry, that unpopular decisions had to be made if Spain wanted to keep its relations with the United Kingdom and the United States intact.[124]

So the policy of repatriation of obnoxious Germans remained in place, the Allies pushed, and Spain returned to a position of reluctance and stalling. In December 1946 Earle Titus, of the U.S. embassy, met with Satorres in Madrid to raise again the issue of police inactivity, especially in Bilbao, Barcelona, and Valencia. Satorres insisted that the reason was no longer a lack of communication between Spanish ministries, as Artajo had suggested in July, but rather that there simply were not enough people to arrest, that the Germans desired by the Americans were gone. Titus concluded that the Spanish Ministry of Foreign Affairs, long thought to be one of the agencies of the government most likely to concede on repatriation, had now decided "to slow up, or even completely stop, arresting Germans for repatriation." What Satorres wanted, according to Titus, was to discuss matters on a case-by-case basis and only deal with those cases from the Allies' top two priority lists.[125] Satorres in fact hoped that evidence of a significant Spanish effort to round up most of the 255 top-priority candidates by early 1947 would allow the two sides to "terminate the repatriation question."[126] This mirrored the position expressed by Satorres's minister, Artajo, that instead of working from the lengthy lists created by the Allies, working from a new "short consolidated list" would be sufficient to wrap things up. Artajo raised the issue with U.S. and British officials for the first time in August and then again in September and late October.

Despite Titus's complaints in December, Artajo's idea was accepted by the Allies, for Victor Mallet, in Madrid, concluded that "it is quite clear that we shall never get rid of all Germans here but by concentrating on the worst specimens we may get some result."[127] Within the British Foreign Office, Derrick Hoyer-Millar expressed the majority opinion when he concurred that the focus should be on removing a select number of "important individuals," not worrying about "the lesser fry," and moving on.[128] The U.S. embassy in Madrid agreed and called for a "fresh evaluation" of the repatriation issue in a telegram to the State Department dated November 18, 1946.[129]

It is important to note that the resignation apparent in the memos of both British and U.S. officials in the autumn of 1946 was not universal. One memo that emerged from within the U.S. embassy in September 1946 argued that the danger of a continued Nazi presence in Spain "cannot be overestimated" and that "Nazis in Spain become a political and economical menace to security" if left alone.[130] Titus, the U.S. embassy official most responsible for repatriation by the end of 1946, was consistent in demanding that the Spanish act more aggressively, as his December meeting with Satorres demonstrated.

Nonetheless, Spain had survived the renewed focus on its German colony in the U.N. Security Council, and by November the Security Council had removed Spain from its agenda, so that the Spanish case would in future be debated only in the less visible forum of the General Assembly.[131] Its position on repatriation thus became one of greater reluctance than at the start of the year.

CONCLUSION

Over the course of 1946 Allied diplomats in Madrid, London, and Washington made a concerted effort to press Spain on the repatriation issue, develop priority lists from the original target of some 1,600 Germans, and provide the means to repatriate these Germans from Spain to the occupied zones. While the Spanish did move and the repatriation of some 170 individuals did occur, more often the gap between Spanish official promises and actions frustrated British and U.S. officials. In the last quarter of 1946 Allied officials began to debate what form repatriation policy might take in 1947 and beyond. While for an individual like Mallet the constant meetings with individuals at the Spanish Foreign Ministry were the source of frustration, Allied consular and embassy officials understood that the real reason why Spain was not arresting and handing over Germans was the dynamics on the ground, within the Spanish police, Spanish communities, and the German colony itself.

4

PETITIONS TO FRANCO

German Activism and the Fight to Stay in Spain

Germans actively engaged in Nazi intelligence operations and official economic or political work in Spain during World War II often were veterans of the Condor Legion or had been involved on the Nationalist side in the Civil War. Others had been resident in Spain from before the Civil War. Appealing to Spanish officials, who ultimately would be responsible for implementing their repatriation to occupied Germany, these Germans used that history to request exemption from repatriation. The memory of the Nationalist cause was invoked by these Germans as a way to detract from or downplay their role in the Nazi cause during World War II. Their ties to Spain were documented in every detail. The archives of the Spanish Foreign Ministry contain hundreds of petitions from Germans seeking exemption. The language and arguments used by these ex-functionaries and agents of the Nazi regime in Spain offer a unique insight into one of the unexplored uses of the memory of the Civil War in Franco's Spain. Unlike Nazis who claimed little affiliation to the hard-core ideology of Hitler, ex-Nazi officials and agents in Spain could argue that they *had* been motivated by ideology and that they had made a political commitment—to Franco. If that was not enough, many argued that through familial relationships, marriage, and attitude they were more or less Spaniards. Some even tried to legally obtain Spanish citizenship. In short, using a variety of means, Germans facing repatriation from Spain drew upon a unique history to advocate for themselves and shape their own postwar future. In seeking to avoid the denazification procedures that would follow deportation from Spain, these ex-Nazis cast themselves as associates and partisans of one of the last remaining dictatorships in Europe.

As noted in the previous chapter, Spanish officials were willing to exempt Germans from repatriation if they concluded that such individuals were "incorporated into Spanish life." Numerous Germans adopted the language of citizenship to request exemption even though actual legal citizenship was rarely possible. Again, Nancy Green's concept of citizenship as a resource, as a means of obtaining protection from the state, is significant. This choice was possible even in an authoritarian state like Franco's, and one made easier by terms defined by Franco and his regime themselves.

How could Germans wanted for repatriation tap into the existing dialogue about belonging in Franco's Spain to protect themselves? If we take Green's idea that citizenship can be interpreted as social, not necessarily legal, or, as Green puts it, as "practiced identity," then it can be found in post–Civil War Spain. There was, in the aftermath of the Spanish Civil War, a clear discourse about what membership in the New Spain meant and what it entailed. Moreover, in the case of these Germans the claim to have been loyal to Franco's Spain was a claim made by choice, or at least cast in the language of choice.

In reality, many of these Germans did not disavow their ties to Nazism and its history while proclaiming their commitment to Franco's Spain. Indeed, the continuation of Nazism remained a prominent part of life in the German colony in Spain. Germans wanted for repatriation pursued a variety of avenues of argument to emphasize their ties to Spain, all of which advanced the claim that these Germans, despite wartime and even postwar activities that associated them with Nazism, wanted to be seen as Spaniards, or at least as allies of the causes Franco had pursued during and after the Spanish Civil War.

THE GERMAN COLONY, NAZISM, AND ALLIED OFFICIALS

When World War II came to an end, the German colony in Spain was large and economically significant. Many of its members had been compromised politically owing to membership in the NSDAP and through service to the German government during the war through official or supposedly covert intelligence operations. As outlined briefly in chapter 2, German commercial activity in Spain had been growing since the turn of the century, as had the size of the German colony. This activity had intensified during the war as Nazi Germany became Spain's primary supplier of industrial goods and Spain sent 30–40 percent of its exports, mainly food, minerals, and other raw materials, to Germany. The Germans who remained in Spain at the end of the war held considerable resources in the chemical, electricity, banking, and security industries.[1] They had ties to many Spaniards and to Spain, as well as fairly secure economic positions. In contrast, if they returned to Germany, they faced guaranteed interrogation by the occupying powers, the possibility of internment and trial, and an uncertain economic future. Thus most had many reasons to stay where they were.

Yet the Germans did not attempt to leave their wartime past behind. Many members of the German colony attempted not only to avoid repatriation but also to continue to develop a Nazi identity within the community. One of the major objectives of Allied intelligence in 1945 and 1946 was to measure the continued existence in Spain of overt Nazi activity. As demonstrated in chapter 2, when the war ended Allied intelligence operatives feared the creation of active Nazi stay-behind, or "werewolf," groups within the German colony. This activity did not diminish with the passage of time and remained a prominent feature of Allied intelligence work and was useful evidence to show why particular Germans remained on the top priority list for repatriation.

One of the most intriguing members of the German colony in Spain was Hans Ziegra, who had been a New York financier in the 1930s and served with the West German Foreign Service in Brazil in the 1960s.[2] Ziegra's U.S. company, the New York Overseas Corporation, was dissolved in 1941 by U.S. law.[3] Prior to coming to the United States he had been a broker in Rio de Janeiro and acquired Brazilian citizenship in 1932. By 1939 he had joined the Gestapo in Norway and Paris, and then he was posted to Lisbon and Rio de Janeiro before being posted to Madrid by the SD in May 1943. His work for the Gestapo in Lisbon in 1941 involved "the handling of accounts for Jews departing from Germany for other countries," especially arranging the transfer of money collected from Jews for emigration from the Reichsbank to other institutions, collecting a broker's fee himself for each transaction.[4] Apparently this personal corruption led to Ziegra's arrest by the Gestapo, but it did not lead to a jail sentence only because he was picked up by the SD for work in Madrid. He was valuable to the SD because it was working to establish solid links between Spain and Latin America under the SD commander in Spain, Karl Arnold.[5] Nonetheless, this work did not last, and he was sent back to Germany in the autumn of 1944, returning to Madrid in April 1945. Living openly in Madrid after the war, Ziegra was the subject of investigations by Allied intelligence for his supposed efforts to create a "new SD." In October 1945 there were reports that he and a number of other former SD agents had left Madrid for a rendezvous in Málaga to discuss this and meet with others from across Spain, although they had all named different towns in Andalusia as their vacation spots when reporting to the Spanish police.[6] Rumors circulated that at the same time that Ziegra was implicated in the effort to form a "new SD," he was trying to negotiate with members of the U.S. intelligence community in Madrid and to deal in South American passports on the black market.[7]

Other supposed werewolf groups, while never large in number nor ever a real threat to the Spanish state or security in general, were nonetheless active as Nazis, as well as on the lookout for favors from the Spanish government and perhaps even influence over the Franco regime on certain matters. Interrogations of former German embassy employees in Madrid revealed that in the last months of the war General Eckard Krahmer, the air attaché, had accumulated some 7–9 million pesetas through the sale of German aeronautical equipment and that the money had been used to fund werewolf activity.[8] Krahmer worked with the former naval attaché at the embassy, Kurt Meyer-Doehner, to establish a group called Kampfgemeinschaft Adolf Hitler. Their base was the Erika Bar in Madrid. Using the funds Krahmer had raised, by July 1946 they had established a list of former Nazis who had cooperated with Allied investigators and targeted them for "liquidations"; how many were actually killed is unclear from the documents.[9] Reports from other sources also indicated the potential role of violence against anti-Nazi Germans within such groups. Former SD agents working with Gestapo and Nazi Party officials had established an "expulsion committee" to denounce anti-Nazi Germans to the Spanish police and have them deported.[10] In May 1946 one of the werewolf groups, Edelweiss 88 (the number 8 represented the letter *H*, so "88" meant "Heil Hitler!"), kidnapped a prominent German outside of Seville, robbed him, and then threatened him with death if he spoke to Allied authorities or to other Germans about the incident.[11]

Over time, as these groups and their sources of money and locations became more established, they moved from clandestine werewolf activities to more open advocacy for their cause. The evidence of this was best summed up by a source working with U.S. intelligence identified only as "Eva," who reported in mid-1946 that "the general tendency of the Nazis during these months has been to work more and more openly and to convince the more moderate or scared Germans that *no pasa nada* from the side of the Allies. I find the situation worse than it was a year ago, when there was a great confusion and a general feeling of insecurity among them [the Nazis]." According to small talk reported to Eva, many Nazis were now willing to advise others to "keep strong because the Allies are in quarrel and our hour is near."[12]

While the violence linked with werewolf activities had a sensational element to it, far more common was the mere Nazi presence within the German colony that "Eva" referred to. For Allied intelligence, monitoring such activity was important and further evidence of the need to follow through with the repatriation policy. The U.S. embassy in Madrid cultivated one informant, a Frenchman named Roger Tur (code-named "RIC"), who had been working for the Allies in the region of Zaragoza since 1944.[13] He continued to report on Nazism within the German colony into the postwar period. Tur had previously been closely affiliated with the Vichy regime in France and had many contacts within Spanish and German circles in Spain.[14] As early as October 1945 he reported that radio contact had been established between pro-Nazi elements in Bavaria and in Zaragoza, and there was general agreement that the German colony should support Franco "in order to annoy the Allies."[15]

These reports from Zaragoza were representative of what was being observed across Spain. Most Allied agents overplayed the initial fear of werewolf activities and by early 1946 came to see much of what was reported from Germans in Spain as "pure bombast and 'wishful thinking,'" not a real threat to peace or security internationally, within Spain, or even locally. Allied officials came to accept that there was no real wireless radio communication with Germany and that the idea of a network of agents linked via radio across Europe was fictitious.[16] Of greater concern was the fact that the longer Germans stayed in Spain, the more their infiltration into Spanish life and the possibility that they would influence important elements of Spanish society and politics grew. This was a fear that such Germans would introduce elements of Nazi ideology into Spain. The involvement of these Germans in the organization of anti-French demonstrations in Zaragoza in February 1946, when France was in the midst of debating its own policy toward Spain domestically and within the United Nations, is one example.[17]

The potential for a Nazi influence in Spain was also seen in the cases of individuals who obtained prominent positions within Spanish institutions and thus began to establish successful postwar careers in Spain. The former cultural attaché of the German embassy, Hans Juretschke, managed to move into education, teaching German at the University of Madrid, where in May 1946 he opened a German library. The majority of the books were relics of the Nazis' Propaganda Ministry collection sent to the embassy in Madrid. The OSS report on Juretschke from late 1946 called him "the link between Nazi *Kultur* and Gestapo" and described his postwar activities as nothing less than a continuation of Nazi cultural propaganda in Spain.[18] In June 1945 Dr. Heinz Franz Josef Schulte-Herbruggen, a lecturer on German language and literature at the University of

Murcia, presented himself to the U.S. embassy in Madrid as an anti-Nazi and informed the embassy of the German influence within the Spanish education system. His own views, well known as anti-Nazi, led to harassment from other Germans participating in the Spanish university system, especially the German lecturer at the University of Madrid, Juretschke.[19]

ALLIED OFFICIALS AND THE SPANISH POLICE

Beyond carrying out investigations into individuals and groups desired for repatriation or to monitor activities that seemed to suggest a continuation of Nazism, U.S. and British consuls in places like Bilbao and Vigo were charged with following up with Spanish authorities on implementation of repatriation, or at the very least reminding Spanish authorities to limit German activity in Spain. If Spain had already agreed to arrest individuals for the purpose of preparing for their repatriation to occupied Germany, it was the job of the consulates to make sure it happened. One of the most significant moments came in the spring of 1946, when ships to be provided by the United States were organized to move Germans from Spain to Germany. In Vigo, even before such publications, U.S. Vice Consul General Donald Marelius reported that Spanish police had personally visited all registered Germans to inform them of this option and that he had offered his intelligence on German residents to police to help them accomplish the task.[20]

Numerous reports suggest that local police often failed to act, or made limited efforts, to arrest Germans desired for repatriation. Foreign Minister Artajo expressed his personal frustration with the police on many occasions, and in mid-1946 he ordered the Interior Ministry to launch a national investigation into local inaction.[21] In February 1946 Harry Hawley, the U.S. consul in Bilbao, reported that he had established a positive working relationship with the local chief of police, who not only carried out arrests but oversaw the German internment camps at Sobrón and Miranda del Ebro.[22] Nothing was permanently resolved, however, for in June Hawley filed a number of complaints with the police on their failure to arrest Germans before they went into hiding or "escaped" police custody.[23] This was followed up by a complaint from the U.S. embassy in August 1946 that although police in Bilbao had issued arrest warrants for seventy-six individuals in the city wanted for repatriation, they had not done so for another eighty-eight in similar circumstances.[24]

In Vigo, the consulate reported on numerous Germans traveling from Galicia across Spain, something forbidden by a decree of the Spanish government; what was worse, many of those desired for repatriation often traveled with Falange identification cards, not German passports.[25] Vice Consul Marelius expressed his frustration that Germans were not being added to the repatriation lists because no Spanish authority or individual was pushing for action. According to Marelius, Germans in Vigo simply denied their involvement in Nazi espionage, pointing to those Germans who had already left as the only culprits, and no Spanish witnesses or Spanish accomplices came forward to verify intelligence reports he was receiving. He concluded that further work on his part would be "useless."[26] The British embassy concurred, filing a complaint with the Foreign Ministry in August 1946 that police in Vigo were deliberately given lists of individuals to be arrested for repatriation that did not live there. As a result, no arrests were carried out in Vigo even though individuals on the Allies' top-priority lists lived there.[27]

In Málaga, U.S. Consul General Harold B. Quarton attempted to ascertain just what orders the police had received regarding local Germans on Allied lists. He determined that by midsummer no arrest orders had been issued despite the fact that it was in the spring and summer of 1946 that the air and maritime transport of repatriates was at its height. At a meeting between officials of the U.S. consulate and the local police in Málaga on August 12 the police produced lists of 74 Germans on Allied lists in the Málaga region, 42 of whom the police had instructed to voluntarily repatriate, with the remaining 32 to be subject to "more special methods" to get them to repatriate. For Quarton such measures fell far short of official arrest orders.[28]

GERMAN ADVOCACY

The earliest investigations were of the most prominent and public individuals associated with Nazi activity in Spain. Many of these individuals, knowing they would be investigated, directly contacted British and U.S. officials in order to plead their cases. The most infamous case in this respect was that of Johannes Bernhardt, the director of Sofindus. Bernhardt was, simply put, the German most engaged in Spain from the beginning of the Spanish Civil War to the postwar period. A member of the Nazi Party's Auslandorganization in Spain, Bernhardt had been instrumental in securing Nazi Germany's assistance in the military rebellion of July 1936.[29] He had gone on to lead HISMA (Hispano-Marroquí de Transportes), which, together with ROWAK, managed all trade between Germany and the Francoist zone during the Civil War. While the majority of HISMA's financing came from Franco's government, ROWAK eventually created eleven different companies and negotiated with Franco to secure 40 percent ownership in the massive MONTANA mineral project, which developed near the end of the conflict. Sofindus was one of the offshoots of ROWAK, created in 1939 to manage all German investments in Spain. Bernhardt was its director from the beginning. Subsequently, during World War II, Sofindus spun off a number of companies, the most significant being Compañía Marítima de Transportes, also known as Transcomar.[30]

Bernhardt worked closely with Hitler's director of the Four-Year Plan, Hermann Göring, in developing German economic plans for Iberia, which often coincided with military-intelligence operations. One prominent example was a German commercial-fishing exploratory mission to the Canary Islands in the summer of 1938 that also sought to assess the islands' potential use as a refueling and supply post for German U-boats.[31] Early on, then, German economic activity in Spain and German espionage were closely linked, and the distinction between private, state, and para-state assets to be examined after the war was rarely clear. This pattern continued, with Bernhardt, Sofindus, and especially Transcomar involved in a number of operations that, ostensibly commercial, were linked to supplying and assisting the German military. One of the largest occurred late in the war and involved German companies in Spain supplying German troops in France from the Cantabrian coast from January to March 1945. Beyond these specific operations, employment with Sofindus and its many subsidiaries often provided cover for SD agents like Walter Mosig. For his wartime service, Bernhardt ended the war with the SS rank of Oberfuhrer.[32]

With the end of the war and the acquisition of official state assets and buildings by the British, French, and U.S. authorities as representatives of the ACC, Bernhardt and Sofindus were of immediate priority to Allied investigators. A full report of Sofindus assets and holdings, with an annex outlining the personal holdings of Bernhardt himself, was issued in July 1945.[33] Although Sofindus was legally registered as a Spanish holding company, the Allies insisted that its offices and assets be considered the equivalent of German state enterprises because of its links with ROWAK, which was an entity of the German government.[34] Meanwhile, in Hamburg Allied investigators pored over ROWAK's books and interrogated ROWAK officials based in Germany.[35]

Later, the former economic counselor in the German embassy in Madrid, Walter Becker, revealed that both the embassy and the central government in Berlin had ran two different accounts, one for Sofindus and one for Bernhardt personally, which again led to the conclusion that Sofindus should not be treated as merely a Spanish enterprise.[36] As a result of Becker's revelations, in June 1945 Bernhardt himself proposed a meeting with Allied officials and offered to assist them in going through Sofindus documents, stating that he feared the cloaking of Sofindus assets in the names of Spaniards would lead to the Spanish government's protecting those assets rather than turning them over to the Allies.[37] Bernhardt worked with the Allies while maintaining a prominent position among Nazis in Spain, as well as with his contacts in the Spanish government. Such offers to assist Allied investigations were not uncommon in Spain or in occupied Germany, where SS members in particular often volunteered their services.[38]

Bernhardt met with U.S. and British embassy officials in Madrid in July 1945. His initial statement to these investigators demonstrates a good deal about the inability of the Nazi community in Spain to separate their work for the German cause, their ties to Spain and the Franco regime, and their fear for whatever fate they might face at the hands of the Allies:

We know that Germany has lost the war; we are without a country and we do not know what the future will bring us. We live in a neutral country to which we have been united for many years in certain common interests and from time to time with certain friendships. Everything we have done here has been done with all due correctness and if occasionally there were certain "actions," it was always done with consent. We dispose of good, proved friendships. We are disposed to place ourselves at your disposition, believing we can be useful. I only request that you not ask things that go against our and my honor. Our idea must be to think, if possible, in a constructive manner so that we not become slaves but can work and be useful in constructive labor in Europe.[39]

Certainly one must take Bernhard's words with a grain of salt. He was, after all, being interviewed by U.S. and British officials as the leading Nazi in Spain. However, his words are representative of important sentiments within the Nazi community in Spain. The end of the war left them, in Bernhardt's description, stateless. In the interwar period numerous states denaturalized various groups, usually for ethnic reasons, as the Nazis did German Jews. Now Bernhardt was claiming statelessness in the minimal sense of losing the state's protection.[40] Of course there was a government in postwar Germany, the Allied Control Council. Yet because Bernhardt did not recognize the Allied occupiers of Germany as the legitimate government there, he considered himself stateless.

Bernhardt and other Germans in Spain had another option besides seeking international protection as stateless, however. There was another state that could protect him—Spain. While acknowledging the lack of any legal tie between Germans resident in Spain and the Franco regime, he used the word *united* to describe the relationship between Germans resident there and the Spanish state. Bernhardt proposed that his personal and other ties in Spain could be used as a basis to stay and thus could be used to reject any consideration of repatriation to occupied Germany. He sought to claim a status that, even if not a legal one, would serve some of the same purposes, especially to protect him from repatriation.

To complain about the role of the occupier in postwar Germany was not new or unique to Germans in Spain. Bernhardt's language is similar to that used by other high-profile Nazis in Germany and elsewhere in their efforts to avoid trials, civilian internment, and other potential impositions on the part of the Allies. Across Germany, Allied occupation and reeducation policies coexisted with a bureaucratic, professional, political, military, and clerical elite that consistently "sought to undermine its [Allied policy's] foundations to the end of creating a 'usable past' on which German national identity could be reconstructed."[41] If one perceives Safe Haven and the search for "obnoxious" Germans in neutral states like Spain as part of a broad denazification program based on JCS 1067, then Bernhardt's interpretation of his position in Spain was simply a different take on the consistent unpopularity of denazification measures inside Germany.[42] As Jeffrey Herf has written about Konrad Adenauer and the emerging Christian Democratic position on denazification in 1946 and 1947, "The best way to overcome Nazism was to avoid a direct confrontation with it."[43] Arguably that sentiment was shared by the so-called obnoxious Germans in Spain, although they could do more than ignore it; as Bernhardt demonstrated, they could draw upon other ties, those with Spain, to divert attention away from the immediate past.

Some Germans decided on their own to return to Germany, where they went through denazification processes as if they had been found there at the end of the war. The British and the Americans established the British-American Repatriation Centre in Madrid to process these cases. However, voluntary repatriation rarely involved those ex-Nazi intelligence agents so desired by the victorious wartime powers. For example, of the 207 Germans who left for Bremen voluntarily on board a U.S. ship in August 1946, only 2 were on the list of those desired for repatriation compiled by the British and the Americans.[44] For many of the Germans most sought by the Allies, the knowledge of repatriation was widespread and the desire to conform was minimal. Germans who either were targeted for repatriation or feared they would be took the initiative of requesting permission to stay in Spain and built upon Bernhardt's initial arguments made in the summer of 1945 by petitioning the Spanish government. In these petitions a number of consistent themes emerge. One of the most striking is the claim that any political, espionage, or related activity was undertaken in the spirit of the Spanish Nationalist cause, not Nazism, and especially not Nazism in a way that harmed Spain during World War II.

SERVICE TO FRANCO:
GERMANS AS NATIONALIST CRUSADERS

Those Germans most likely to take up the pen in their own defense were those who knew they were on the priority lists for repatriation, those who had been the most active Nazis during the war—agents and party and diplomatic officials. Before examining the words of these Germans themselves, it is important to look at the Francoist discourse of the time about the Civil War, for this discourse was the most commonly employed by Germans seeking to stay in Spain. As Paloma Aguilar has written, examining official discourse allows us "to study the kind of version of the Civil War that the regime wished to convey to the generation that had not lived through the war, as well as to those that had taken part in it."[45] German veterans of the Civil War could use that discourse to shape their own defense against Allied demands for their deportation back to occupied Germany.

Aguilar argues that the key to early use of the war's memory came in Franco's argument that his coup and the subsequent civil war had been necessary to provide legitimacy to government, a legitimacy that he believed the Second Republic had failed to produce. In the view of Franco and his movement, because the Second Republic did not contain political violence, defend the church, and protect the unity of national territory, it was illegitimate. The fact that the right wing saw the influence of outsiders, especially the Soviets, as part of the Second Republic's makeup only added to the charges against it. Even if civil war was necessary, however, and not a choice, it was nonetheless purifying, and the total defeat of the enemy renewed Spain. The language associated with such depictions of the war included such phrases as *crusade, war of national liberation,* and *glorious uprising.* As Aguilar concludes, "It was a matter of good against evil, of Spanishness against anti-Spanishness, of believers against atheists, of law-abiding people against anarchists, of reason against barbarians."[46]

It is useful to consider the initial post–Civil War period, roughly 1939–47, as a revolutionary transitional era, one in which the state was engaged in significant nation building. There were aspects of social engineering in an attempt to purge the state of the those who had been on the losing side in the Civil War and to assert new ideas of citizenship and patriotism. Such ideas were present in the concentration camps established by Franco after 1939, called the "laboratories of the New Spain" by the historian Javier Rodrigo.[47] The concentration camps were set up to punish and in many instances kill opponents of the regime, but they also had a "social function of indoctrination [and] re-education."[48] This moment of great focus on establishing a "New Spain" could easily be tapped into by others, such as the Germans facing repatriation. In textbooks used in the education system and in the public celebrations of the war's key dates, July 18, 1936 (the beginning of the coup against the Second Republic), and April 1, 1939 (the end of the war), such language and imagery were prevalent in Spain in the 1940s. Commitment to this memory of the conflict was especially strong among Nationalist military officers, with whom the German military attachés and intelligence agents had considerable contact.[49]

Antonio Cazorla-Sánchez has built on these ideas in describing what Spaniards understood as citizenship in the late 1940s. As he writes, "nationalism and dictatorship were used interchangeably" in official language. Citizens accepted the regime's argument that democracy meant a return to chaos and civil war, and they supported the regime in mass demonstrations when the United Nations condemned it in December 1946. As Cazorla-Sánchez writes, "Spaniards may or may not have completely believed these assertions, but the mere possibility of again falling into civil strife drove ordinary people to support the notion that peace could only be preserved by Franco."[50] Thus Spaniards reinterpreted what it meant to be a Spanish citizen, and many did indeed participate in the regime's projection of community and identity.

Just as Spaniards participated in this time of upheaval and redefinition of loyalty and citizenship, so too did their German neighbors in seeking to defend themselves from the threat of repatriation. First they underlined their service in the Condor Legion during the Spanish Civil War as a service to Spain, not to Germany. Many people could justify this claim with evidence of direct service to Franco in addition to service in the Condor Legion. One such person was Max Nutz, a former employee of the German embassy who served as an interpreter for the air attaché in Madrid from 1939 to 1943. Nutz had come to Spain in 1926, after serving in Morocco with the Spanish Foreign Legion. He settled in Alicante, where he was an active member of the German colony, and joined the NSDAP in 1935. During the Civil War he had served in the Condor Legion. He argued, however, that any service to the Nazi cause was only based on "patriotism and obligation"; the work that had most inspired him was service in Morocco and in the "War of Liberation," fighting for Spain.[51] Similarly, Alfred Giese, who had resided in Spain for twenty years, wrote that he considered Spain "my second country"; and he said that his work in the Condor Legion during the "war of liberation" had led to his being awarded two Spanish military medals, the Cruz de Caballero de Isabel la Católica and the Cruz de Caballero de la Orden de Mehdauia. His wartime service was to a private German firm in Málaga, Casa

Scholtz Hermanso, and thus he found his arrest in 1945 shocking, especially considering his "service to Spain."[52]

Meino von Eitzen was a top target for U.S. and British intelligence. Arrested by Spanish authorities in December 1944 based on U.S. evidence that he was a German intelligence agent, he was one of the last internees held by the Spanish in the Caldas de Mallavella camp, until mid-1946.[53] Spanish Foreign Minister Lequerica considered von Etzen to be too "political" to be granted special consideration and released.[54] In his bids for early release from internment, von Eitzen sent records of his Condor Legion membership, his military awards from Spain, and his membership in the Falange, which went back to 1936. Von Eitzen also had letters of support from the head of the civil government in Vigo confirming no German political activity on his part, as well as from the office of Francisco Franco himself verifying von Eitzen's military and political service to Spain.[55] Eventually the minister of the navy, Admiral Salvador Moreno, advocated on von Eitzen's behalf, underlining not only his service in the Condor Legion but his service to the Spanish navy in Vigo as well.[56]

Similarly, Alfred Genserowsky emphasized his service to Spain. Identified by the OSS as the leading Abwehr agent in San Sebastian, Genserowsky played a prominent role in coordinating Abwehr naval intelligence activity in northern Spain with agents of the Spanish military, especially the Spanish High Command.[57] His name first appeared on Allied lists for expulsion in March 1944.[58] Orders were issued for his internment in Caldas de Malavella in May 1945, and one of his collaborators within Spanish Military Intelligence, or SIM, José Jiménez y Mora, was arrested by Spanish officials for being too close to Nazism.[59] In appealing his own order for internment, Genserowsky requested an exemption owing to his wife's ill health and asked to be permitted to reside in Segovia, where his wife was receiving medical treatment. He also noted that he was "an ex-combatant in the Spanish Crusade of the Nationalist columns."[60] His petition was supported by General Martinez de Campos, of the Spanish High Command, who emphasized that Genserowsky had been injured during the Spanish Civil War, when he acted as a translator for the Condor Legion, and that he was "un mutilado."[61] Although Genserowsky eventually decided to conform and was voluntarily deported to Germany in August 1946, he was not arrested while in Spain, and he was permitted to settle in Segovia until he left. He returned to Spain in April 1948.[62]

As early as 1944, before the war ended, investigations into potential German agents carried out by the Dirección General de Seguridad were constrained if the persons in question had served in the Civil War. One of the earliest investigations of Germans based on U.S. and British accusations of spying was of three individuals—Hans Kellner, Ricard Herberg, and Alfred Klaevisch. None of these men was deemed a spy; and mentioned most prominently were, first, their time of residence in Spain, which in all cases had began in the 1920s or earlier, and second, their service to the Nationalist cause in the Civil War. Klaevisch worked for the Spanish Red Cross during the Civil War and then for the Naval Ministry; Herberg aided Spanish refugees in Germany during the Civil War; and Kellner not only served in the Condor Legion but acted as a liaison between the Legion and the Spanish air force, and he trained pilots for the Spanish air force after the Civil War.[63]

In the case of Otto Hinrichsen, the most notable German activist in Bilbao during the war, his long residency in Spain and his service in the Condor Legion led to a position within the Spanish army itself. Owing to this and to his subsequent work in Bilbao, he was, in the eyes of one member of the Spanish Foreign Ministry, an "ideological enthusiast" for the Franco regime, who said that Hinrichsen's inclusion on Allied repatriation lists was an "injustice."[64]

The arguments that one might expect to have been presented in 1944 were still being put forward by the Spanish much later. In 1947 the U.S. and British embassies, facing the real failure of the repatriation program in terms of numbers actually deported from Spain, came up with a final list of 104 Germans wanted for deportation.[65] The Political Economy Department of the Spanish Ministry of Foreign Affairs divided these individuals into three categories: intelligence agents, most of whom probably would have to go; friendly Germans, who could be forced out if the British and the Americans became insistent; and Germans to be protected without question. In this third group there were certainly many Germans who had been, and continued to be, leaders in industry, such as Karl Albrecht of AEG, Karl Andress Moser of Merck, and Johannes Bernhardt, the former head of Sofindus. However, also appearing prominently on the list were those with ties to the Condor Legion, for example, Erich Gabelt and Alfred Menzell.[66] Of course these figures were of economic and/or political importance within the German colony, and all had Spanish defenders, but the fact that their service in the Condor Legion would be mentioned as late as 1948 demonstrates the success of treating prominent Nazi activists and diplomats as Spanish veterans of the Civil War.

GERMANS AS NATIONALISTS AND ANTI-COMMUNISTS

While explaining Nazi and German activity during the war as service to Spain was the most common tactic taken by Germans wanted for repatriation, the more overtly political manner in which Franco cast the Civil War after the conflict was not absent. In particular, this meant depicting one's service to Spain not only as part of the Nationalist "crusade" but as a crusade against Communism. As the international political environment changed following World War II, and the Cold War conflict between the United States and the Soviet Union, between democratic capitalism and totalitarian Communism, emerged, Franco was quick to articulate his regime's anti-Communism.[67] Indeed, Franco had begun making such arguments to officials from the United States even before the war ended. In March 1945 he had told the new U.S. ambassador to Madrid, Norman Armour, that Spain accepted the defeat of the Nazis but refused "to be indifferent to the dangers presented by communism in postwar Europe."[68] Even earlier, in October 1944, Franco had written a personal letter to British Prime Minister Winston Churchill expressing his fear that the end of the war would bring a massive expansion of Bolshevism and Soviet hegemony in France and Italy.[69] And even before the end of the Civil War, "deMarxification" had been an important element of Franco's prison system.[70]

Franco's identification of service to Spain as service against Communism went back to his interpretation of the Civil War as a crusade not only against "anti-Spain" but in particular against Communism in Spain. Similar arguments were put forth by many Germans with a history of service in Spain during the Civil War. Take, for example, the petitions of Friedhelm Burbach, the former consul general in Bilbao, which had a significant German population. It was difficult for Burbach to convince others that he had not acted as the official representative of the Nazi regime. However, like many other Germans, he had a history in Spain, having been awarded the Imperial Order of the Yoke and Arrow by Franco, so he petitioned Franco directly as "Head of State and Grand Master of the Order." A resident of Spain before the outbreak of the Civil War, he was connected with Johannes Bernhardt in 1936 as part of the group of Germans who assisted Franco's rebellion. In 1946 he argued that rather than Germans getting involved in the internal affairs of another country, their role in the Spanish Civil War had been justified because it was not a purely civil war but a "dispute between nationalism and the ideas of order and civilization against Communism." In a second statement, Burbach outlined his role at the outbreak of the Civil War, in 1936, in the Basque region, where he coordinated the evacuation of the German colony from Republican territory; he claimed to have been personally responsible for moving some seven thousand Germans by ship back to Germany to escape "red" zones and stated that more than one thousand Spaniards also had been saved in this way. He requested that Franco and the Spanish government interpret his actions to assist Spaniards as a "humanitarian labor of saving Spaniards persecuted and condemned to death" by the Communist-Republican side.[71]

Significantly, in Burbach's petition to Franco he never sought to distance himself from Nazism or its positions. He once stated that he had never interfered with any Jewish refugees who came to Bilbao from France permitting Spanish authorities to deal with Jewish refugees as they wished. He also never claimed that service to Nationalist Spain overrode his service to Germany as consul general since 1936. What he did do was argue that the battle against Communism united Nationalists and Nazis and that his service must be interpreted in that light. A Nazi acting as a Nazi therefore requested Franco's assistance in resisting the U.S. order for his repatriation as an "unjust situation."[72] It is worth noting that Burbach made similar arguments in petitions to the U.S. embassy, with the difference that he highlighted his opposition to anti-Semitism and the absence of any Nazi racial policy in Spain alongside his anti-Communism. Yet the anti-Communist element remained strong, for Burbach emphasized in a letter to Hawley that his work in evacuating Germans and Spaniards from Bilbao in 1936 could only be interpreted as "the humanitarian work of all the nations we call civilized" given the fate that awaited those "politically condemned by Spanish reds."[73]

One of the most notorious cases was that of Kurt Meyer-Doehner. In petitioning the Spanish Ministry of Foreign Affairs to prevent his deportation from the village of Pozuelo de Laracon, outside Madrid, Meyer-Doehner referred to his appointment as naval attaché to the Condor Legion at the end of 1936, which had first brought him to Spain. Like others, he characterized his service as service not to Germany but to Spain and listed all of the Spanish (but not German) military awards he had won during the Civil War. He then emphasized that he had brought his family to Spain in 1938, before the end of the conflict, and not only raised his four German-born children in Spain but had three more once in Iberia. Since he had had no contact with family members in Germany, except being notified that his mother had died and that his family home had been bombed by the Allies, he had no desire to return to Germany. Most significant for this analysis, however, is his argument that returning to Germany with young children would mean a return to the Soviet zone, where his family residence was, and that this would expose him and his children to a leftist government and education system. His desire "to maintain my family and educate and baptize my children" could only be realized in Spain.[74] Implicit in Meyer-Doehner's petition are suggestions not just of exposure to leftist ideas but also that Communist regimes would remove children from their families and prevent religious education and practice. This mirrored the conceptualization of the Republican movement present in Spain at the time, which was portrayed as not only leftist but also foreign.[75]

A connection of the Spanish Civil War and World War II as fights against the same Communist enemy is clear in the petition for exemption from deportation made by Richard Enge in April 1946. Enge had been employed by the German embassy in Madrid during the war on a contract basis, as an assistant to the commercial counselor. His experience in Spain, where he had lived since 1919, was primarily with the Banco Alemán Transatlántico, a leading German investment firm. His petition for assistance to avoid deportation mentioned the loss of his home and personal assets during the Spanish Civil War on account of an attack by "reds" in Madrid, and he noted that what family he had left in Germany lived in the "red" zone of occupation.[76] Without explicitly saying so, Enge was implying that he would suffer the same fate twice if repatriated. And it wasn't necessary to be blunt about what a terrible fate it would be to be under Communist rule.

The public projection of the Franco regime as having emerged from civil war to conquer a foreign, atheist socialism consistently shaped the rhetoric of the period from the end of the Civil War to after World War II.[77] It is thus unsurprising that the Spanish government responded favorably to Germans wanted for repatriation when they applied elements of the general Francoist argument to their own situation. Their commitment to fighting "reds" was compatible with the mission of the Spanish government; it made them, in essence, good Nationalists in the present as well as in the past. Alfred Menzell combined past and present when he explained his decision to fight in the Spanish Civil War in the Condor Legion as a result of his having lived in "red Barcelona" for a year after the outbreak of the conflict.[78]

Another target of the Allies, Walter Leutner, who was arrested and interned from late 1944 to mid-1946, highlighted not only his many years of residency in Spain but also his service in the Condor

Legion in the "war of liberation" and the fact that this experience had led him to be hired by the Spanish army as an instructor. He considered these two different deployments as one common experience, serving Spain in its "Glorious Moment," and he said that he was most comfortable in the uniform of Spain.[79] He urged the Spanish government to consider these facts, rather than his work for the German embassy in 1940 and 1941 and for the German consulate in Barcelona from 1941 until his arrest in November 1944.[80]

CATHOLIC, NOT NAZI

Leutner also employed another line of argument commonly used by Germans threatened with repatriation to add to their credentials as loyalists in the service of Franco. He underlined the fact that he had never been involved in either the SS or the Gestapo and that he was a "good Catholic."[81] Indeed, he went so far as to state that membership in the NSDAP would have been "absolutely incompatible with my religion."[82] Implicit here was that devotion to Catholicism showed a commitment to Franco's Spain rather than to Hitler's Germany. The archbishop of Toledo, Cardinal Enrique Pla y Daniel, built on such arguments and created a list of German Catholics to be protected from repatriation that he sent to the Spanish government.[83] Similarly, Gottfried von Waldheim, formerly the German consul general in Barcelona, noted his support by German Catholics to imply his opposition to Nazism. In his efforts to document that he was not a member of the Nazi Party and therefore did not deserve deportation despite his prominent diplomatic position, Waldheim petitioned not only the Spanish Foreign Ministry but also the U.S. embassy in Madrid, sending on testimonies from German Jews and Catholics within and outside Spain.[84]

The use of one's Catholicism to distance oneself from the NSDAP and/or to justify one's actions as service to Spain was similar to the role of Catholicism in Francoist memory of the Civil War. Catholicism's concept of sacrifice and martyrdom fit well with Francoist rhetoric about coming through a "crusade."[85] Francoist propaganda proposed that the state's support for the Catholic Church was just as important as its focus on Franco as Caudillo (Leader) and its promotion of Spanish nationalism. Indeed, in many prison camps the celebration of the anniversary of Franco's coup, July 18, was followed on July 19 by ceremonies and discussions of "La Religión y la Patria."[86] Thus Catholicism was used by Germans in Spain in two contexts, to downplay their commitment to Nazism and, and more importantly, to reinforce their loyalty to Franco's Spain.

Many Germans sought for repatriation stated that they were Catholic on the assumption that this made it impossible to be considered a Nazi. José Lipperheide Henke, a prominent Bilbao mining-company executive, expressed surprise at the Anglo-U.S. request for his repatriation to Germany since he was "a Catholic by birth and conviction," which explained why he had never been involved with the NSDAP.[87] His brother and business partner, Federico Lipperheide, was president of the Association of German Catholics in Spain and also a "fervent Catholic," according to the archbishop of Toledo.[88] While the association was created for community-building purposes, its use in the defense of Germans threatened with repatriation suggests that German Catholicism could be politicized to distance Germans from Nazi activities. Both brothers were on the Allied lists for repatriation, Federico especially for his ties to Nazi propaganda agents and for importing of German propaganda films into Spain during the war.[89] In the case of Federico, the many letters of support received on his behalf by the Spanish Ministry of Foreign Affairs and the U.S. embassy in Madrid almost always mention his Catholicism as evidence of his anti-Nazi stance, despite Allied evidence to the contrary. Lipperheide himself sent the U.S. embassy personal testimonies from the president of the Bilbao Chamber of Commerce, Pedro Galindez, mentioning his Catholicism and his anti-Nazism, and from the president of the Bank of Vizcaya, Pedro Cereaga, who called him an "anti-Hitler German."[90] Most significantly, Father José María Huber, head of the Association of German Catholics in Northern Spain, wrote that Allied accusations against Lipperheide were false in large part because Nazism "would not be compatible with his catholic convictions, demonstrated by his incorporation into the movement *Acción Católica*."[91]

Similarly, Georg Wolfgang Scuebel, former head of the Reichsbahn in Spain and the German tourist office in Barcelona, explained in his interrogation that since he was Catholic, he was only a "nominal" member of the NSDAP, joining in 1938 for employment purposes.[92] Initially arrested by Spanish authorities and held in Yserias prison for repatriation before being released, Antonio Oboril mentioned his Catholicism as well as that of his wife and two children.[93] In all of these cases there was an implicit assumption that being Catholic would be interpreted as incompatible with being a Nazi. Therefore, they believed that proof of a commitment to Catholicism would be enough to exempt them from denazification and, in these cases, deportation from Spain.

The use of Catholicism was not simply common among individuals; it was also a strategy used by church leaders and encouraged by many within the German colony. The dispatch of German Catholic priests to Spain in the summer of 1945, primarily through religious orders, and their involvement in linking the Catholic Church and Germans was another concerning trend, remarked upon by the Allied informant Roger Tur.[94] Similar reports came from Bilbao, where prominent priests in the German community, such as Father Lang, had taken residence in convents, and a source reported that plans might be in the works to hide fugitive Germans within religious orders.[95]

A number of prominent priests played significant roles in the advancement of Catholicism as a defense in the face of repatriation. The two most notable were Father José María Huber, head of the Association of German Catholics in Northern Spain, and Father José Boos, head of the Association of German Catholics, based in Barcelona. When the war ended, the archbishop of Cologne appointed Father Johann Leukering to head the German Catholic community in Madrid. Leukering, like the head of the German Catholic community in Barcelona, Father Boos, was a member of the order of the Hiltruper Missionsgellschaft. Earle Titus, of the U.S. embassy in Madrid, discovered that Leukering was himself actually on the Allied repatriation list in Lisbon, Portugal, where he had served during the war.[96] Luekering was close to Father Boos, who was officially Luekering's superior as rector in both Barcelona and Madrid, recognized by the papal nuncio and the archbishops in Spain in this capacity. Boos took it upon himself to argue against repatriation as an overarching policy, writing to the Foreign Ministry in Spain that his role was solely a "moral one" to advocate against the separation of families if fathers and husbands were on the repatriation list and to act to prevent German Catholics in Spain from being exposed to "the material and moral misery" of occupied Germany.[97] Father Huber also defended German Catholics against repatriation. Both Huber and Boos drew support from the church hierarchy, most notably Cardinal Enrique Pla y Daniel, archbishop of Toledo.[98] The cardinal wrote in praise of the work of Boos and Huber in defending Catholics from repatriation, calling on Foreign Minister Artajo to call on his own "sentiments of justice and Christian charity" in defense of "our German co-religionists."[99]

The activism of Boos and Huber typically involved sending lists of names of persons to be exempted from deportation to Spain's Ministry of Foreign Affairs.[100] Boos used a number of arguments linked to religion to justify his requests that repatriations not be carried out in the cases of the men he defended. He wrote that in all cases he was involved with, the separation of a father from the family should be reason enough to exempt an individual from repatriation, for material reasons but also to avoid the "disgrace" that would fall upon single mothers in Spain's Catholic communities. He also stated that it was his "moral obligation" as a Catholic leader to advocate the exercise of international law, which allowed for the "defense of each individual person."[101]

In addition to arguing against repatriation, church leaders such as Boos and Huber played a significant role in supporting those Germans interned at Caldas de Malavella and other camps through fundraising. Ostensibly, the purpose of such activity was to provide food and clothing for those interned at places like Caldas de Malavella. This work grew out of similar activities during wartime, when the

German Red Cross in Spain had collected roughly 1 million pesetas each year and the Nazi Party had collected the same amount through its "Winter Aid" program, Winterhilfawerk.[102] Housed in the Banco Germánico de la América del Sur, such funds were secretly transferred to Spaniards in 1945. After the war, such fund-raising activities continued and drew upon the leaders of the Nazi community in Spain. One such figure was Karl Albrecht, the head of AEG in Madrid, described as "one of the most dangerous Germans in Madrid from the political and party point of view."[103] In the autumn of 1945, accompanied by two priests, he began to visit many pro-Nazi members of the German colony in Madrid seeking donations for Germans held in Spanish custody; those priests were Boos and Huber, who were central to all fund-raising efforts for the German colony.[104] Indeed, the largest fund, the Correa Fund, based in Barcelona, was set up and administered by Boos. Early intelligence reports in 1946 suggest that the funds raised within the German colony, were used to support not only internees in the Spanish camps but also, primarily, the wives and families of interned Abwehr members.[105]

Allied officials were eager to learn about the role of such Church-sponsored activities within the German colony. Perhaps U.S. officials' most important contact within the German colony was Pastor Bruno Mohr, the head of the German Protestant Church in Madrid. Mohr was a close friend of the former German embassy employee Hans Rothe. Rothe regularly passed on to U.S. embassy officials what Mohr had told him, making Mohr, in the words of Earle Titus, "indirectly very useful" to the United States.[106] In 1947, when Rothe left for the United States, Mohr was put in direct contact with the U.S. embassy and continued to supply intelligence on Nazism within the German colony. As the leader of the German Protestant Church in Spain, Mohr visited Germans held in Spanish internment camps while their repatriation status was being investigated. On one of these trips, in January 1946, to the camp at Carranza, which held four hundred internees, Mohr observed how monies raised for the maintenance of internees, often by Catholic priests, were directed to the more vocal pro-Nazis. Thus, not only were such monies linked to charity but they were distributed with the intent, in Rothe's words, "to animate political life within the camps."[107] More and more, the focus on Nazi activism in Spain was directed toward the role of German Catholic leaders, who worked openly within the broader Catholic institutions in Spain. Moreover, the focus was not on political ideology but rather on the continued existence of Nazi cells working together to benefit one another and maintain a presence in Spain, even if it was a presence without overt political or espionage goals.[108]

Allied intelligence had contacts not only with Pastor Mohr but also within the Catholic community, most notably with Father Conrad Simonsen, of the Order of Capuchins in Madrid. Simonsen reported to Earle Titus on the role of church leaders in the process of developing arguments that used Catholicism as a defense against repatriation, and he believed that many Nazis were finding refuge within the Catholic community, regardless of their personal views on religion.[109] Such organized activities, approved by the church and by civil authorities in Spain, suggested the acquiescence of the Spanish government in assisting or at least facilitating the networks of support that emerged in the aftermath of World War II. To Simonsen, this amounted to "considerable mischief" that went beyond simply supplying internees with food and other goods, and he implied that the continuation of Nazi identity, now within the framework of the Catholic Church, was really what was happening. One such instance Simonsen reported on came from the internment camp at Carranza, where ultimately internees were divided along Nazi and anti-Nazi lines, which resulted in the arrest and removal of internees denounced to Spanish officials as "Communists" and their imprisonment in regular Spanish prisons.[110]

Fearful that German Catholics and Nazis would become compatible in people's minds, Father Simonsen and other prominent German Catholics actively worked with the U.S. embassy and created a group of anti-Nazi German Catholics to advocate on their own behalf with both the U.S. and Spanish governments.[111] This group did not achieve the same significance as established groups, however, and did not win the support of leading church officials in Spain. They preferred to continue to use Catholicism to protect Germans from Allied policies. Titus found this compatible with other reports he had received from across Europe, which suggested that many former Nazis favored such a strategy because it "enable[d] them to have the protection of the church by posing as the defenders of Catholicism against Bolshevism."[112] Titus was correct, for such a strategy was well under way across Europe, not only in Spain. In Italy many former Nazis were rebaptized as Catholics, even though it was against canon law, in the belief that it might help them to hide; Gerald Steinacher has called this a form of "church denazification."[113] Moreover, many leading priests in Rome and other parts of Italy were deeply involved in the hiding of wanted German war criminals in monasteries and other church properties.[114]

Simonsen, although concerned about the politicization of Catholicism as a defense against Nazism, was not immune to making the same arguments himself. He did so in the case of Baron Joaquim von Knoblach, the honorary German consul in Alicante during World War II and earlier. Writing on his behalf, Simonsen underlined that von Knoblach's primary work as honorary consul before the war had been to organize the evacuation from Alicante of Germans and Francoist supporters in 1936, when the Republicans attacked. He had then joined the Francoist side and had subsequently been transferred to the Condor Legion at the end of 1936. However, he was never a member of the Nazi Party, and he had attempted to resign his consulship, but the German government had refused to accept his resignation.[115] Luis Carrero Blanco, under secretary of the government and later Franco's hand-picked successor (named prime minister in 1973 before being assassinated), characterized von Knoblach's actions as "great service to Spain," not as activism in favor of Nazi Germany.[116]

Carrero Blanco's interpretation of von Knoblach's actions suggested a second use of the Catholic argument. Rather than simply arguing that Catholicism made it impossible to be a Nazi, many Germans in Spain went further and argued that their commitment to Catholicism also demonstrated their loyalty and service to the Franco regime. In many cases, as in von Knoblach's, Germans' religion was combined with their service during the Civil War to make a complete argument about their loyalty to Franco's Spain. Herbert Hahn, an SD agent arrested by the Spanish in May 1945, as the war was ending, and still in prison at Yserias in March 1946, wrote to appeal his own deportation, signing his appeal "an admirer of Spain and a fervent Catholic."[117] The bringing together of his being pro-Spanish and Catholic was more deliberate than simply stating that one's Catholicism made it impossible to be a committed Nazi. Moreover, this led naturally to claiming that one was better categorized as "Spaniard" than as "German." Catholic piety as asserted by these Germans dovetailed perfectly with the Franco regime's official self-portrayal as a state characterized by "national Catholicism" in the immediate postwar era.

GERMANS AS SPANIARDS

The final strategy for Germans defending themselves against the threat of repatriation, those who spoke up and tried to shape their own fate in the face of U.S. policy and the Spanish government's response, was to be even more blunt than the petitioners already examined and simply argue that they were, in effect, Spaniards. For the most part they were Germans who had lived in Spain since before the Nazi rise to power in 1933. Most had come to Spain for business, not becoming involved in politics and service to the Nazi state until much later. Most of them had married Spanish women and had children born in Spain. These people, however, made up the core of the Abwehr in Spain, which by 1944 employed 220 people directly and more than 1,000 agents, most of whom came from the German colony already in existence in Spain or were employees of German businesses that developed in Spain after 1936.[118] Friedrich Burkhardt cited his conversion to Catholicism, his first marriage to a Spaniard, his service in Franco's army, and his residence in Spain since 1913 to declare Spain as "my second country." He claimed to have done only a little work for the German embassy during the war and viewed what had happened to Germany under Nazism as "a Spaniard."[119] According to OSS records, Burkhardt had served the Abwehr in Seville, where he was based, from 1943 on.[120]

Marriage was the primary basis on which the claim to be effectively Spanish was made, with length of time in Spain usually also mentioned. In most cases these two circumstances went hand in hand. This was true whether the petitioner was on one of the top-priority lists and his arrest was potentially imminent or whether he was on a lower-priority list and the U.S. and British embassies had simply contacted him to ask him to consider voluntary repatriation. Wilhelm Meyer, who was a higher-priority candidate for repatriation, protested the Spanish order to intern him at Caldas de Malavella in May 1945 based on his thirty-two years' residency in Bilbao, his twenty-four-year marriage to a Spanish woman, and the fact that his only political activity had been not as a German but as a Spaniard, as a member of the Falange during the Civil War.[121] Max Ludwig Muller-Bohm, a lower-priority candidate, received requests for voluntary repatriation from his local police in Barcelona and from the British-American Repatriation Centre in February 1946. He protested these requests based on his residency in Spain since 1930 and his marriage to a Spaniard. He also noted that his two children had been born in Barcelona and baptized in the Sagrada Familia Cathedral. To him, these facts mattered more than his absence from Spain to work in Germany during the Republican period in Barcelona, his work in Tetuán, Spanish Morocco, from 1938 to 1943, or his membership in the German Labor Front (Deutsche Arbeitsfront, or DAF) of the Nazi Party.[122]

These arguments also proved to be the most convincing to Spanish officials, many of whom used the same arguments in petitioning their Ministry of Foreign Affairs to protect their German friends, saying that whether these Germans were actual Spanish citizens did not matter. This was the argument on behalf of Germans "incorporated into Spanish life," as described in chapter 2. In the case of Alfred Menzell, formerly of the German naval attaché's office, one of the leading figures in the Spanish government, Luis Carrero Blanco, wrote to Artajo with Francisco Franco's approval. He advocated that

Menzell be exempted from repatriation based in part on his residency in Spain since 1918, his marriage to a Spaniard in 1925, and the birth of three children on Spanish soil. These facts, argued Carrero Blanco, meant that Menzell's inclusion on a repatriation list could only be a "bureaucratic error."[123] However, the U.S. embassy made the protection of Menzell by Spanish officials, including the security services, a major point of complaint in a subsequent meeting with Artajo, suggesting that Menzell was in fact one of the prominent targets for repatriation.[124]

A number of Germans took the most direct step to protect themselves from repatriation and attempted to acquire Spanish citizenship in the aftermath of World War II. The leading German in Spain, Johannes Bernhardt, made his application directly to Francisco Franco on April 15, 1946. By May the Ministry of Foreign Affairs and the Ministry of Government had expedited the request.[125] Many agents who feared internment had applied for citizenship much earlier, before the war ended. Such was the case of Anton Paukner and Alfred Radeke, who acquired citizenship in the summer and fall of 1944, respectively, but still were identified on the Allied priority list as German agents. The Ministry of Foreign Affairs decided to arrest them and intern them at the Caldas de Malavella camp in October 1945, only to be informed by the Dirección General de Seguridad that these men were Spanish citizens.[126] Paukner had been attached to the naval office in the German embassy in Madrid and acquired citizenship shortly after leaving his post.[127] The result was a coordinated effort by the Ministry of Foreign Affairs, the Dirección General de Seguridad, and the Ministry of Justice to prevent Germans from acquiring citizenship.[128]

The U.S. government feared that Germans' acquiring Spanish citizenship would constitute the sort of "creeping tactic" that many German officials had employed in the early days of the postwar era, when Germans refused to turn German schools over to the Allies, arguing that schools were not the same as embassy property.[129] Citizenship, argued LaVerne Baldwin, of the U.S. embassy, would not only allow Germans to stay, but would put them in a position to continue to influence the Franco regime in years to come.[130] Here again the concern was raised not just about avoiding repatriation but about the longer-term consequences for national security and U.S. relations with Spain. From the immediate end of the war on, the U.S. embassy repeatedly protested to the Ministry of Foreign Affairs against the potential acquisition of Spanish citizenship by German agents, and U.S. intelligence documented specific cases where possible.[131]

In reality, this tactic continued among many Germans and met with some success within various agencies of the Spanish government. U.S. intelligence, for example, documented the efforts of Eduard Bunge, former German consul in Bilbao, as he attempted to acquire citizenship in the face of a repatriation order in April 1946.[132] José Lipperheide Henke, from Bilbao, admitted that he had not sought Spanish citizenship until he was informed of the repatriation order in mid-1946, but he argued that the "special circumstances" of his case, namely, his twenty-two years' residency in Spain and his marriage to a Spaniard, qualified him for citizenship.[133] By 1948 Spain had removed 45 individuals from the list based on their Spanish citizenship.[134]

CONCLUSION

U.S. and British officials, especially in intelligence agencies, tracked ex-Nazis in Spain following World War II in an effort to eradicate the last vestiges of Nazism, to detach the Spanish dictatorship from any Nazi influence, and to ensure that German economic penetration of the Iberia Peninsula did not return. The raw intelligence information collected, now available to researchers, tells us a great deal about the extensiveness of Nazi activity in Spain after May 1945, as well as the response of the Spanish government to the emerging situation. In a variety of cases, a small number of Nazi activists continued to organize themselves as Nazis and to seek a place within the German colony.

More significant was the broader movement of Germans sought for repatriation who attempted to recast themselves as Francoists.

While some of these individuals actively sought out Spanish citizenship, it is more important to see this movement as an effort to achieve "social" citizenship, membership in the "New Spain," not legal status. Whether they drew upon service in the Condor Legion, the war, as Francoists or as anti-Communists, whether they described themselves as Catholics or outright Spaniards, they sought to use their political beliefs and values to claim membership in the nation Franco was still in the midst of building. Very few presented themselves as humanitarian refugees; they were political activists who desired to stay in Spain and play a future role. They sought to use the language provided to them by the Francoist state to cast themselves as patriots. While much of this activity appears in the form of individual petitions, it was in fact organized within the German colony. These Germans actions varied from fund-raising and assistance to internees to hiding from Allied officials and the police, but they all sought to do so as advocates who retained a connection to their Nazi past and sought continued participation in a Francoist future.

The atmosphere in Spain encouraged such continuity from war to postwar, something simply not likely in occupied Germany or elsewhere in Europe. At almost every stage, however, the support of key figures from the Spanish government was essential. When challenged by the Allies to repatriate these Nazis, the Spanish government generally refused to comply.[135] More directly, as Nazi groups attempted to establish themselves in Spain and make arguments for a sustainable future, numerous forces inside the government assisted them in or facilitated their work. In this regard, U.S. and British officials were correct in their assessment that the potential for a Spanish regime that continued to be influenced by Nazis and Nazi ideology remained after V-E Day.

5

THE FATE OF REPATRIATION IN GERMANY, SPAIN, AND BEYOND, 1947–1948

The main actors in the history of Allied repatriation policy were the intelligence and diplomatic agents of the United States and the United Kingdom in Spain, the Spanish government, and the German colony. However, the occupation authorities in the U.S. zone of Germany, where all successfully repatriated Germans were sent, also played their part. Moreover, once a decision was made not to deport an individual, neither Spanish officials nor the German colony ceased their activities. Where, when, if, and how Germans moved around Europe did not change with the declining focus on repatriation in 1947 and 1948. Some who stayed in Spain grew weary and sought other places to live, such as Argentina; some who had been removed from Spain were released in Germany and sought ways to return to Spain or to travel to Argentina; some even remained in Germany. All of these movements are part of the history of repatriation of "obnoxious Germans" from Spain.

REPATRIATES IN OCCUPIED GERMANY

The vast majority of those who returned to occupied Germany from Spain were sent to, or were transferred to, the U.S. zone of occupation. A very few who arrived on the British ship *Highland Monarch* were detained in the Neuengamme civilian internment camp in the British zone, while others were transferred to the U.S. zone.[1] In the case of the *Marine Perch,* which sailed from Bilbao in June 1946, military guards on board came from the U.S. army force in occupied Germany and were accompanied by State Department officials.[2] Repatriates were then investigated by various authorities in Germany, who used transcripts of previous interviews conducted by U.S. embassy, consular, and intelligence officials in Spain, as well as documents found in Spain and in Germany. Generally there were three teams of investigators, one from the Allied Control Council's Finance Division, one from the British Foreign Office, and one made up of representatives from both the U.S. State Department and U.S. Army intelligence.[3]

A basic intelligence interrogation for screening purposes was conducted upon arrival, and then the repatriate filled out the standard denazification questionnaire, the Fragebogen, which was given to all civilian internees in Germany.[4] If all was fine, plans were made to release the repatriate from civilian internment; if not, interrogations by some or all of the various Allied agencies were scheduled. In practice, all internees from Spain were sent to the U.S. zone of occupation, so British interrogations beyond initial intelligence screenings were rare. The primary interrogators of intelligence and diplomatic personnel were members of the Office of the Political Advisor in Germany, led by the State Department. The two main interrogators were DeWitt Poole and Wendell Blancke, who concerned themselves with assessing Nazi Germany's diplomatic and intelligence relationship with Franco's Spain and with assessing connections developed by Nazi intelligence from Iberia, especially to the Western Hemisphere.

In order to understand the relationship between Spain and Nazi Germany, the Allies interviewed not only repatriates but former diplomatic personnel who had returned to Germany before the war ended and often had not been interned. One such former diplomat was Ilse Koch, former secretary to the Luftwaffe intelligence unit in Madrid, who was repatriated on the *Marine Perch* in June 1946 and then released after initial interrogation in the British zone. While there, she was required to report to British authorities weekly while awaiting paperwork to allow her to rejoin her family in the Soviet zone. Koch was considered a lower-level bureaucrat and thus was not held, but the fact that she was officially interrogated by the British on August 24, 1946, before they would grant her permission to leave their zone demonstrates how extensive the operation was in occupied Germany, even in the case of someone not considered worth holding. Her testimony gave British intelligence a sense of the extent of the agent network in Spain run by Koch's superiors.[5]

DeWitt Poole's November 1945 visit to the Black Forest home (in the French zone of occupation) of former German ambassador to Spain (1943–44) Hans Heinrich Dieckhoff, provided useful information, even though the French, who did not participate in the repatriate program, had not interned him. Dieckhoff was a career diplomat who became frustrated by the dominance of the Nazi intelligence apparatus in Spain. He recalled that during his time in Madrid, only a year, there were 160 regular Foreign Ministry officials at the German embassy, compared with 484 party, Abwehr, and other military officials. Similar disproportions existed in the primary consulates general in Algeciras, Barcelona, Valencia, and Bilbao.[6] The interrogation of Walther Giese was similar in its initial significance. Giese was the former head of the Abwehr in the region of Galicia, an early repatriate sent directly to U.S. authorities at the Berlin Interrogation Center. His October 1945 interrogation has been assessed by Javier Rodríguez González as vital to the U.S. understanding of just how deeply Nazi intelligence was implanted in Spain.[7] Of great significance was the flow chart Giese supplied to U.S. officials, outlining the structure of the Abwehr in Spain before its absorption by the SD in 1944.[8] Such information reinforced the general direction of the repatriation policy, which was primarily to list party and intelligence agents in Spain as the top-priority targets for repatriation.

Interrogation procedures and significant questions for German officials repatriated from neutral states were developed in the summer of 1945 by the Office of the Political Advisor in Germany, led by Robert Murphy, and the OSS. Chief among the concerns was the role of the Nazi Party and its Auslandorganisation in the workings of the foreign-policy apparatus and the linkages between the party and cultural organizations in Spain and elsewhere, such as the Ibero-American Institute, the Germans schools, and so on. It was most important to question officials about personnel and plans for remaining in Spain and continuing to develop Nazi ideas in some cultural, economic, or political context, including in the local press.[9] As noted in chapter 1, while the concern about Nazi stay-behind networks was overblown in these early days of the postwar period, they are none-theless significant in demonstrating the very direct linkages between denazification in occupied Germany and the repatriation campaign in neutral states.

Early repatriates like Walther Giese were taken from Spain to Berlin and interrogated at the Berlin Interrogation Center established by U.S. Army intelligence. Poole and Blancke conducted their own inter-rogations of these early repatriates, as well as the relevant top party and intelligence leadership under arrest in Berlin, such as Wilhelm Hoettl and Walter Schellenberg, interrogated in October 1945 about the connections between SD operations in Spain and Latin America organized by Karl Arnold from 1943 on.[10] At the end of 1945 it was decided that repatriates from all neutral countries would be interned together at Civilian Internment Enclosure No. 76, in Hohenasperg, Germany. Hohenasperg was a fifteenth-century citadel.[11] It had been used as a prison since the eighteenth century, and the Nazis used it as a transit camp for Roma and Sinti on their way to Auschwitz from 1940 to 1943.[12] After the war, it was under the command of the U.S. Third and Seventh armies.

Beginning in the summer of 1946, U.S. military and civilian au-thorities in occupied Germany began to review the cases of those still interned, with the goal of closing the civilian internment camps and transferring authority to local German officials.[13] The U.S. Third Army, responsible for a series of camps in the Ludwigsburg region, including Hohenasperg, released some 1,295 internees in the month of August alone, although it is impossible to say how many were in-dividuals from Hohenasperg who had been repatriated from Spain.[14] By September 1946 the U.S. authorities in Baden-Wurttemberg had well-developed plans to turn most of the civilian internment camps, including the one at Hohenasperg, over to local German authorities. A detailed plan for the transfer of all camps in the region was drawn up and approved by Third Army authorities on September 21, 1946.[15] In October, 23,939 internees in Baden were turned over to regional authorities, leaving 34,827 in U.S. hands; by the end of November the United States had only 17,295 internees under its control.[16] The United States retained control of a few larger camps, including Enclosure No. 74, at Ludwigsburg, to which repatriates at Hohenasperg who were still of interest to U.S. investigators were moved.[17] In the case of Hohenasperg, the first transfer of control to German guards and camp leadership occurred on October 20, 1946, and on November 30 final orders to remove U.S. personnel were approved. By December 12, 1946, Hohenasperg was entirely under German control.[18] Following this transfer, the local panels for German denazification, *Spruchkammern,* were carried out as the internment camp at Hohenasperg was gradually being wound down.[19] The local government in Ludwigsburg had removed the remaining internees from the camp by the end of 1947 and transformed it into two separate entities, a medical prison for criminals with tuberculosis and a juvenile prison.[20]

Following the transfer of Hohenasperg to German authorities, anyone repatriated from Spain was still sent to Baden-Wurttemberg and placed in the custody of the Third Army at Civilian Internment Enclosure No. 74, Ludwigsburg. There initial intelligence interrogations were held, and those deemed subject to "automatic arrest," namely, SS and SD members, were transferred to a camp under German command, while others were generally released to their homes unless desired for further interrogation. Again, the Americans kept only those of high interest to intelligence operations. After their release, most were interrogated through the *Spruchkammern* process and then went on with their lives.[21]

From the summer through the fall of 1946 the bulk of interrogations took place at Hohenasperg as the repatriation program was implemented by air and sea. While Blancke or Poole was often involved here, many of these interrogations were carried out by intelligence officers of the Third Army, which administered the camp. However, even in these cases the interrogations had been requested by the Office of the Political Advisor, and certain lines of questioning were pursued as developed by U.S. officials in Madrid.

One such case was that of Alfred Muller-Thyssen, interrogated at Hohenasperg on July 5, 1946. Muller-Thyssen, an Abwehr agent from Pamplona, was placed, along with his brother Walter, on the initial repatriation lists by local U.S. agents in September 1945. Walter Muller-Thyssen was suspected of wolfram smuggling and having ties to the Gestapo, his brother of being the head of the German Abwehr in Pamplona.[22] In Pamplona the two ran an import-export firm, and both had been born in Spain to parents who arrived from Germany in the 1880s. Walter visited the pro-Allied informant Hans Rothe in January 1946 to protest the brothers' inclusion on the list, simply stating that his wartime business had been to sell sardines to the German army in France.[23] Pastor Bruno Mohr, another Allied contact, however, described the family's prominence within the Nazi establishment in Spain.[24] Walter Muller-Thyssen also protested to LaVerne Baldwin at the U.S. embassy in February 1946.[25] Alfred was repatriated to Germany by plane on May 10, 1946.[26] In his July interrogation, conducted by Earl H. Look, Alfred admitted to helping German intelligence on small matters but stated that he had never been an agent or head, claiming that the German colony in Pamplona had comprised only eleven people.[27] There is no evidence that Walter was ever repatriated. In late 1946 Alfred was released, likely around the time the Hohenasperg camp was turned over to German authorities. By the spring of 1947 he was back in Spain, and in June he established a leather-manufacturing company in Pamplona, linked to his brother's firm, which was now located in San Sebastian.[28]

In reading a series of these interrogations, it becomes clear that on the ground in Germany there was little consensus about what the internment of repatriates from Spain and other neutral states was meant to achieve. Earl Look questioned the purpose of his job in his interview with Wilhelm Lampe, who operated radio communications for the Abwehr at the Seville airport from January 1942 to May 1945, then moved to Madrid, where he was arrested in April 1946 by Spanish police and repatriated to Enclosure No. 76 at Hohenasperg. Lampe was a key target of U.S. investigators not only because of his Abwehr work but also because he had been a member of four NSDAP organizations. Nonetheless, Look reported that all Lampe's testimony did was reassert what was already known—that the Spanish had provided all the facilities and cover for the Seville operation and that "the use of Spanish properties and manpower in behalf of German success in arms can hardly be construed as neutrality." Look concluded that there was no intelligence value to holding Lampe any further nor any reason to suspect that he would be a security risk within Germany.[29] Similarly, Ernst Schultze, the former head of the Abwehr post at Algeciras, was deemed to be of no further interest to authorities once he provided details of his operations to Blancke during three interrogations in September 1946.[30]

A lack of clarity about the reasons for holding Germans in confinement can also be seen in the case of German von Wenckstern, the head of the Luftwaffe's intelligence service in Spain until August 1944, then assistant air attaché at the embassy in Madrid. Von Wenckstern was on the Allied list of agents compiled before the war ended. He was arrested by Spanish police and interned at Caldas de Malavella in May 1945, then given top priority and repatriated by air to Germany on January 29, 1946.[31] Once in Germany, however, he sat in internment for nearly one year before being interrogated by U.S. Army intelligence on December 26, 1946, when he provided details about the organization of the Luftwaffe intelligence services across Spain and Gibraltar. The result of this interrogation was a simple statement that he should be released, since "the prisoner is very anxious to help and his information appears reliable."[32] The very rapid downgrading of the von Wenckstern case from one of top priority to one on the back burner suggests that U.S. officials in Germany did not share the same perspective on repatriates as those who created the lists and pressured the Spanish regime in Madrid. Similar conclusions were reached in the interrogations of numerous Abwehr agents, especially those responsible for tracking Allied shipping, running radio transmitters, and so on. In the case of the Abwehr operative Ernst Schultze, the conclusion reached by Wendell Blancke was that ""his espionage activities were very limited and local."[33] The path of Alfred Muller-Thyssen from repatriation to interrogation, release, and return to Spain suggests the same.

More focused interrogations were carried out by the investigators from the Finance Division of the military government in Germany with the aim of obtaining information about the cloaking of German assets to be used in negotiations with the Spanish government related to Safe Haven. Hans Loetsch, repatriated via the SS *Marine Marlin* in September 1946, provided the names of a number of firms in Bilbao that were officially transferred from German to Spanish ownership in the months from January to May 1945 but remained essentially under German control.[34] Other focused interrogations often involved identifying leading party members in a region who did not hold consular or intelligence positions that the United States already knew about. This was the focus of the interrogation of Herbert Richter, a career foreign-service officer who served as consul general in Tetuán, Spanish Morocco, from 1939 to 1945.[35] Nonetheless, a reading of any series of interrogations suggests that once repatriates were in Germany and answered questions developed by U.S. intelligence and embassy officials in Madrid, they became of less value as civilian internees and informants.

The result was that over time those Germans from Spain were released from internment. This was in part a result of turning over camps like that at Hohenasperg to German authorities. In other instances, officials from the Political Division of the occupation government in Germany simply did not see the significance of these individuals and did not dedicate resources to implementing the policy of long-term internment. Byron Blankinship, of the U.S. embassy in Madrid, traveled to occupied Germany in August 1946 and was appalled at what he saw. The Office of the Political Advisor did not employ a particular person dedicated to the repatriation issue, so that when interrogation queries and background information such as those files prepared by Gillie Howell, of the Madrid embassy, arrived in occupied Germany, they were simply filed away.[36]

All of this prompted the U.S. embassy's Earle Titus to ask in January 1947 whether the authorities in occupied Germany actually agreed with the U.S. embassy in Madrid that released internees should not be allowed to return to Spain if they saw, as he did, that what it meant was "the danger of their establishing nuclei of resistance."[37] It seems that in most cases officials in occupied Germany did not agree with Titus's blanket assessment regarding these Germans. The case of Oswald Langenheim is one example. Langenheim was a member of the Abwehr in Tetuán, Spanish Morocco, where his family owned property, who traveled to Germany to join the war effort in late 1942 or early 1943. Spanish authorities had removed both his brother and his father from Tetuán during the war for being Abwehr agents, although Oswald's brother, Heinrich, continued to be paid by the German embassy until the end of the war.[38] They were held first in Caldas de Malavella and then under supervised house arrest in Málaga. Oswald was interned in Germany. On June 24, 1946, Oswald Langenheim was released from the Dachau Civilian Internment Enclosure by the U.S. Third Army; by July 24 he had returned to Spain, where he was interned at Miranda del Ebro for a brief period before being released to live in Málaga with his family by August 2. The U.S. authorities concluded that there should be no reason not to allow the family to return to Tetuán and their property there since there was no point in repatriating them to Germany even though the father, Adolf, and his son Heinrich remained on repatriation lists.[39]

In most instances U.S. and British authorities wanted repatriates to stay in Germany. As early as the summer of 1946 both Allied powers raised the specter of released repatriates returning to Spain. The British embassy, in reply to a query from the Foreign Office in London, stated that it was "very anxious to prevent the return of individuals who, although they may have some title to Spanish nationality or have family or other ties to Spain, are German or German by origin or have married Germans or have in some way participated in the German war effort."[40] Titus documented numerous cases of returnees in 1947, particularly emphasizing transport from Italy to Spain after the internees left Germany for Genoa.[41]

Once individuals were released from internment camps in Germany, and once Germans were in charge of internment camps and authorizing releases of their own, it was extremely difficult to track individuals and prevent their return to Spain. Titus attempted to work with officials in occupied Germany to establish tighter control, and by January 1947 the U.S. Third Army had instituted new procedures for repatriates from Spain within Civilian Internment Enclosure No. 74 at Ludwigsburg. If repatriates were not held in Ludwigsburg after interrogation, they were refused travel documents upon release and sent to be denazified by local hearing panels, the *Spruchkammern*, in their towns of origin.[42] Nonetheless, a British Foreign Office adviser within the German Department wrote, "I doubt if 5 or 10 years hence we will be able to forbid movement back to Spain. . . . I cannot see that these people are likely to do much harm in Spain or anywhere else unless they are in communication with a revived, powerful and aggressive Germany, in which case we'll have plenty of other things to worry us."[43]

Even in the case of successful repatriates, trying to put into words the ultimate aim of the repatriation policy took the wind out of the Allies' sails. Removing them from Spain was achieved, but did it mean forever? As Titus discovered when he traveled to Germany in March 1948, little effort was being put into controlling the movement of Germans once they were released from internment camps. He concluded that it was easier for officials there "to disregard any obligation ACC may have assumed in its character as the Government of Germany," including the control of movement by German citizens.[44] Of course, by 1948 the same dynamic was occurring in the implementation of denazification overall. The primary result of the repatriation policy was that the majority of those desired for repatriation were not sent to Germany; the secondary result was that of those sent back, most were not held for extensive internment, and many could not be prevented from returning to Spain. Together both foreshadowed the end of the policy generally.

It was acknowledged that most returnees were not intent on continuing pro-Nazi activities. As R. A. Burroughs, of the German Department in the British Foreign Office, indicated, "Nothing could be reported from Germany sufficiently useful to induce Germans to return from Spain."[45] For most of these Germans, who had been active in business in Spain before the war or even before the Spanish Civil War, their contacts were there, not in Germany; their families were there, not in Germany; and thus their prospects for rebuilding an apolitical life were better in Spain than in Germany. That said, the increasing rate of formerly repatriated Germans illegally entering Spain by 1947 was enough of a concern for Phillip Crosthwaite, of the British Foreign Office, to declare repatriation a failure and raise the fear that "Germans in Spain are just as dangerous to us as Russians would be."[46] A subsequent report from Madrid indicated that 96 former repatriates had returned to Spain over the course of 1947.[47] In 1948 there was a veritable flood. One report by Titus stated that "almost the whole German colony, pre-war, is back in Valencia."[48] By June 1948 the German colony was estimated to number nearly 15,000, up from the 12,000 or so estimated in mid-1947. One of the sources within the colony told Titus that the increased numbers were "stimulating the growth of an already active Nazi mentality here."[49]

The flood of returnees by late 1947 and 1948 raises the question who the Germans were that remained in U.S. custody. Which Germans did the United States deem so dangerous that they were transferred from Hohenasperg to Ludwigsburg once the former camp was turned over to German officials just so they could remain in U.S. custody and then stayed in custody into 1947 and in some cases 1948? One of these was Walter Eugen Mosig, the former SD agent in Madrid. Mosig was primarily responsible for the establishment of the Restaurant Horcher in Madrid as a cover for SD operations and for the transfer of black-market funds from Germany, Switzerland, and other places.[50] He was on the Allied repatriation lists from 1944 but remained in Spain after the war, when he even was employed by Spanish military intelligence for a brief time.[51] Mosig was repatriated by air in August 1946 and interrogated by Wendell Blancke at Hohenasperg in September 1946. When control of Hohenasperg was turned over to the Germans, Mosig was moved to Civilian Internment Enclosure No. 74 in Ludwigsburg, where he remained. He was interrogated again in August 1947 by U.S. Army intelligence officer

Arnold Silver, who found no new information but recommended continued internment. One of the primary reasons for Mosig's continued internment, despite his openness with U.S. officials in all his interrogations, was that he had obtained the rank of SS Sturmbrunnfuehrer by the end of the war, which even in late 1947 put him in the category of automatic arrestees, although his interrogators did not believe him to be an ideological Nazi in any way.[52]

BACK IN SPAIN

Of course many of those desired for repatriation and interrogation remained in Spain. In these cases intelligence gathering by U.S. and British officials continued as they sought to pressure the Spanish regime to arrest and add these Germans to the repatriation flights. By mid-1946 many of these individuals were in hiding. As 1946 turned into 1947, what came to concern the Allies more was the reemergence of overt pro-Nazi activity within the German colony as some repatriates returned to Spain and others concluded that they would not be deported.

Within the U.S. embassy, the counterintelligence agents Medalie and Titus were responsible for maintaining files on these individuals and gathering new information from a variety of intelligence sources. Near the end of 1946 embassy secretary Gillie Howell compiled a collective portrait of those still desired and their activities, bringing together all the information collected by Medalie and Titus by that time. This report demonstrates all the aspects of the repatriation campaign—extensive U.S. and British intelligence work, a lack of Spanish response and even Spanish assistance, and the inability to actually repatriate many of the top-priority candidates on Allied lists. It includes cases such as those of Karl Andress, an Abwehr agent in the war under cover of the Merck Company, who some informants suggested was also in the SS. Listed on all Allied repatriation lists since May 1945, he remained active in Barcelona after the war, hired a Spanish police officer to let him know if an arrest order was ever issued, and went into hiding sometime after October 1946. Wilhelm Beisel Heuss, the Nazi Party chief in San Sebastian during the war, remained at large, living with his Spanish-born wife, despite being named on Allied expulsion lists before the war ended, in February 1945.[53]

José Boogen, from Bilbao, reportedly served the Abwehr there, and some thought he was the Gestapo chief for the city. He had come to Spain in 1929, served in the Condor Legion, and remained following the Spanish Civil War, operating a commercial firm representing German businesses in Bilbao and the north. The Spanish government initially agreed to arrest him in May 1944, when the Allies first presented his name to them as a German agent, but this order was suspended in September 1944 and never reissued. Also in Bilbao was Eduard Bunge, the Spanish manager of a German firm during the war and an NSDAP member. Bunge had withdrawn all of his money from Bilbao banks after the war ended and pursued the acquisition of Spanish citizenship to avoid repatriation, which was demanded by the United States in a note to the Spanish Foreign Ministry in April 1946. Alfred Menzell was the former assistant naval attaché at the German embassy in Madrid, believed to be connected to naval intelligence during the war. He was on the Allied air priority repatriation list and agreed to be repatriated on the May 10, 1946, airlift to Germany. He then claimed to be ill and missed the flight. After that he lived openly without fear of arrest. His two sons, born in Spain in the 1920s, when Menzell first showed up there, had returned to Germany and were held as members of the NSDAP until one escaped and returned to Spain.[54]

This random sampling of the more than one hundred cases presented in Howell's report reveals that most of the repatriates, regardless of their role during the war, had had previous ties to Spain and drew upon these ties to make their case to stay even if they could not obtain Spanish citizenship. As outlined in chapter 4, Menzell petitioned the Foreign Ministry on the basis of his time in Spain before and after the Civil War and also drew upon the support of prominent individuals in the Franco regime such as Luis Carrero

Blanco. This sampling also demonstrates that while some prominent Germans went into hiding, many in fact could and did live openly in Spain without fear of arrest by the end of 1946. The increased fear of repatriation within the Germany colony that occurred in the summer of 1946 seemed to have subsided by autumn.

Another significant factor that emerged as 1946 turned into 1947 was the growing intelligence from a variety of sources suggesting that prominent former Nazis were resuming their leadership activities within the German colony. For Earle Titus this only reinforced the need to continue the repatriation policy. In 1947 Titus reported on a series of informants who suggested that former leaders of the colony were returning to prominence. The most significant sign of such a change was the more public activities of the Catholic charitable organizations in the camps where Germans were interned. What began as fund-raising for German internees within the German colony became more public as the fear of repatriation faded. By 1947 several leading members of the German community—Clarita Stauffer, Father José Boos, and Herbert Hellman of AEG—had formed a new Hilfsverein (Aid Agency) to raise funds for Germans still interned, to officially advocate for the release of those Germans who remained interned, and to find homes for those Germans upon their release and otherwise assist them, including helping them move to the Western Hemisphere. Initially Boos had sought to launch the group publicly, but this was denied by the civil governor of Barcelona on the advice of the U.S. and British consulates there.[55] Nonetheless, its establishment was tolerated by Spanish officials, and by April and May 1947 the group was able to promote its fund-raising efforts via radio and newspaper ads, although it used the term *Central Europeans* rather than *Germans* on the advice of the Spanish foreign minister and the papal nuncio.[56]

Titus believed that the purpose of the group, beyond its aid activities, was "fostering German nationalism and that Junker spirit of imperialism which has largely been the cause of the European disaster," and he believed that its leadership, "known Nazi sympathizers that we have in Madrid and Barcelona," would lead the group to become "an opposition which may eventually become dangerous."[57] The success of the Hilfsverein is best measured in terms of its impact on Spanish authorities. At the start of 1947 Spain continued to intern Germans. While Caldas de Malavella had ceased to be a central camp for these internees, other prisons around Spain continued to hold populations of Germans. One of the largest was at Nanclares, which held 67 Germans on July 7, 1947.[58] Germans who had crossed from France into Spain clandestinely following the war continued to be held at the northern camp of Miranda del Ebro, numbering approximately 160 by February 1947.[59] Finally, the prison at Salamanca held 26 German internees; that at Lerida, 46, and that at Pamplona, 9. The Hilfsverein put pressure on the Foreign Ministry regarding all of these prisons, as well as the one at Nanclares. In the early months of 1947, a Hilfsverein campaign to secure the gradual release of prisoners not at Nanclares was largely successful.[60] Following their release, these individuals were sent, via the Hilfsverein, to live with other pro-Nazi families in various Spanish cities.[61]

In Bilbao, a group similar to Boos's Hilfsverein was established under Father José María Huber, head of the Association of German Catholics in Northern Spain; the group sought to advocate for the release of those in the camp at Miranda del Ebro.[62] Just as Boos and Huber had been crucial in 1946 in mobilizing petitions directed to the Foreign Ministry, they became important leaders in the efforts in 1947 to release the remaining German internees and move others to Argentina. The British embassy in Madrid considered the Hilfsverein network to be the most significant example of Nazi influence on the Franco regime, even as it acknowledged that Spanish military intelligence and the Falange were still under the spell of the Nazi model. While Germans' overall influence in Spain had declined, the existence of this group and similar groups in Barcelona and Bilbao meant that it was "unwise to discount the possibility of its revival."[63]

Beyond the activities of these individuals in the Hilfsverein, Earle Titus saw signs of a Nazi revival within the German colony in the activities of other formerly prominent community members. For example, Ernst Jaeger, former head of the German Chamber of Commerce in Spain, had resumed traveling around the country to visit businesses in the company of other known Nazi sympathizers.[64] Jaeger had used the chamber for many pro-Nazi propaganda initiatives during the war, and in October 1947 he was campaigning for reelection to its board.[65] Titus also noted that Pastor Bruno Mohr, the Lutheran leader in Madrid who had assisted the Allies and had a strong anti-Nazi reputation, in 1947 was being openly criticized by many former Nazis in his parish for reading U.S. Lutheran materials to his congregation instead of German materials, which he took as a sign of the more public face of a Nazi revival.[66]

A source of grave concern to Titus was the German colony's effort to reopen the German schools in Spain. Early on in the repatriation campaign the U.S. embassy in Madrid made it clear that all employees of German schools that operated under Nazism would be considered officials of the German government.[67] In 1945 the British-American Trusteeship had seized the buildings of all German schools, which were considered part of the German government property that the trusteeship took over as the Spanish representative of the ACC in occupied Germany. By 1947 many of those buildings had been repurposed; in Bilbao, for example, the trusteeship had given the German school to the French government, which opened the first French school in the city there.[68] A committee led by Eugen Armbruster, also a member of the Hilfsverein, emerged within the Madrid colony in the spring of 1947 to petition the Spanish Foreign Ministry to allow the school there to resume its role in educating the expatriate colony.[69] In Barcelona, where the Allies had turned the former German school there into an "International School," a private German school opened in the spring of 1947 and was reported by fall to be "a social and cultural center for the German colony," which Titus feared would make it "a future nucleus of German nationalism."[70] A formal appeal to the U.S. embassy to open a German school in Madrid was made by Father Boos in January 1948.[71]

GERMAN UNDERGROUND AND ESCAPE ACTIVITY:
RATLINES IN SPAIN

As time went on, the Spanish government made it clear that while it tolerated the presence of many Germans desired for repatriation, it was not in a position to employ them. As a result, a transformation of organized activities within the German colony occurred. Whereas in 1945–47 the colony had focused on general organization, establishing a presence, providing assistance to internees, and fighting off repatriation, by 1947 and 1948 it sought primarily to assist those sought for repatriation by not only getting them released from internment but ultimately hiding them and, in many cases, helping them leave Spain for greener pastures. In his book *The Real Odessa*, Uki Goñi outlines what this meant in the case of the Belgian collaborator Pierre Daye, who had lived comfortably in Madrid until May 1946, when his Spanish contacts informed him that Foreign Minister Artajo was willing to hand him over if the Belgian government requested it.[72] Although it was never a consistent Spanish policy to repatriate individuals, subtle changes on a case-by-case basis created an atmosphere in which hiding and escape seemed more reasonable to many of the most prominent Germans and other collaborators like Daye. Although he did not leave Madrid until May 1947, the process was set in motion in mid-1946.[73]

The person who most exemplified the transformation of community activism from fund-raising and material assistance to hiding and escape activities was Clarita Stauffer. A woman of Hispano-German background, Stauffer carried a German passport and was a national secretary of the Sección Femenina of the Falange.[74] She emerged in the fall of 1945 as one of the leaders of the Hilfsverein, collecting clothes and food packages for Germans held at the Spanish internment camp of Sobrón. She also attempted to find employment for many Germans within the Falange. Before long she was linked with Father Boos, the rector of the German Catholic community in Madrid and Barcelona. As noted above, Stauffer, Boos, and Herbert Hellman were members of a new Hilfsverein created in 1947 as a public organization. This organization soon moved from assistance and fund-raising to more clandestine activities, namely, hiding Germans wanted for repatriation in Spain and helping them move to the Western Hemisphere. This group developed close ties with a series of pro-Nazi officials in the Dirección General de Seguridad, especially the head, Rodríguez. It petitioned officials at Seguridad to release Germans still interned in Spanish camps, including the ten released from Salamanca in March 1947. These individuals then proceeded to Stauffer's apartment in Madrid and from there to private homes or to Stauffer's own pension in Oviedo, which she rented from the Falange Femenina. The private homes were those of former Nazis, such as Alfred Muller-Thyssen in Pamplona, Father Boos himself in Barcelona, or friendly Spaniards such as Castilda Cardenal of the Falange Femenina in Madrid.[75]

While Allied intelligence was interested in the group because of its clandestine activities, Titus, the U.S. embassy official responsible for repatriation policy in Madrid, drew special attention to the ideology for which the group advocated. Even as late as 1947 what motivated these groups intellectually recalled Bernhardt's early statement to Allied officials at the end of the war and resonated with the nationalistic rhetoric employed inside Germany to reject Allied denazification policy as reeducation. Titus quoted a slogan from the Hilfsverein's own materials stating that its goal in serving the community was to "Let all Germans unite; forget the past; [and] let us preserve our German nationalism."[76]

Generally speaking, Germans did not decide to go into hiding and use these developing networks until mid- to late 1946. For many Germans who went into hiding, the decision was reached only after all other avenues had been exhausted. For many, avoiding repatriation involved multiple strategies, including pleading their cases with U.S. embassy officials; petitioning the Spanish Foreign Ministry and calling on friends within the Spanish government; surviving internment and requesting release; and going into hiding if all other options failed. Based in Madrid, Stauffer by mid-1946 was active in establishing a series of hiding places for Germans around Santander.

One such case was that of the head of AEG in Spain, Karl Albrecht. Albrecht, like Bernhardt, was a Nazi Party member with purported ties to German intelligence activities.[77] Ultimately AEG Iberica was shut down by the Spanish government in 1948 as part of its settlement with the ACC over German para-state companies with ties to Nazism.[78] However, when the war ended, Albrecht continued to live openly in Madrid and run the company. In addition to leading AEG, he was president of the German Chamber of Commerce in Spain from 1941 to 1944 and head of the German schools' funding agency, which was a chief arm of Nazi propaganda in Spain during the war and was believed to have taken in Nazi assets as the war ended.[79] After the war, he continued to lead AEG in Madrid until pressures from U.S. investigators to meet drove him into hiding, reportedly in a monastery, in early 1946.[80] In July 1946 the AEG Iberica board of directors officially dismissed him from his post as president for being absent for the previous six months.[81]

Others in hiding included Fritz Ehlert, formerly head of the German Labor Front in Spain, who disappeared from Madrid in November 1945 and reportedly was living near Torrelavega; Robert Baalk, a former Gestapo agent sent to Spain in the spring of 1944, in hiding near Vigo; and the former air attaché General Eckhard Krahmer, who initially lived openly in Madrid following the war but went into hiding in February 1946.[82] Krahmer was wanted not only for his military activities but also for the transport from France to Spain in October 1944 of some two hundred works of art stolen in the name of Hermann Göring.[83]

U.S. intelligence was well aware that Spain would attract not only those former Nazis already there but also those who had managed to hide elsewhere in Europe and who faced potential war-crimes charges within Germany. As early as 1946, U.S. agents in Spain continually reviewed intelligence gathered from German contacts and others in order to prepare lists of war criminals that might have entered Spain.[84] Many of these individuals were immediately interned by Spanish officials in a number of camps. What these fugitives found when they arrived in Spain, however, was that the preexisting network of support that had originated in the werewolf and Hilfsverein groups had expanded greatly and was there to serve them as well as longer-term, Spanish-based Germans. Beneficiaries of material support and cash from the Nazi self-help groups, these individuals as well as others already in Spain would receive additional help in finding a way out. Besides Stauffer's assistance organization, the other main player in Spain was the Argentinian Charles Lesca (or L'Escat). Lesca had spent most of the war in Paris, working in Nazi propaganda operations, and then had gone to Berlin when France fell. In December 1944 he arrived in Madrid, where he became the main person behind the effort to move German intelligence officials to Argentina.[85]

In October 1947 Titus reviewed a report concerning a Major Brohmann, who had arrived in Spain from Germany in February 1947, via Paris. Traveling on a Lithuanian passport, he and his family were based at a home in Madrid known to be a residence for German military officers with false papers. While he sought ultimate refuge in either Venezuela or Argentina, for the time being Stauffer had arranged for his employment in the Spanish Ministry of War.[86] It is certainly likely that this individual was fleeing potential prosecution for war crimes. More notorious was the case of Walter Kutschmann, head of the Gestapo in Poland during the war, who entered Vigo via Italy at the end of the conflict and remained until 1947 under the alias Ricardo Olmo before moving on to Argentina, where he was discovered in the 1980s by the Nazi hunter Simon Wiesenthal.[87]

U.S. intelligence was aware of the potential movement of Spanish-based Germans to Argentina, and at Hohenasperg they questioned the former SD agent Herbert Senner on the matter. Senner had been in the process of discussing movement to Argentina with Otto Horcher, the owner of the infamous pro-Nazi restaurant in Madrid, when he was arrested and subsequently repatriated to Germany on May 10, 1946. Movement to Argentina grew naturally out of the hiding that Boos and others were facilitating. Senner was familiar with Lesca and spoke of plans for a coordinated movement of those in hiding to Argentina from Cádiz that began to take shape at the time Senner was arrested.[88] Senner reported that the movement of

Germans planned for the second half of 1946 was "so closely tied up with the Spanish authorities—police and army—that the tactic used so far [by the Allies], to obtain an arrest by giving the address to the police, is no longer of use."[89]

For most Germans seeking refuge, Argentina was the location of choice. There was already an active German community there, and the government of Juan Perón encouraged German and Italian immigration following the end of the war in Europe, especially of those with technological skills.[90] Horst Carlos Fuldner, a German-Argentine who had been in the SS in the 1930s and later had been connected with Sofindus in Madrid, first established the escape routes through Spain, aided by Lesca. Following Perón's election as leader of Argentina in March 1946, real plans for movement began to form, and Lesca himself was the first to depart, leaving Spain in August 1946.[91]

Simultaneously, the Catholic leadership in Argentina began to make connections in Rome and to foster the movement of French war criminals.[92] What are commonly called "ratlines," used to allow top Nazis to escape to South America after the war, originated in a complex web of Hispano-Argentine and Vatican diplomacy during the latter half of the war. The historian Michael Phayer has shown that one purpose of these escape lines via Spain was to permit European Catholics to flee if indeed the Nazis triumphed and the church came to face more intense persecution. However, the first escape lines over the Pyrenees from France into Spain, linked with the church, soon were exploited by German intelligence, especially the SD under the leadership of Walter Schellenberg. The movement of Germans from France as the Nazi occupation was collapsing soon grew into a broader program of movement.[93] Coincidentally, relations between Perón and Franco warmed considerably, and the April 1946 visit to Spain of the Argentine cardinal Antonio Caggiano cemented the tie.[94]

By the end of 1947 the Stauffer group was involved not only in hiding people like those described above but also in facilitating their movement via the routes already established by Lesca, Fuldner, and others. It has been shown that Boos was the leader of the Spanish ratline that took war criminals from Italian territory to Spain and then on to Argentina.[95] Generally speaking, among the German colony in Spain those already in hiding easily were persuaded to consider moving to Argentina even after the general fear of repatriation began to diminish in 1947. Titus wrote that by 1948 Stauffer's charity work had transformed into "a front for facilitating release from concentration camps of Nazi-minded Germans and their eventual departure for the Western hemisphere."[96]

Spanish assistance in this effort was vital. Just as many Spaniards had written against repatriation in 1946, assisting their German friends, they became involved in hiding and escape as well. The civil governor of Valencia, Ramón LaPorta, proved to be of immense help to Boos in establishing a route to Argentina from his port, which twenty to twenty-five Germans had used by April 1948.[97] Other, similarly organized efforts to move Germans to Argentina were found in Cartagena and Mallorca.[98] Among those thought to have moved to Argentina by early 1948 were the former AEG head Karl Albrecht and the air attaché Krahmer.[99] Krahmer reportedly received an appointment as a "professor of military aviation strategy" with the Argentine Air Ministry.[100] Although the U.S. government had no evidence that the Spanish government had an official policy of assisting such movement, the rumors circulating throughout Spain "would appear to lend some credence to the belief that a concerted plan may be in operation."[101] Titus, for one, wanted the issue of potential support for this movement by the police and army to be raised with the Spanish foreign minister.[102]

There is no doubt that the Argentine government was formally involved in the movement of Germans from Spain and was especially interested in military and intelligence personnel or that the entire policy was driven from the top, by President Perón.[103] Before long the Nazi groups in Spain became involved. Stauffer managed to make contact with a member of the Argentine Air Ministry, who arranged for work visas for Germans from December 1947 on.[104] Moreover, in February 1948 Carl Schulz, an Argentine, was dispatched to Spain to make contact with Boos and recruit former Nazis from security services for work in the Argentine army.[105] Schulz was instructed to make use of the German Catholic movement in Spain to facilitate his work.[106] U.S. intelligence estimated that by June 1948 some seven hundred Germans had entered Spain with the intent of moving to South America via the Stauffer or Boos network.[107] Estimates of the number of war criminals who entered Argentina vary, from as low as 180, estimated by the Commission for the Clarification of Nazi Activities in Argentina (CENEA), to as many as 300, estimated by the journalist Uki Goñi.[108] It is impossible to determine how many former Nazis in the "obnoxious German" category also went to Argentina and how many of those went there from Spain. It is clear, however, that some did.

What did the activities of someone like Stauffer mean to the United States and the United Kingdom by 1947 or 1948, when the lack of support from Spain for repatriation clearly meant the inevitable failure of that policy? Earle Titus wrote in early 1948 that Stauffer's activities were so well organized that the Spanish government had to be doing more than merely tolerating her activities. "There is too much smoke in all this business not to have fire somewhere," wrote Titus.[109] Earlier, in June 1947, Douglas Howard, of the British embassy in Madrid, wrote that while the Germans no longer had economic power in Spain, Stauffer's network represented the "biggest threat" from a security perspective if Spain decided to return to more pro-Nazi activities.[110] Even if ex-Nazis could not practically be returned to occupied Germany, the Western Allies still feared that they might influence Spanish policy or the Argentinian government. In London, one member of the Foreign Office commented on Stauffer by writing, "Germans in Spain are just as dangerous to us as Russians world be, as I think even the Americans must admit."[111]

ENDING REPATRIATION

Despite extensive Allied intelligence concerning ratlines and the work of groups like those led by Boos and Stauffer, an increase in hiding and movement coincided with diminishing enthusiasm for repatriation as the solution to the persistent German and Nazi influence in Spain. As early as August 1946, rumors circulated that the British were losing their enthusiasm for repatriation.[112] Indeed, Peter Garran, of the Foreign Office, had noted even earlier, in June, that the British government "do not attach very great importance to getting these undesirable Germans back to Germany, with the exception of a small number of very bad cases. The U.S. Govt, however, attach more importance to this than we do, and, from the point of view of solidarity on the Control Commission we want to back the Americans up over this."[113] Ambassador Mallet, in Madrid, wrote that many Spanish national as well as local officials "dislike it on human grounds and all down the line persons of influence are ready to protect individual Germans either because they are known to them or their friends or for ideological reasons of for some financial inducement. . . . I can think of no sanction the threat or use of which would accelerate matters. . . . There seems no alternative therefore to continuance of our present policy of exhortation and nagging."[114]

Spain was eager to capitalize on this situation. Roberto de Satorres, of the Spanish Foreign Ministry, raised the issue of ending repatriation with a final, smaller list of desired repatriates in a meeting with Miles Bond, of the U.S. embassy, and John Galsworthy, of the British embassy, on August 8, 1946.[115] The very next day, Martín Artajo suggested to the U.S. chargé, Phillip Bonsal, that there was no precedent in international law for what the Americans were doing, that they were lucky to get the Spanish cooperation that they had, and that it would be easier to get other Spanish ministries to cooperate if the end were in sight.[116] Artajo did get the Spanish cabinet to agree to more repatriation on August 10, 1946, focusing on the remaining thirty-two agents from the top-priority list.[117] Then in September he officially asked the United States when the policy would end.[118]

A number of arrests of prominent Germans occurred after the August 10 cabinet decision, and on August 23 a flight left Madrid for Germany with some of the most notorious repatriates forced out of Spain yet, including the SD agents Karl Arnold and Walter

Eugen Mosig. Flight X, as it was called, was welcomed by Bonsal, even though it carried only sixteen of the thirty-two top-priority Germans the Spanish had agreed to repatriate.[119] Bonsal was growing frustrated with the process, however. He and others came to believe that use of large lists was pointless and that a narrower focus on certain individuals should become the new policy, for "quality is more important than quantity and . . . if we can get even small number of important Germans, project will be worthwhile." Bonsal and others thus proposed considering 100–200 of the remaining 600 names, and a revision process began at the end of September 1946.[120] Bonsal suggested that U.S. policy needed to shift from removing Germans from Spain to simply making sure they did not excessively influence the Spanish government, since it appeared likely that most would stay.[121] He was certainly pressured on this by the Spanish government, and in November Artajo asked Bonsal directly if he could, "with my hand on my heart, tell him that the Germans remaining in Spain really constitute a potential danger to the security of the United Nations."[122] In conversation, Bonsal defended the policy and responded in the affirmative, but in reality he did not believe it. Three days later he wrote to Washington that despite the success, and despite his intention to continue to press the Spanish government, "we have reached point where fresh evaluation of problem and policy decision are required."[123]

By November 23, 1946, a total of 245 individuals from all the Allied lists submitted to Spain (numbering over 800) had been repatriated.[124] By January 1947 the British embassy in Madrid had to admit that more Germans were returning to Spain from occupied Germany than were being sent there.[125] As a result, the idea of ending the policy had gained even greater prominence than before. In the Foreign Office, R. Sloan wrote in January 1947 that "there is no point in exerting future pressure on the Spanish Govt for the moment; we lose nothing by waiting a little before returning to this charge."[126] In November 1946 both the British and U.S. embassies proposed a "fresh evaluation" of the situation on the ground and reconsideration of what was and was not possible.[127] In Portugal the Allied powers had decided upon a final, consolidated list, smaller than the initial lists drawn up immediately after the war. The impetus for this was the end of Allied control over exits from Germany, to occur as of September 30, 1946.[128] The same idea was suggested in Spain.

The culmination of this line of thinking came with a U.S. proposal in May 1947 to create a final, "hard-core" list of some 175 names of Germans desired for repatriation and present it to the Spanish government.[129] This was followed, however, by an augmentation; in July 1947 the United States insisted on 201 names.[130] Meanwhile, the Spanish were shutting down prison camps and releasing most of the Germans who remained in prison.[131] Then on July 10, before a formal request had been made to Spain, the Spanish government suggested a shorter list, of perhaps 100 names. The total number of repatriates at the time was 265, and the Spanish, according to Sator-res, sought a "final and definitive effort to comply" with the Allied demands.[132] The Spanish government indicated that it would seek to exclude any Germans who had acquired Spanish citizenship or who had "integrated into Spanish life through long-existent local ties."[133] Once again the United States and the United Kingdom sought to comply and shorten the list. Chargé d'Affaires Paul Culbertson admitted that the best result would be for the Spanish government to agree to arrest the seventy Germans it had already indicated should leave the country who remained free.[134]

The only debate among the Allies was whether the final effort should be publicized; the United States thought it should, while the United Kingdom and Spain disagreed.[135] From August 1947, then, there was an effort to create a final list, and the Spanish were told that the issue would end with the final repatriation of the individuals on that list. On October 22, 1947, a final list of 104 names was given to the Spanish government, names of persons described as "the most objectionable of the German nationals still in this country. . . . Their presence here continues to constitute a very real menace to those objectives for world peace for which the Allied nations fought and defeated Germany."[136] Since 1945 the United States and the United Kingdom had demanded the repatriation of 811 Germans; 265 had been repatriated, and 546 remained, of which the Allies were now asking for just 104. Moreover, the list of 104 included the names of 44 persons whom the Spanish had already agreed to repatriate.[137] By that time Spain was the only formerly neutral country that had not completed a repatriation program, and the United States suggested that anything short of complete compliance would "justify a change in orientation" on the part of the State Department toward Spain on all fronts.[138]

The Spanish government did not immediately respond to the list of 104 until March 23, 1948. At that time José Sebastian de Erice, the director general of the Ministry of Foreign Affairs, stated that Spain had agreed to round up and repatriate 59 of the Germans on the list but that the others should be exempted because they were Spanish citizens or had significantly integrated themselves into Spanish life. Culbertson said that this was fine with him, and he tried to convince Washington "that we should either give oral acceptance to the Spanish proposal or drop the whole thing."[139] The British in general agreed, and Randolph-Rose, in the Foreign Office, wrote that most of the 59 named constituted "a good percentage of the more dangerous Nazis with certain less important ones as make-weights."[140] The British embassy in Madrid agreed with Culbertson, and Douglas Howard wrote that he and Culbertson were united in thinking that to argue with the Spaniards now would "prolong the stalemate ad infinitum and repatriation would remain a constant sore."[141] However, the Foreign Office refused to completely give up on the others, and the State Department disagreed with the idea; so Culbertson and Howard responded on June 1 that this was unacceptable.[142] De Erice then said that it was up to the United States and the United Kingdom to agree on just 50 names, for some of the 59 had left Spain, or else forget the matter entirely. Culbertson and Howard believed that this represented the end of repatriation, with no agreement on the final list.[143] The only remaining communication from the Spanish government was a note explaining why they had exempted 45 names.[144]

There is no indication that any other negotiations took place or that any of the remaining 104 individuals were ever repatriated from

Spain. Indeed, in February 1948 one German on the previous list but not on the final list of 104, Reinhardt Mey, requested that the Spanish Foreign Ministry remove all restrictions against him, and this was granted.[145] Others on the list, such as Kurt Bormann, petitioned the Spanish government to remove them.[146] The United States and the United Kingdom listed Bormann as a Gestapo agent who had used his insurance business as a cover for espionage during the war.[147] Other Spanish government agencies chimed in, such as the Ministry of Air, under Eduardo Gallarza, who requested that Franz Bey be removed from the list because of his service in the Spanish Civil War and his time assisting the Spanish air force as adjunct air attaché in the German embassy during World War II.[148] A process of clearing the list through any means except repatriation was under way. The result was an effective end to repatriation, without any final statement, announcement, or definitive conclusion.

On the side of the U.S. government, the lead taken by the head of the embassy, Paul Culbertson, appointed in 1947, was crucial. He noted in response to the Spanish proposal for a final list in July 1947 that his wish was for "a speedy winding-up of this long-drawn out affair."[149] In discussions with Artajo in the summer of 1947, he suggested that the Spanish might repatriate at most a dozen or so, for they did not care about the rest and were not going to go out of their way for the sake of the United States. Culbertson wrote that "the chances of obtaining the repatriation of around two hundred Germans are equal to the chances of the proverbial snowball."[150] This echoed his predecessor, Bonsal, who had initiated the reduction of the repatriation list based on what Spain might actually do. More significant was Culbertson's own opinion on the matter. In a July 1947 letter to the secretary of state, he wrote that "I find it difficult to go along with this 'dangerous' German business since it seems to me that the German danger, if it exists, will develop in Germany. . . . A handful of Germans outside Germany won't amount to much from the standpoint of danger."[151]

As noted above, when the Spanish agreed to remove 59 names from the list of 104 in March 1948, Culbertson was quick to say that this was good enough. He went on to state that the repatriation issue as a whole was "a rather useless point of difference between us and the Spaniards" and that the Spanish offer was "the best we are going to get" and would "close out a rather minor war hang over."[152] Culbertson's views were echoed by those serving the United States in occupied Germany. When Earle Titus visited the U.S. zone in Germany in February 1948, he found a "relative disinterest" in the activities of Germans outside Germany and noted that "it does not seem to make much difference whether we continued to control Germans in Spain or not." Only the State Department continued to press for repatriation and control of German movement outside Germany.[153]

So Culbertson set out to do an end run around the State Department. In May 1948 he withheld an instruction that was to be sent to the Office of the Political Advisor in Germany stressing the need to prevent Germans from moving back to Spain. Within the U.S. embassy he argued that the return of Germans to Spain, even those who had been repatriated, was "amazing," but "I don't view it with concern."[154] On September 30, 1948, Culbertson suggested that any travel restrictions on Germans returning to Spain be dropped even if the German in question had been a repatriate. Knowing the history of repatriation and the support it still had in some quarters, Culbertson's deputy, J. Y. Millar, suggested the change be made quietly, without informing the State Department or the Spanish Foreign Ministry. The reason for this was that even as late as September 1948 the ongoing discussions with Spain concerning the final list of 104 had not ended, and there was a risk that if this policy change got out, it would impact the repatriation talks. But Millar added the qualification, "If repatriation might really take place." Millar wrote to Culbertson, "While I understand that you wish to abolish all controls, someone in the Department might get peeved on this point."[155] Culbertson pressed on quietly, and by December 1948 the British in Madrid had agreed to similar measures, and all travel restrictions on Germans coming to Spain were ended, with the exception of the 104, who had to consult with the Allies if they wished to leave Spain.[156]

Culbertson was questioned about his approach to the topic within his own embassy, most notably by Titus, who had come to Spain with the OSS and stayed on in the embassy to direct the repatriation campaign. Titus prepared a series of memos for Culbertson in 1948 in which he argued for Culbertson to keep pressure on the Spanish government concerning repatriation. His memos from this time include one arguing that Spain should be demanded to act to prevent the movement of Germans to Argentina and take action against Clarita Stauffer;[157] he also wrote a memo outlining the return of Germans to Spain from Germany, which he argued was "destroying our prestige" in Spain.[158] Also advocating for more activism on repatriation was Hudson Smith, who had been responsible for running the British-American Repatriation Centre, which coordinated the air and maritime movement of Germans out of Spain in 1946.[159]

CONCLUSION

Titus and Smith, long consumed with repatriation, were ultimately fighting a losing battle. By the end of 1948, especially once Spain and the Allies had come to an agreement on German assets in Spain, repatriation was a fading memory. There was a discussion in the autumn of 1948 about linking repatriation to the assets agreement by forcing Spain to freeze the assets of those on the list of 104, or at least those of the 59 Germans Spain had already agreed to deport.[160] Phillip Crosthwaite, formerly in the British embassy in Madrid and at the time of the discussion in the Foreign Office, argued that such a linkage at least gave the Allies the chance to defend the policy from a moral point of view, and "decency should overrule expediency."[161] His colleague John Russell responded that Crosthwaite's views, "which have considerable moral force," had to be overruled by "other, earthier forces."[162] Even the State Department came to embrace the end of repatriation.[163] The British embassy in Madrid rejected linking repatriation to the assets agreement, calling repatriation "a dead issue."[164] And so it was.

CONCLUSION

The United States struggled to find the proper way to deal with General Francisco Franco's dictatorial regime after World War II. Both at the Potsdam Conference in July 1945 and in the Tripartite Statement of March 4, 1946, the United States condemned the Franco regime as incompatible with the emerging postwar order and took the lead in releasing captured German documents that demonstrated Spain's close relationship with the Nazis.[1] The United States removed its ambassador to Madrid, Norman Armour, in December 1945 and replaced him with only a chargé d'affaires, Phillip Bonsal, who was followed by Paul Culbertson in 1947. This was in line with the U.N. condemnation of Franco's regime; while diplomatic relations were permitted, they should not be at the highest level. The United States did not send another ambassador to Madrid until Stanton Griffis was appointed in February 1951. However, the United States never sought to overthrow Franco, despite tentatively broaching the idea Franco's retirement with elements of the Spanish army, the anti-Franco opposition, and the dictator himself in spring 1947.[2]

The complexity of the relationship between the Western Allies and Franco's Spain became increasingly clear as the Cold War developed in Europe. There were growing fears that any upheaval in Spain, or even any effort at the United Nations or elsewhere to discuss the Franco regime, would benefit the Soviet Union. While there was no fear of a Soviet invasion in Spain, when France and then Poland brought the issue to the United Nations in 1946, it was seen as a great propaganda victory for the Soviets, for it meant that the United States had to either agree with the Soviets that the Franco regime was an illegitimate vestige of Fascism or state that it was perfectly legal, which would put the United States clearly on the antidemocratic side of the ledger. Eventually the United States just had to admit that it accepted Franco. The most notable move in this direction was the adoption of a document prepared by the State Department's Policy Planning Staff in October 1947 calling for a "normalization" of relations between the United States and Spain.[3]

The State Department document reflected the fact that Spain was seen by the United States less as a country that was home to spoiler Nazis and more in the context of the Cold War with the Soviet Union. While some policies against Franco remained in place, such as Spain's exclusion from Marshall Plan aid, relations were gradually normalized. Soon after Marshall Plan aid was cut, the Truman government worked to facilitate private credit for Spain, and U.S. military planners began to explore the issue of military aid for Spain and the possibility of building U.S. military bases there.[4] These bases were agreed to in an accord signed in 1953. As Angel Viñas has written, the "exigencies of *Realpolitik*" came to determine the direction of policy.[5] The realism of 1945, characterized by a fear of Nazism, was replaced by that of 1947, with its sense of a clear Soviet threat in Europe.

Another victim of the Cold War was the deep commitment to denazification. While U.S. authorities began to investigate rumors of escape routes for former SS members from Italy via Spain to Argentina in 1946, by 1947 they had decided to use them themselves. Once the war ended, U.S. intelligence was interested in interviewing any Nazi intelligence agents who had worked with anticommunist networks across Europe. By 1947 almost any former Nazi with anticommunist experience was eligible for a job with U.S. intelligence.[6] Once these former Nazi intelligence agents were identified, U.S. intelligence used existing networks of movement, or "ratlines," to help get people with whom they wanted to work out of hiding. Other U.S. agencies similarly recruited top German experts, especially in scientific fields. The most infamous of these were Wernher von Braun and other rocket scientists recruited under Operation Paperclip, but hundreds were actually recruited to serve in a Cold War capacity. Many other former Nazi intelligence agents, scientists, and technicians went to Argentina, a fact that the United States knew well but one that it overlooked during the early 1950s.[7] In light of these efforts by the United States, the repatriation campaign in Spain seemed anachronistic by 1947. Once Spain had more fully joined the Western defense system by allowing U.S. bases to be built there, repatriation was dated.

From 1945 to 1948 the United States and the United Kingdom demanded the repatriation of 811 Germans. Of these, 265 were repatriated, although many subsequently returned to Spain; 546 remained, of which the United States and the United Kingdom asked for only 104 in October 1947, but none of these were ever deported.[8] Thus, most Germans on the repatriation list remained in place. In this respect the repatriation effort was a failure. However, assessing the effort from a variety of different perspectives complicates such a conclusion.

Of those Germans who wanted to stay in Spain, most were able to. In the city of Bilbao, for example, the German colony continued to play an important economic role in the city and surrounding region, as it had before the Civil War. Germans had settled in the industrial city in the years before and after World War I, establishing a prominent business community there led by Friedrich Lipperheide Henke, founder of the plastics firm Lipperheide y Guzman. Among other leading businessmen from the 1920s and early 1930s was Josef Boogen.[9] From 1933, and especially with the start of the Civil War in 1936, these individuals became active in the Nazi Party and in Spanish politics, often combining the two. Boogen, for instance, settled in Bilbao for business reasons in the 1920s and served in the Spanish Civil War as a member of the German Condor Legion, sent to assist the rebellion of General Francisco Franco.[10] Josef (José) Boogen reportedly served the Abwehr in Bilbao during the war, and some thought he was the Gestapo chief for the city. He had come to Spain in 1929, served in the Condor Legion, and then remained following the Spanish Civil War, operating a commercial firm representing German businesses in Bilbao and the north. The Spanish government initially agreed to arrest him in May 1944, when the Allies first presented his name to them as a German agent, but this order for arrest was suspended in September 1944 and never reissued.[11] His movements were restricted, and for most of the first half of 1945, based on accusations of espionage from the United States and the United Kingdom, Boogen was required by the Spanish government to remain within the city of Vitoria and regularly check in with police.[12]

Boogen pled his case with the U.S. embassy and the Spanish Foreign Ministry. To the United States he wrote that he had been in Spain since 1929 but acknowledged his Civil War service in the Condor Legion and his membership in the NSDAP dating from 1935. But he argued that his main role had been to unify all elements of the German colony and that his main allegiance had been to the Catholic Church and related organizations such as the German Catholic Association of Bilbao. He concluded that none of his wartime activities had been in contradiction to Spanish neutrality.[13] To the Spanish he wrote numerous times, insisting again on his Catholicism and his adherence to Spanish law and emphasizing his long residency and the fact that his three children had been born in Spain, as well as outlining his willingness, beginning in October 1945, to sit down with U.S. officials and answer their questions.[14] Prominent Spaniards, such as the vice secretary of the Falange movement, also wrote to the Ministry of Foreign Affairs on his behalf.[15]

Boogen's appeals proved successful, and he was allowed to leave Vitoria to return to his home in Bilbao. Then in August 1946 his name was removed from the repatriation lists by Spanish authorities, although it is unclear who exactly ordered this.[16] U.S. complaints that a warrant for his arrest was never issued fell on deaf ears.[17] He remained on Allied lists for repatriation as a top-priority candidate and was among the last 104 individuals listed for repatriation by the Allies in October 1947, their final demand to Spain that it act against "the most objectionable German nationals still in this country."[18] Boogen was considered an important German in Bilbao, but in March 1948 the Spanish decided that he was part of a group they were willing to kick out of Spain if the Allies insisted upon action on the final list of 104 (while there were some 45 names the Spanish refused to act upon).[19] The Allies never did insist, however, and

Boogen remained in Spain. He was not immune from monitoring, however, and the U.S. consulate in Bilbao stepped in in April 1947 to prevent Boogen's firm from acquiring the rights to represent a group of Dutch firms in Spain.[20]

In April 1949 Boogen again wrote the Spanish Foreign Ministry to request that any remaining restrictions on him be removed. The Spanish directed him to Hudson Smith, a U.S. diplomat in Madrid who represented the Allied Control Council in Germany. Apparently Boogen met with Smith and was informed that all restrictions had been removed by the United States and the United Kingdom.[21] Boogen remained in Bilbao operating his business, which eventually was passed on to his son. He died there in 1985.[22] Today one of Boogen's heirs, Horst-José Boogen Heudorf, serves as the honorary consul for Germany in Bilbao.[23]

Federico (Friedrich) Lipperheide established himself in Bilbao in 1921 along with his brothers in order to become involved in the mining business.[24] During the war, using his contacts in Germany, Lipperheide added to his mining business by creating one of the largest industrial groups in the chemical industry.[25] Although he had a well-publicized falling out with Johannes Bernhardt, Lipperheide was a member of the NSDAP from 1934, and according to U.S. intelligence sources, he purportedly smuggled German propaganda films into Spain throughout the war,[26] as well as doing extensive business in the mining and chemical areas with Nazi Germany. He vigorously resisted repatriation, contacting both the Foreign Ministry in Madrid and the U.S. consulate in Bilbao.[27] Although the Allies vetoed his purchasing of chemical companies being sold after the war as German assets, he stayed in Spain and negotiated a series of agreements with Bayer and other companies that allowed him to build two of the largest Spanish chemical companies in the autarkic era of Franco's Spain.[28] Both Lipperheide and Boogen became Spanish citizens, as did their children.[29]

From all accounts, these men thrived under the long life of the Franco regime. Like many of their compatriots, they sought to be part of the regime that Franco was still in the process of building as World War II ended. Social citizenship and value-based identities mattered to these men. They succeeded in becoming part of Franco's "New Spain." That they may have had to wait for official legal citizenship was less important in the late 1940s than their argument that their role in the Spanish Civil War and World War II, when they worked mostly for the German government in Spain, had given them a loyalty and commitment to Franco's new vision. All they asked for in return was a place. They adopted the language of patriotism given to them by Franco's regime and used it to prepare for a postwar future. For these Civil War veterans, partisans of a renewed and Catholic Spain, and anti-Communists, their Nazi and Francoist commitments were linked. The continuation of the Franco regime after World War II allowed them to make such connections and commitments the basis for avoiding denazification.

Over time, their residency in Spain and their protected status under Franco's regime made them increasingly Spanish, a fact officially recognized with formal citizenship. And like other Spaniards, they found ways to thrive in the period of transition following the war and in the Spanish democracy that followed Franco. Thus while it may appear that these former Nazis in Spain succeeded and the United States failed in repatriation, the primary U.S. fear, that spoilers would continue to spread Nazism and lead a movement that could be influential in Spain, did not come to pass. German industry remained prominent even after many companies were seized and sold as part of the Allied Safe Haven program; indeed, Spain was the only country in the world that maintained an active German chamber of commerce in the years 1945–50.[30] The healthy and active Germany colony established in Spain before the Nazis' rise to power, which was mostly engaged in business, resumed after their collapse. Those who desired continued involvement in intelligence and military affairs made their way to Argentina, for the most part. Those who stayed in Spain replicated the German colony that had existed in Spain in the 1920s.

Nazism did not disappear from the German colony or from the larger realm of Franco's Spain, and it would be incorrect to assert that everyone simply became apolitical. As Joan Cantarero makes clear in his recent study of neo-Nazism in Spain, members of the old Nazi espionage and diplomatic services, along with members of the Falange and veterans of the División Azul, Spanish fighters on the Eastern Front during World War II, made up the core of the Círculo Español de Amigos de Europa (CEDADE), the first legal neo-Nazi association in Europe, founded in Madrid in 1966. Key figures in this group included the Austrian SS commander Otto Skorzeny and the former Belgian Fascist leader Léon Degrelle, who entered Spain after the war and remained until they died, in 1975 and 1994, respectively. Others, like Herbert Heim, a SS doctor at the Mauthausen concentration camp, also settled in Spain for most of their remaining years. Indeed, Heim was part of an active German community in the region of Valencia, which, along with Málaga and Palma de Mallorca, became a center of continued Nazi activity after World War II, aided by people like the former German consul in Málaga, Hans Hoffmann, and his counterpart in Palma de Mallorca, Hans Dede.[31] Some Nazis who escaped persecution for war crimes also became part of this community. One such was Paul (Pablo) Hafner, who served the SS on the Finnish-Soviet border and later as one of the last SS squad commanders in Germany. He lived in Austria and Italy before coming to Spain in 1954, eventually opening a Tyrolean performance space in Madrid, where he lived until his death in 2010, proclaiming Hitler's greatness and denying the Holocaust right to the end.[32]

There were others who definitely had more influence over Spanish life than these Nazi retirees. One of the most prominent was Hans Juretschke, the scholar who served as cultural attaché in the German embassy. After the war, in 1946, he moved to the Universidad Complutense de Madrid to establish a German cultural library and academic program. He served in Spain's Consejo Superior de Investigaciones Científicas (CSIC) from 1946 to 1974, directing its research on German literature and on the linkages between German and Spanish romanticism. In 1974 he was a founder of the Institute for Modern Languages and Translation at the Universidad Complutense and taught German literature there before his death in 2004.[33]

Most of those who wanted to continue to be active in the realms of military service and intelligence work did not find a place in Spain. If they did, it was in 1945 or 1946, but not for long. For example, Walter Eugen Mosig served briefly with Spanish Military Intelligence (SIM) before being arrested in 1946 and turned over to the Americans for repatriation. Major Eckhardt Krahmer, formerly the air attaché at the German embassy in Madrid, was active in the postwar werewolf organization centered on the Restaurant Horcher in Madrid, and he was reportedly active in intimidating anti-Nazis within the German colony after the war.[34] He maintained close ties with the Spanish Air Ministry and others in the Spanish military, especially those who had been responsible for the dispatch of Franco's troops to the Eastern Front in the División Azul.[35] Consistently one of the top-priority candidates for repatriation for the United States, he was arrested and held for a brief time in 1946 before escaping from Yserias prison, outside Madrid, in early 1946.[36] By early 1947 he had gone into hiding.[37] Any rumor relating to the inability of Spanish police to carry out his arrest was closely tracked by U.S. officials.[38] Soon he, like others interested in continuing their careers as government officials, decided that it was best to leave. Krahmer ended up in Buenos Aires as a professor of military-aviation strategy for Argentine military officers.[39]

In cases like Eckhardt Krahmer's and Walter Mosig's, although repatriation clearly failed, it can be argued that the main goal of the United States, to limit or even eliminate the influence that former Nazis might have on the Spanish government, was achieved. Although the ambitions for the repatriation program, like so much linked to denazification in general, were grand, too grand to be fully implemented, their main fears about spoilers and lasting influence were addressed; active Fascists such as the Belgian Rexist Degrelle remained on the fringe of postwar politics in Spain. Certainly justice was not done, and many people who should and could have been more definitively denazified got away without ever having to testify about their wartime involvement. The continued presence of U.S. and British intelligence in Spain in the years following World War II lay bare the frustration many felt over the gap between ambition and reality. That frustration and the Franco regime's failure to conform to expectations after the war only made relations between Franco and the United States and the United Kingdom more difficult.

Repatriation failed in large part because of the activism of the German colony. The role individuals and groups had in shaping their own postwar destinies and not conforming to contemporary expectations of the defeated needs to be explored further. Yet repatriation ended because other concerns, such as the Cold War, emerged and because, as Paul Culbertson and other U.S. officials came to recognize, the Nazis had little influence over Franco and were off to Argentina if they wanted to be involved in something more directly militaristic.

The repatriation of Nazis from Spain was a hunt that both failed and succeeded. Although Franco's regime remained a repressive, dictatorial one until its end in 1975, it did so on its own terms. Hunting Nazis in Spain may not have yielded great numbers, but it did achieve some of what it set out to do.

NOTES

INTRODUCTION

1. Interrogation of Walter Eugen Mosig, Final Interrogation Report 164, U.S. Army European Command Investigation Center, 22 Aug. 1947, copy in KV 2/3574, National Archives of the United Kingdom, Kew (hereafter cited as NA).

2. D. I. Ferber, transcript of interrogation of Germans at Yserias Prison, Spain, 21 Aug. 1946, RG 226 Entry 210, Box 35, National Archives and Records Administration II, College Park, MD (hereafter cited as NARA).

3. Uki Goñi, *The Real Odessa: How Perón Brought the Nazi War Criminals to Argentina*, rev. ed. (London: Granta Books, 2003), 74.

4. Interrogation of Walter Eugen Mosig, Final Interrogation Report 164, 22 Aug. 1947, U.S. Army European Command Investigation Center, copy in KV 2/3574, NA.

5. Wendell Blancke, Office of the Political Advisor, Germany, to State Department, 1 Oct. 1946, RG 84, Entry 2531B, Box 167, NARA.

6. Memo, U.S. Military Intelligence Company 7827 (Ludwigsburg), 7 Apr. 1948, RG 84, Entry 2531B, Box 167, NARA.

7. Deputy Director of Plans, CIA, to Deputy Assistant Secretary for Security, State Department, 6 Sept. 1972, RG 65, Box 215, NARA.

8. Paul Preston, *The Spanish Holocaust: Inquisition and Extermination in Twentieth Century Spain* (New York: Norton, 2012), 471.

9. See, for example, Javier Tussell, *Franco, España y la II Guerra Mundial: Entre el eje y la neutralidad* (Madrid: Temas de Hoy, 1995); Christian Leitz, *Economic Relations between Nazi Germany and Franco's Spain, 1936–1945* (Oxford: Oxford University Press, 1996); and Wayne H. Bowen, *Spaniards and Nazi Germany: Collaboration in the New Order* (Columbia: University of Missouri Press, 2000).

10. Antonio Marquina, "The Spanish Neutrality during the Second World War," *American University International Law Review* 14, no. 1 (1998): 171–72.

11. Christian Leitz, *Nazi Germany and Neutral Europe during the Second World War* (Manchester: Manchester University Press, 2000), 115.

12. José María Irujo, "Los espías nazis que salvó Franco," *El País*, 26 Jan. 2003.

13. José María Irujo, *La lista negra: Los espías nazis protegidos por Franco y la Iglesia* (Madrid: Aguilar, 2003). Irujo's writings in *El País*, especially in 1997, which served as the basis for his book, are also relevant.

14. "Costa Blanca's Hidden Nazis," *Guardian*, 10 Aug. 2010.

15. Herron Adams to Allan Fisher, 6 July 1945, RG 260, Entry 421(1), Box 585, NARA.

16. U.S. Embassy, Madrid, to State Department, 1 July 1945, RG 226, Entry 127, Box 2, NARA.

17. ACC, Directorate of Prisoners of War and Displaced Persons, "Procedure for Returning German Nationals from Neutral Countries," 27 Dec. 1945, FO 371/55343, NA.

18. Memo, Economic Warfare Division, Foreign Office, 8 May 1946, FO 371/55350, NA.

19. Minutes of the Thirty-Fourth Meeting of the ACC Political Directorate, 26 June 1946, FO 945/642, NA.

20. Political Directorate, ACC (British Element), to German Department, Foreign Office, 17 Oct. 1946, FO 371/55356, NA.

21. Tony Judt, *Postwar: A History of Europe since 1945* (New York: Penguin, 2005), 2.

22. Memo, U.S. Military Intelligence Company 7827 (Ludwigsburg), 7 Apr. 1948, RG 84, Entry 2531B, Box 167, NARA.

23. William Wyndham Torr to MI.3, 22 Feb. 1945, copy in War Office to Foreign Office, 12 Mar. 1945, FO 371/49548, NA.

24. Feargal Cochrane, *Ending Wars* (Cambridge: Polity Press, 2008), 110.

25. Lisa J. LaPlante, "Transitional Justice and Peace Building: Diagnosing and Addressing the Socioeconomic Roots of Violence through a Human Rights Framework," *International Journal of Transitional Justice* 2 (2008): 354.

26. Stephen Stedman, "Spoiler Problems in Peace Processes," *International Security* 22, no. 2 (1997): 10.

27. Ibid.

28. Brewster Morris, Office of the Political Advisor, Germany, to Chandler Morse, OSS, 21 May 1945, RG 84, Entry 2531B, Box 27, NARA.

29. Memo by Western Department, Foreign Office, 4 Dec. 1946, FO 371/55359, NA.

CHAPTER 1

1. ACC, Directorate of Prisoners of War and Displaced Persons, "Procedure for Returning German Nationals from Neutral Countries," 27 Dec. 1945, FO 371/55343, NA.

2. Ibid.

3. Perry Biddiscombe, *The Denazification of Germany: A History, 1945–1950* (Stroud, UK: Tempus, 2007), 7.

4. Valerie Geneviève Hébert, *Hitler's Generals on Trial: The Last War Crimes Tribunal at Nuremberg* (Lawrence: University of Kansas Press, 2010), 11.

5. Frank M. Buscher, *The U.S. War Crimes Trial Program in Germany, 1946–1955* (New York: Greenwood, 1989), 7.

6. Henry Morgenthau Jr., "Memorandum for President Roosevelt," 5 Sept. 1944, in *The Nuremberg War Crimes Trial, 1945–46: A Documentary History*, ed. Michael Marrus (Boston: Longman, 1997), 24–25.

7. Tom Bower, *The Pledge Betrayed: America and Britain and the Denazification of Postwar Germany* (New York: Doubleday, 1982), 101–2.

8. Ibid., 102.

9. Biddiscombe, *Denazification of Germany*, 21; Hébert, *Hitler's Generals on Trial*, 12.

10. Biddiscombe, *Denazification of Germany*, 21.

11. Buscher, *U.S. War Crimes Trial Program*, 13.

12. Biddiscombe, *Denazification of Germany*, 33.

13. Ibid., 19, 26.

14. Ibid., 27.

15. William I. Hitchcock, *The Bitter Road to Freedom: A New History of the Liberation of Europe* (New York: Free Press, 2008), 3, 126–27.

16. Ibid., 178.

17. Quoted in Biddiscombe, *Denazification of Germany*, 29.

18. Buscher, *U.S. War Crimes Trial Program*, 21.

19. Hébert, *Hitler's Generals on Trial*, 29.

20. Buscher, *U.S. War Crimes Trial Program*, 19.

21. Biddiscombe, *Denazification of Germany*, 39.

22. Lisa Yavnai, "U.S. Army War Crimes Trials in Germany, 1945–1947," in *Atrocities on Trial: Historical Perspectives on the Politics of Prosecuting War Crimes*, ed. Patricia Heberer and Jurgen Matthaus (Lincoln: University of Nebraska Press, 2008), 49.

23. Toby Thacker, *The End of the Third Reich: Defeat, Denazification and Nuremberg January 1944–November 1946* (Stroud, UK: Tempus, 2006), 152.

24. Konrad H. Jarausch, *After Hitler: Recivilizing Germans, 1945–1995* (Oxford: Oxford University Press, 2006), 25, 74.

25. Hilary Earl, *The Nuremberg SS-Einsatzgruppen Trial, 1945–1958: Atrocity, Law and History* (Cambridge: Cambridge University Press, 2009), 40.

26. Hitchcock, *Bitter Road to Freedom*, 202–8.

27. Biddiscombe, *Denazification of Germany*, 62, 63, 72–73, 65.

28. Ibid., 9.

29. Thacker, *End of the Third Reich*, 153.

30. John Gimbel, *The American Occupation of Germany: Politics and the Military, 1945–1949* (Stanford, CA: Stanford University Press, 1968); Lutz Niethammer, *Entnazifizierung in Bayern: Sauberung und Rehabilitierung unter amerikanischer Besatzung* (Frankfurt am Main: S. Fischer, 1972); Bower, *Pledge Betrayed;* James Tent, *Mission on the Rhine: Reeducation and Denazification in American-Occupied Germany* (Chicago: University of Chicago Press, 1982).

31. Hitchcock, *Bitter Road to Freedom*, 202.

32. Gimbel, *American Occupation of Germany*, 101, 103, 104.

33. Earl, *Nuremberg SS-Einsatzgruppen Trial*, 25–30.

34. Edward N. Peterson, *The American Occupation of Germany: Retreat to Victory* (Detroit: Wayne State University Press, 1977), 141, 145, 146.

35. Jill Jones, "Eradicating Nazism from the British Zone of Germany: Early Policy and Practice," *German History* 8, no. 2 (1990): 145, 149–51, 159.

36. Devin O. Pendas, "Seeking Justice, Finding Law: Nazi Trials in Postwar Europe," *Journal of Modern History* 81 (June 2009): 354, 356, 359, 360.

37. Grant to Argus, 28 Aug. 1944, RG 226, Entry 127, Box 23, NARA.

38. Note, 11 May 1945, RG 226, Entry 127, Box 27, NARA.

39. Political Directorate, ACC, 15 Jan. 1946, FO 371/55344, NA.

40. Lord Halifax to Foreign Office, 23 Jan. 1946, FO 371/55344, NA.

41. Brigadier J. M. Hailey, Office of the Deputy Military Governor, Berlin, to Granville Smith, Control Office for Germany and Austria, 14 Mar. 1946, FO 371/55350, NA.

42. Memo, State Department to Office of the Political Advisor, Germany, 3 May 1946, RG 260, NARA.

43. Denis Smyth, *Diplomacy and Strategy of Survival: British Policy and Franco's Spain, 1940–41* (Cambridge: Cambridge University Press, 1986), 6.

44. Denis Smyth, "Les chevaliers de Saint-George: La Grande-Bretagne et la corruption des généraux espanols (1940–1942)," *Guerres Mondiales et Conflits Contemporains* 162 (1991): 29–54.

45. Paul Preston, *Franco* (London: Fontana, 1994), 500; Manuel Ros Agudo, *La guerra secreta de Franco (1939–1945)* (Barcelona: Crítica, 2002), 331.

46. On the extent of German involvement in Spain, see Ros Agudo, *La guerra secreta*. On the activities of pro-Nazi Spaniards, see Bowen, *Spaniards and Nazi Germany*.

47. William Z. Slany, *U.S. and Allied Wartime and Postwar Relations and Negotiations with Argentina, Portugal, Spain, Sweden, and Turkey on Looted Gold and German External Assets and U.S. Concerns About the Fate of the Wartime Ustasha Treasury; A Supplement to Preliminary Study on U.S. and Allied Efforts to Recover and Restore Gold and Other Assets Stolen or Hidden by Germany During World War II* (Washington, DC: Department of State, 1998), ix.

48. William Z. Slany, *U.S. and Allied Efforts to Recover and Restore Gold and Other Assets Stolen or Hidden by Germany During World War II* (Washington, DC: Department of State 1997), 15.

49. Secretary of State to All Diplomatic Missions, 19 Aug. 1944, in U.S. Department of State, *Foreign Relations of the United States, 1944* (Washington, DC: U.S. Government Printing Office, 1967), 2:218 (hereafter cited as *FRUS, 1944*).

50. "United States Proposal for Allied Economic Policy Toward Neutral Countries," 8 Dec. 1944, in ibid., 2:148.

51. Assistant Secretary of State Dean Acheson to British Minister in Washington Ronald Campbell, 12 Sept. 1944, in ibid., 2:140.

52. Egon Guttman, "The Concept of Neutrality since the Adoption and Ratification of the Hague Neutrality Convention of 1907," *American University International Law Review* 14, no. 1 (1998): 55–56.

53. Marquina, "Spanish Neutrality," 184.

54. Carlos Collado Seidel, *España: Refugio nazi* (Madrid: Temas de Hoy, 2005), 161.

55. Carlos Collado Seidel, "España y los agentes alemanes 1944–1947: Intransigencia y pragmatism político," *Espacio, Tiempo y Forma, Serie V* 5 (1992): 436.

56. Leonard Horwin to U.S. Consular Conference, 27 Oct. 1945, RG 226, Entry 127, Box 5, NARA.

57. Memo, Economic Warfare Division, Foreign Office, 25 May 1946, FO 371/55350, NA.

58. Leitz, *Economic Relations*, chap. 5; Leitz, "Nazi Germany's Struggle for Spanish Wolfram during the Second World War," *European History Quarterly* 25, no. 1 (1995): 71–92. See also Klaus-Jorg Ruhl, "L'alliance à distance: Les relations economiques germano-espagnoles de 1936 à 1945," *Revue d'Histoire de la Deuxieme Guerre Mondiale* 118 (1980): 69–102.

59. Leitz, "Nazi Germany's Struggle for Spanish Wolfram," 78.

60. Denis Smyth, "Franco and the Allies," in *Spain and the Great Powers in the Twentieth Century,* edited by Paul Preston and Sebastian Balfour (London: Routledge, 1999), 188, 186.

61. David A. Messenger, "Fighting for Relevance: Economic Intelligence and Special Operations Executive in Spain, 1943–1945," *Intelligence and National Security* 15, no. 3 (2000).

62. James W. Cortada, *United States–Spanish Relations, Wolfram and World War II* (Barcelona: Manuel Pareja, 1971), 22–23, 28.

63. Collado Seidel, "España y los agentes alemanes," 447.

64. LaVerne Baldwin, U.S. Embassy, Madrid, to Privy Council Office, London, 5 Dec. 1944, RG 226, Entry 210, Box 35, NARA.

65. Memo of meeting with Roberto de Satorres, Ministry of Foreign Affairs, Spain, 28 Dec. 1945, FO 371/55343, NA.

66. Minutes of Thirty-Fourth Meeting of the ACC Political Directorate, 26 June 1946, FO 945/642, NA.

67. Memo, Madrid X-2, 3 Aug. 1945, RG 226, Entry 127, Box 5, NARA.

68. Memo, Economic Warfare Division, Foreign Office, 25 May 1946, FO 371/55350, NA.

69. Memo to T. E. Bromley, Foreign Office, 18 Jan. 1946, FO 371/55344, NA.

70. Sir Owen St. Clair O'Malley (British ambassador to Portugal) to Ernest Bevin (foreign secretary), 13 Mar. 1946, FO 371/60301, NA.

71. Memo to T. E. Bromley, Foreign Office, 18 Jan. 1946, FO 371/55344, NA.

72. Christian Leitz, "Nazi Germany and the Luso-Hispanic World," *Contemporary European History* 12, no. 2 (2003): 194.

73. Leitz, *Nazi Germany and Neutral Europe,* 153.

74. Memo by Western Department, Foreign Office, 4 Dec. 1946, FO 371/55359, NA.

75. Franklin D. Roosevelt to Norman Armour, 10 Mar. 1945, in U.S. Department of State, *Foreign Relations of the United States, 1945* (Washington, DC: U.S. Government Printing Office, 1967), 5:667 (hereafter cited as *FRUS, 1945*).

76. Mark Byrnes, "Unfinished Business: The United States and Franco's Spain, 1944–1947," *Diplomacy & Statecraft* 11, no. 1 (2000): 137.

77. Andrew Buchanan, "Washington's 'Silent Ally' in World War II? United States Policy towards Spain, 1939–1945," *Journal of Transatlantic Studies* 7, no. 2 (2009): 107.

78. Enrique Moradiellos, "The Potsdam Conference and the Spanish Problem," *Contemporary European History* 10, no. 1 (2001): 76–77.

79. Byrnes, "Unfinished Business," 137.

80. Moradiellos, "Potsdam Conference," 82, 88.

81. Buchanan, "Washington's 'Silent Ally,'" 108.

82. Ernest Bevin, 20 August 1945, *Parliamentary Debates,* Commons, 5th series (1909–80).

83. For Attlee's views, see Florentino Portero, "Spain, Britain and the Cold War," in Preston and Balfour, *Spain and the Great Powers,* 211–18.

84. CAB 128/129 45(45), 23 Oct. 1945, in United Kingdom, Cabinet Office, *Cabinet Papers: Series Three, CAB 128/129, Parts I and II* (London, 1996).

85. Bernard Hardion (Madrid) to European Department, Foreign Ministry, Paris, 15 Dec. 1945, Série Z/Europe 1944–1949/Espagne, Box 66, Archives de la Ministère des Affaires Etrangères, Paris.

86. Sir Victor Mallet to Bevin, 3 Dec. 1945, FO 425/423/34176, NA.

87. F. J. Shuman, U.S. Embassy, London, to Peter Garran, Western Department, Foreign Office, 23 Apr. 1946, FO 371/60434, NA.

88. Minute by Derrick Hoyer-Millar, 21 Jan. 1946, FO 371/55345, NA.

89. Mallet to British consuls general in Spain, 1 Apr. 1946, FO 371/60434, NA.

90. William Strang, Political Advisor in Berlin, to Foreign Office, 8 May 1946, FO 371/55350, NA.

91. Memo, Economic Warfare Division, Foreign Office, 25 May 1946, FO 371/55350, NA.

92. Perry Biddiscombe, *WERWOLF! The History of the National Socialist Guerilla Movement, 1944–1946* (Toronto: University of Toronto Press, 1998), 6.

93. Jeffrey Herf, *Divided Memory: The Nazi Past in the Two Germanies* (Cambridge, MA: Harvard University Press, 1997), 202.

94. Norbert Frei, *Adenauer's Germany and the Nazi Past: The Politics of Amnesty and Integration,* trans. Joel Golb (New York: Columbia University Press, 2002), xiii.

95. Donald Bloxham, "The Genocidal Past in Western Germany and the Experience of Occupation, 1945–6," *European History Quarterly* 34, no. 3 (2004): 307.

96. Memo, Economic Warfare Division, 25 May 1946, FO 371/55350, NA.

97. Commercial Attaché, British Embassy, Madrid, to Economic Warfare Division, Foreign Office, 10 Jan. 1946, FO 371/55345, NA.

98. British Embassy, Madrid, to B. A. B. Burrows, Foreign Office, 30 Aug. 1946, FO 371/55354, NA.

99. Political Directorate, ACC (British Element), to German Department, Foreign Office, 17 Oct. 1946, FO 371/55356, NA.

CHAPTER 2

1. Preston, *Franco*, 404.

2. Elena Hernández-Sandoica and Enrique Moradiellos, "Spain and the Second World War, 1939–1945," in *European Neutrals and Non-Belligerents during the Second World War*, ed. Neville Wylie (Cambridge: Cambridge University Press, 2002), 251–53.

3. Javier Rodríguez González, "El espionaje nazi," in *War Zone: La Segunda Guerra Mundial en el noroeste de la península ibérica*, ed. Emilio Grandío Seone and Javier Rodríguez González (Madrid: Eneida, 2012), 209.

4. Tussell, *Franco, España y la II Guerra Mundial*, 13.

5. Ronald C. Newton, "The United States, the German-Argentines, and the Myth of the Fourth Reich, 1943–47," *Hispanic American Historical Review* 64, no. 1 (1985): 85–86.

6. Núria Puig, "La conexión alemana: Redes empresariales hispano-alemanas en la España del Siglo XX," *VIII Congreso de la Asociación Española de Historia Económica* (2005), 4, www.usc.es/estaticos/congresos/histeco05/b12_puig.pdf.

7. Magali Romero Sá and André Felipe Candido da Silva, "La *Revista Médica de Hamburgo* y la *Revista Médica Germano-Ibero-Americana*: Diseminación de la medicina germánica en España y América Latina (1920–1933)," *Asclepio: Revista de Historia de la Medicina y de la Ciencia* 42, no. 1 (2010): 9.

8. Christopher C. Locksley, "Condor over Spain: The Civil War, Combat Experience and the Development of Luftwaffe Airpower Doctrine," *Civil Wars* 2, no. 1 (1999): 69.

9. Stefanie Schüler-Springorum, *Krieg und Fliegen: Die Legion Condor im Spanische Bürgerkrieg* (Paderborn: Ferdinand Schöningh, 2010), 225–28.

10. Leitz, *Economic Relations*.

11. Leitz, "Nazi Germany's Struggle for Spanish Wolfram," 73.

12. Rodríguez González, "El espionaje nazi," 211.

13. Ros Agudo, *La guerra secreta*, 209–17.

14. Denis Smyth, *Deathly Deception: The Real Story of Operation Mincemeat* (Oxford: Oxford University Press, 2010), 213.

15. Transcript, interrogation of Walther Giese, 11 Oct. 1945, Berlin Interrogation Center, U.S. Army G-2, RG 84, Entry 2531B, Box 28, NARA.

16. Transcript, interrogation of Richard Molenhauer, 3 Oct. 1946, RG 84, Entry 2531B, Box 87, NARA.

17. Memo by Gillie Howell, "Germans for Repatriation," 27 Feb. 1946, RG 226, Entry 190A, Box 23, NARA. Although I refer to this document as a memo dated Feb-

ruary 1946, in actual fact it is an ongoing file on prominent German targets of OSS investigations in Spain kept by Gillie Howell, of the U.S. embassy in Madrid. Reports on individuals in the file date from about October 1945 through early 1947. The date 22 February refers to the first compilation circulated to others in the embassy.

18. Haig Files, 31 Jan. 1946, RG 226, Entry 127, Box 28, NARA.

19. Ros Agudo, *La guerra secreta,* 191–201.

20. For one such case of an agent under cover in a trading firm, that of SD agent Walter Schwedke and the Hamburg-based business Harder & De Vose, see the series of OSS memos beginning 11 July 1946, RG 226, Entry 190A, Box 24, NARA.

21. Memo, "Meeting with A," 11 May 1945, RG 226, Entry 127, Box 27, NARA.

22. Memo, "German Espionage in Spain and Portugal," 29 May 1945, RG 226, Entry 127, Box 27, NARA.

23. Junior to SAINT, 7 Aug. 1945, RG 226, Entry 127, Box 28, NARA.

24. Katrin Paehler, "Foreign Intelligence in a New Paradigm: Amt VI of the Reich Main Security Office (RSHA)," in *Secret Intelligence and the Holocaust,* ed. David Bankier (Jerusalem: Yad Vashem, 2006), 279.

25. Robert H. Whealey, *Hitler and Spain: The Nazi Role in the Spanish Civil War* (Lexington: University Press of Kentucky, 1989), 96.

26. Sigismund von Bibra, interview, 31 Jan. 1946, RG 226, Entry 127, Box 28, NARA.

27. Collado Seidel, "España y los agentes alemanes," 436.

28. Memo, 28 Sept. 1946, RG 226, Entry 127, Box 3, NARA.

29. Messenger, "Fighting for Relevance."

30. Smyth, *Diplomacy and Strategy of Survival,* 3–4.

31. Denis Smyth, "Screening 'Torch': Allied Counter-Intelligence and the Spanish Threat to the Secrecy of the Allied Invasion of French North Africa in November, 1942," *Intelligence and National Security* 4, no. 2 (1989): 342.

32. Michael Alpert, "Operaciones secretas inglesas en España durante la Segunda Guerra Mundial," *Espacio, Tiempo y Forma, Serie V* 15 (2002): 459.

33. Ralph Erskine, "Eavesdropping on 'Bodden': ISOS v. the Abwehr in the Straits of Gibraltar," *Intelligence and National Security* 12, no. 3 (1997): 110–29.

34. Ibid., 123.

35. Kim Philby, *My Silent War,* introduction by Phillip Knightly, foreword by Graham Greene (New York: Modern Library, 2002), 56, 57.

36. Anthony Cave Brown, *"C": The Secret Life of Sir Stewart Graham Menzies, Spymaster to Winston Churchill* (New York: Macmillan, 1987), 295.

37. W. J. M. Mackenzie, *The Secret History of SOE: The Special Operations Executive, 1940–1945* (London: St Ermin's, 2000), 241; M. R. D. Foot, *SOE in France: An Account of the Work of the British Special Operations Executive in France, 1940–1944* (London: HMSO, 1966), 94.

38. F. H. Hinsley and C. A. G. Simkins, *British Intelligence in the Second World War,* vol. 4, *Security and Counter-Intelligence* (New York: Cambridge University Press, 1990), 161.

39. For more on this area of SOE activities, see David A. Messenger, "Against the Grain: Special Operations Executive in Spain, 1941–1945," in *The Politics and Strategy of Clandestine War: Special Operations Executive, 1940–1946*, ed. Neville Wylie (London: Routledge, 2007), 177–92.

40. "Draft Directive for Future Policy," 25 July 1943, HS 6/963, NA.

41. Messenger, "Fighting for Relevance," 40–41.

42. "Draft Directive for Future Policy," 25 July 1943, HS 6/963, NA.

43. Richardson to Deputy Chief of SOE, 9 Sept. 1943, HS 6/963, NA.

44. Earl of Selborne (Roundell Cecil Palmer) to Hugh Ellis-Rees, 10 Sept. 1943, HS 6/963, NA.

45. Richardson to P. Mandestan, 9 July 1943, HS 6/981, NA.

46. Record of meeting between SIS and SOE, 29 June 1944, HS 6/982, NA.

47. Morris to Richardson, 7 Feb. 1944, HS 6/981, NA.

48. Hinsley and Simkins, *British Intelligence*, 159–62, 204–6.

49. VS to Morris, 18 June 1944, HS 6/982, NA.

50. Memo, "Wolfram Coup," 25 July 1944, HS 6/982, NA.

51. Report for the Secretary of State, 1 Apr. 1944, Entry 99, Box 20, NARA.

52. Frank T. Ryan, "OSS Activities in the Iberian Peninsula, Apr. 1944–July 1945," 11 Oct. 1945, RG 226, Entry 210, Box 313, NARA.

53. William Donovan to the President, 24 July 1944, RG 226, M1642, Reel 24, NARA.

54. David J. Dunthorn, *Britain and the Spanish Anti-Franco Opposition, 1940–1950* (London: Palgrave Macmillan, 2000), 37.

55. Ryan, "OSS Activities in the Iberian Peninsula, Apr. 1944–July 1945," 11 Oct. 1945, RG 226, Entry 210, Box 313, NARA.

56. Morris to R. G. Head, 21 June 1944, HS 6/982, NA.

57. VS to Morris, 4 July 1944, HS 6/982, NA.

58. Leitz, *Economic Relations*, 180; W. N. Medlicott, *The Economic Blockade*, vol. 2 (London: HMSO, 1959), 559–60.

59. Leitz, *Economic Relations*, 190; Medlicott, *Economic Blockade*, 563–76.

60. For the best accounts of the Allied wolfram campaign, see Leitz, *Economic Relations*, chap. 5; Cortada, *United States–Spanish Relations*; Medlicott, *Economic Blockade*, 305–13, 557–81; and Preston, *Franco*, 502–12.

61. Medlicott, *Economic Blockade*, 579.

62. Collado Seidel, "España y los agentes alemanes," 447.

63. Haig to SAINT, 30 Apr. 1945, RG 226, Entry 127, Box 2, NARA.

64. Agent 23715/C, report, 23 Apr. 1945, RG 226, Entry 127, Box 2, NARA.

65. British Embassy, Madrid, to Ministry of Foreign Affairs, Spain, 16 Mar. 1944, R 2159/1, Archivo General del Ministerio des Asuntos Exteriores, Madrid (hereafter cited as MAE).

66. U.S. Embassy, Madrid, to Ministry of Foreign Affairs, Spain, 26 May 1945, R 2159/3, MAE.

67. SAINT BC 012 to SAINT BC 001, 31 Aug. 1945, RG 226, Entry 127, Box 1, NARA.

68. SAINT BC 001, report, 31 May 1945, RG 226, Entry 127, Box 1, NARA.

69. Alfred Genserwosky to Martín Artajo, 28 May 1945, and Dirección General Seguridad to Dirección General Política Exterior, Ministry of Foreign Affairs, Spain, 8 Aug. 1945, both in R 2159/3, MAE.

70. Carlton Hayes to Secretary of State, Coordinated Military Intelligence Report—Iberia, 24 May 1944, RG 59, 740.0011EW/34495, NARA.

71. Hayes to Secretary of State, Coordinated Military Intelligence Report—Iberia, 29 May 1944, RG 59, 740.0011EW/34495, NARA.

72. Sir Samuel Hoare to Anthony Eden, 10 June 1944, copy in J. Rives Childs to Secretary of State, 15 Aug. 1944, RG 59, 740.0011EW/8-1544, NARA.

73. Memo, OSS, 29 Sept. 1944, RG 226, Entry 210, Box 9, NARA.

74. "Germany: Who's Who," vol. 1, "The German Intelligence Services," 1 Aug. 1944, National Security Agency Library, RG 457, NARA.

75. Head to Eric Mockler-Ferryman, 18 Aug. 1944, HS 6/929, NA.

76. Ibid.

77. Ellis-Rees to Geoffrey Gibbs, MEW, 21 Aug. 1944, HS 6/929, NA.

78. Head to Mockler-Ferryman, 14 Sept. 1944, HS 6/929, NA.

79. The best description of Safe Haven and its creation is the account by the State Department's historian, published in the aftermath of the Swiss gold scandal of the 1990s, Slany, *U.S. and Allied Efforts*, 15–48.

80. Notes of meeting, 16 Sept. 1944, HS 6/929, NA.

81. Morris to Head, 17 Oct. 1944, HS 6/929, NA.

82. See Donald P. Steury, "The OSS and Project SAFE HAVEN," *Studies in Intelligence* 9 (Summer 2000).

83. Whitney Shepardson to Spencer Phenix, private correspondence, 11 July 1945, RG 226, Entry 106, Box 29, NARA.

84. Agent 983 to Elton, 2 June 1945, RG 226, Entry 99, Box 20, NARA.

85. David Stafford, "Secret Operations versus Secret Intelligence in World War II: The British Experience," in *Men at War: Politics, Technology and Innovation in the Twentieth Century*, ed. T. Travers and C. Archer (Chicago: University of Chicago Press, 1982), 132.

86. Colin Gubbins to Blake, 19 July 1945, HS 6/929, NA.

87. Record of OSS-SIS meeting, 20 Mar. 1945, RG 226, Entry 127, Box 27, NARA.

88. Michael Salter, *Nazi War Crimes, US Intelligence and Selective Prosecution at Nuremberg: Controversies Regarding the Role of the Office of Strategic Services* (New York: Routledge, 2007), 2, 310, 313.

89. Agent 983 to Armour, 11 May 1945, RG 226, Entry 127, Box 23, NARA.

90. The best study of the Safe Haven investigations into state and para-state assets in Spain is Collado Seidel, *España: Refugio nazi*.

91. Baldwin to Walton Butterworth and Armour, 3 May 1945, RG 84, Entry 3163, Box 2, NARA.

92. Memo, 8 May 1945, RG 226, Entry 127, Box 1, NARA.

93. Agent 983 to Elton, 2 June 1945, RG 226, Entry 99, Box 20, NARA.

94. Ibid.

95. Armour to Secretary of State, 5 May 1945, RG 84, Madrid, Entry 3162, Box 66, NARA.

96. Collado Seidel, *España: Refugio nazi*, 54.

97. Armour to Secretary of State, 5 May 1945, RG 84, Madrid, Entry 3162, Box 66, NARA.

98. British Embassy, Madrid, to Butterworth, 5 Mar. 1945, RG 84, Madrid, Entry 3162, Box 68, NARA.

99. Haig to SAINT (copy to OSS), 30 Apr. 1945, RG 226, Entry 127, Box 27, NARA.

100. Memo, 8 May 1945, RG 226, Entry 127, Box 1, NARA; U.S. Embassy, Madrid, to U.S. Consulate, Bilbao, 7 July 1945, RG 226, Entry 127, Box 2, NARA; Armour to all U.S. Missions in Spain, 7 July 1945, RG 84, Entry 3162, Box 75, NARA.

101. Baldwin to Butterworth, 19 June 1945, RG 226, Entry 127, Box 5, NARA.

102. Memo, 28 Sept. 1946, RG 226, Entry 127, Box 3, NARA.

103. Irujo, *La lista negra*, 88, 89, 151.

104. Agent 23715/C to agent 23700, 21 Sept. 1945, RG 226, Entry 127, Box 2, NARA.

105. U.S. Consulate, Bilbao, to U.S. Embassy, Madrid, 12 June 1945, RG 226, Entry 127, Box 2, NARA.

106. White to Legion, 16 Mar. 1945, RG 226, Entry 127, Box 2, NARA. See also Eduard Rolland, *Galicia en guerra: Espías, batallas, submarinos e volframio; do desfile da Wehrmacht en Vigo á fuxida dos criminais nazis* (Vigo: Edicións Xerasi, 2006).

107. Rolland, *Galicia en guerra*, 37–38.

108. SAINT, Bilbao, to SAINT, Madrid, 14 Apr. 1945, RG 226, Entry 127, Box 1, NARA.

109. SAINT, Bilbao, to SAINT, Madrid, 16 Apr. 1945, RG 226, Entry 127, Box 1, NARA.

110. Memo by Howell, "Germans for repatriation," 27 Feb. 1946, RG 226, Entry 190A, Box 23, NARA.

111. U.S. Consulate, Bilbao, to U.S. Embassy, Madrid, 12 June 1945, RG 226, Entry 127, Box 2, NARA.

112. Agent 23715/C to agent 23700, 21 Sept. 1945, RG 226, Entry 127, Box 2, NARA.

113. Memo for SAINT, 31 Jan. 1946, RG 226, Entry 127, Box 28, NARA.

114. Friedhelm Burbach to Armour, via U.S. Consulate, Bilbao, 21 Jan. 1946, RG 84, Entry 3162, Box 105, NARA.

115. Andrew Wardlaw to Phillip Bonsal, 21 May 1947, RG 84, Entry 3175, Box 22, NARA.

116. Memo by Howell, "Germans for repatriation," 27 Feb. 1946, RG 226, Entry 190A, Box 23, NARA.

117. Herman Kuhne, statement attached to Donald Marelius to Butterworth, 30 Jan. 1946, RG 84, Entry 3162, Box 99, NARA.

118. Memo of conversation with Gustav Draeger and Hans-David Ziegra, 12 June 1945, RG 84, Entry 3162, Box 75, NARA.

119. Marelius to Butterworth, 30 Jan. 1946, RG 84, Entry 3161, Box 99, NARA.

120. Final Interrogation Report, Walter Eugen Mosig, U.S. Army European Command Intelligence Center, 22 Aug. 1947, KV 2/3574, NA.

121. For intelligence on Mosig and his SD activities in Spain, see Junior to SAINT, 7 Aug. 1945, and on the interview with Mosig, see memo to SAINT, "Walter Eugen Mosig," 4 Sept. 1945, both in RG 226, Entry 127, Box 28, NARA.

122. Memo to SAINT, with W. O. Frohberg signed statement of 19 Oct. attached, 22 Oct. 1945, RG 226, Entry 127, Box 28, NARA.

123. Memo to SAINT, 18 Sept. 1945, RG 226, Entry 127, Box 28, NARA.

124. Agent 23715/C to agent 23700, 4 Dec. 1945, RG 226, Entry 127, Box 2, NARA.

125. Memo by Howell, "Germans for repatriation," 27 Feb. 1946, RG 226, Entry 190A, Box 23, NARA.

126. SAINT BC 012 to SAINT BC 001, 12 and 17 May 1945, RG 226, Entry 127, Box 1, NARA.

127. Memo by Howell, "Germans for repatriation," 27 Feb. 1946, RG 226, Entry 190A, Box 23, NARA.

128. Ibid.

129. Ibid.

130. British Embassy, Madrid, to Ministry of Foreign Affairs, Spain, 7 Sept. 1945, FO 371/49550, NA.

131. Memo by Howell, "Germans for repatriation," 27 Feb. 1946, RG 226, Entry 190A, Box 23, NARA.

132. David A. Messenger, "'Our Spanish Brothers' or 'As at Plombières': France and the Spanish Opposition to Franco, 1945–1948," *French History* 20, no. 1 (2006): 61.

133. Memo by Howell, "Germans for repatriation," 27 Feb. 1946, RG 226, Entry 190A, Box 23, NARA.

134. David A. Messenger, *L'Espagne Républicaine: French Policy and Spanish Republicanism in Liberated France* (Brighton, UK: Sussex Academic, 2008), 44–45.

135. Marelius to U.S. Embassy, Madrid, 7 July 1945, RG 84, Entry 3161, Box 73, NARA.

136. Rodríguez González, "El espionaje nazi," 225–32.

137. Marelius to Armour, 9 Nov. 1945, RG 84, Entry 3162, Box 75, NARA.

138. Haig to SAINT (copy to OSS), 30 Apr. 1945, RG 226, Entry 127, Box 27, NARA.

139. Torr to Major L. C. Gane, War Office, 15 June 1945, FO 371/49550, NA.

140. Biddiscombe, *WERWOLF!*, 8.

141. Memo by Baldwin, 7 May 1945, RG 226, Entry 190A, Box 24, NARA.

142. Memo by Howell, "Germans for repatriation," 27 Feb. 1946, RG 226, Entry 190A, Box 23, NARA.

143. SAINT BC 012 to SAINT BC 001, 18 May 1945, RG 226, Entry 127, Box 1, NARA.

144. Egon Olivier, *Mémoire sur l'impossible extradition de Léon Degrelle* (Brussels: privately printed, 2010), 25.

145. Martin Conway, *Collaboration in Belgium: Léon Degrelle and the Rexist Movement, 1940–1944* (New Haven, CT: Yale University Press, 1993), 281.

146. Memo by Howell, "Germans for repatriation," 27 Feb. 1946, RG 226, Entry 190A, Box 23, NARA.

147. Memo by agent 23732/C, 17 Apr. 1945, RG 226, Entry 127, Box 27, NARA.

148. Memo by Howell, "Germans for repatriation," 27 Feb. 1946, RG 226, Entry 190A, Box 23, NARA.

149. Ibid.

150. Baldwin to Armour, 1 Sept. 1945, RG 226, Entry 127, Box 5, NARA.

151. Memo by Baldwin, 25 Sept. 1945, RG 226, Entry 127, Box 5, NARA.

152. Baldwin to Armour, 1 Sept. 1945, RG 226, Entry 127, Box 5, NARA.

CHAPTER 3

1. British Passport Control Officer to British Chancery, 27 June 1946 (copy to U.S. Embassy, Madrid), RG 226, Entry 210, Box 35, NARA.

2. Memo, Dirección General Política Exterior, Ministry of Foreign Affairs, Spain, 26 Nov. 1945, R 2160/4, MAE.

3. Civil Governor of Gerona to Dirección General Seguridad, enclosed in Dirección General Seguridad to Ministry of Foreign Affairs, Spain, Dirección General Política Exterior, 13 Feb. 1946, R 2159/6, MAE.

4. British Embassy, Madrid, to Ministry of Foreign Affairs, Spain, 25 Jan. 1945, R 2159/3, MAE.

5. Ministerio de Gobernación to José Félix Lequerica, 5 Jan. 1945, R2159/3, MAE.

6. Dirección General Política Exterior, Ministry of Foreign Affairs, Spain, to Minister of Foreign Affairs, 23 Oct. 1945, R 2159/4, MAE.

7. Notes, Ministry of Foreign Affairs, Spain, 23 Nov. 1944 and 23 Aug. 1945, R 2160/3, MAE; British Embassy, Madrid, to Ministry of Foreign Affairs, Spain, 23 Feb. 1946, R 2159/6, MAE.

8. Memo for SAINT, 12 Dec. 1945, RG 226, Entry 127, Box 28, NARA.

9. British Passport Control Officer to British Chancery, 27 June 1946 (copy to U.S. Embassy, Madrid), RG 226, Entry 210, Box 35, NARA.

10. Agent 23715/C to agent 23700, Folder "Incoming British," RG 226, Entry 127, Box 2, NARA.

11. Memo to D. P. Medalie, Byron Blankinship, Milton, and Tennant, U.S. Embassy, Madrid, 7 Sept. 1945, RG 226, Entry 127, Box 26, NARA.

12. Agent X to Baldwin, U.S. Embassy, Madrid, 28 Nov. 1945, RG 226, Entry 127, Box 28, NARA.

13. Note of meeting between Artajo and von Bibra, 14 Nov. 1945, R 5161/19, MAE.

14. Jill Edwards, *Anglo-American Relations and the Franco Question, 1945–1955* (Oxford: Clarendon, 1999), xiv.

15. "The Vesting of German Assets in Spain," FEA Enemy Branch, July 1945, RG 169, Entry UD 10, Box 2, NARA.

16. Secretary of State to John Winant (U.S. ambassador to the United Kingdom), 24 Aug. 1944, in *FRUS, 1944*, 2:222.

17. Armour to Secretary of State, 30 Sept. 1945, in *FRUS, 1945*, 5:689.

18. Collado Seidel, *España: Refugio nazi*, 161.

19. Slany, *U.S. and Allied Efforts*, 52.

20. See the text of ACC Law No. 5 in *FRUS, 1945*, 3:836–45.

21. Asesoria Juridica Internacional to Bloqueo, Ministry of Foreign Affairs, Spain, 14 Dec. 1945, R 005477/7, MAE.

22. Seymour J. Rubin, "The Washington Accord Fifty Years Later: Neutrality, Morality and International Law," *American University International Law Review* 14, no. 1 (1998): 67.

23. Ministry of Foreign Affairs, Spain, to British and U.S. embassies, Madrid, 22 Feb. 1946, R 005477/1, MAE.

24. Slany, *U.S. and Allied Wartime and Postwar Relations*, 81.

25. Francisco Gómez-Jordana to Hoare, 20 June 1944, R 2159/1, MAE.

26. British Embassy, Madrid, to Ministry of Foreign Affairs, Spain, 29 Sept. 1944, R 2159/1, MAE.

27. Memo, 18 Nov. 1945, R 5161/19, MAE.

28. Dirección General Política Exterior, Ministry of Foreign Affairs, Spain, to Minister of Foreign Affairs, 23 Oct. 1946, R 2159/4, MAE.

29. Memo, Dirección General Política Exterior, Ministry of Foreign Affairs, Spain, 10 July 1946, R 5161/19, MAE.

30. Satorres, note on meeting with Baldwin and Bramwell, 28 Dec. 1945, R 5161/19, MAE.

31. Christopher Bramwell, notes of meeting with Satorres, 28 Dec. 1945, FO 371/55343, NA.

32. Dirección General Política Exterior, Ministry of Foreign Affairs, Spain, to Artajo, 23 Oct. 1945, R2159/4, MAE.

33. Ibid.

34. Nancy L. Green, "Americans Abroad and the Uses of Citizenship: Paris, 1914–1940," *Journal of American Ethnic History* 31, no. 3 (2012): 7.

35. Brian C. J. Singer, "Cultural versus Contractual Nations: Rethinking their Opposition," *History and Theory* 35, no. 3 (1996): 310.

36. Ibid., 313.

37. See ibid., 324.

38. Immanuel Wallerstein, "Citizens All? Citizens Some! The Making of the Citizen," *Comparative Studies in Society and History* 45, no. 4 (2003): 651.

39. Artajo to Blas Perez Gonzalez, 14 Nov. 1946, R 5161/19, MAE.

40. Eduardo Merello to Tomas Suñer, 7 Feb. 1946, R 2159/6, MAE.

41. Francisco Rodriguez Martínez to Perez Gonzalez, 18 Nov. 1946, R 5161/19, MAE.

42. U.S. Embassy, Madrid, to State Department, 7 Jan. 1946 (copy to British Embassy, Washington, DC), 14 Feb. 1946, FO 371/55348, NA.

43. Transcript, interrogation of Walther Giese, 11 Oct. 1945, Berlin Interrogation Center, U.S. Army G-2, RG 84, Entry 2531B, Box 28, NARA.

44. Marelius to Bonsal, 27 May 1946, RG 84, Entry 3162, Box 101, NARA.

45. Memo for SAINT, 30 Nov. 1945, Haig Files (Incoming British), RG 226, Entry 127, Box 28, NARA.

46. Marelius to Butterworth, 15 Feb. 1946, RG 84, Entry 3162, Box 97, NARA.

47. Marelius to Butterworth, 30 Jan. 1946, RG 84, Entry 3162, Box 99, NARA.

48. Minute by J. M. K. Vyvyan, 28 Dec. 1945, FO 371/55343, NA.

49. Minute by Garran, 28 Dec. 1945, FO 371/55343, NA.

50. British Embassy, Madrid, to German Department, Foreign Office, 3 Jan. 1946, FO 371/55343, NA.

51. Baldwin to British Embassy, Madrid, 7 Jan. 1946, FO 371/55343, NA.

52. W. A. Brandt, MEW, to U.S. Embassy, London, 2 Jan. 1946, FO 371/55343, NA.

53. German Department, Foreign Office, to British embassies, Madrid and Lisbon, 19 Jan. 1946, FO 371/55343, NA.

54. Memo by Earle Titus, 3 May 1946, RG 226, Entry 190A, Box 24, NARA.

55. Memo by Baldwin, 5 May 1946, Entry 190A, Box 24, NARA.

56. Memo by Howell, 1 Nov. 1948, RG 226, Entry 190A, Box 24, NARA.

57. Medalie to Bonsal, 1 Mar. 1946, RG 226, Entry 194, Box 66, NARA.

58. Medalie to Bonsal and Baldwin, 27 Feb. 1946, RG 226, Entry 194, Box 66, NARA.

59. British Embassy, Madrid, to German Department, Foreign Office, 3 Jan. 1946, FO 371/55343, NA.

60. Bramwell, notes of meeting with Satorres, 28 Dec. 1945, FO 371/55343, NA.

61. U.S. and British embassies, Madrid, to Ministry of Foreign Affairs, Spain, 15 Mar. 1946, R 2159/6, MAE, reprinted in document dated 4 Apr. 1946, RG 226, Entry 210, Box 35, NARA.

62. British Embassy, Madrid, to German Department, Foreign Office, 3 Jan. 1946, FO 371/55343, NA.

63. See Foreign Office to Christopher Steel, British Political Advisor in Germany, 19 Jan. 1946, FO 371/55343; Brown, Secretary to ACC Political Directorate, to Foreign Office, 15 Jan. 1946, FO 371/55344; and Steel to Foreign Office, 24 Jan. 1946, FO 371/55344, all in NA.

64. Foreign Office to British Embassy, Madrid, 22 Jan. 1946, FO 371/55344, NA.

65. Minute by Hoyer-Millar, 21 Jan. 1946, FO 371/55345, NA.

66. Mallett to Foreign Office, 5 Feb. 1946, FO 371/55346, NA.

67. Butterworth to State Department, 2 Jan. 1946, RG 84, Entry 3162, Box 99, NARA.

68. Minute by R. Sloan, 8 Feb. 1946, FO 371/55346, NA.

69. British Embassy, Madrid, to German Department, Foreign Office, 4 Feb. 1946, FO 371/55346, NA.

70. Hoyer-Millar, minute on meeting with Satorres, 31 Jan. 1946, FO 371/55345, NA.

71. Bercomb to TROOPERS, 15 Feb. 1946 (copy to Foreign Office), FO 371/55345, NA.

72. Memos, OSS Madrid X-2 and SI, 29 Jan.–23 Aug. 1946, RG 226, Entry 127, Box 4, NARA.

73. Mallett to Bevin, 5 Mar. 1946, FO 371/60434, NA.

74. British Embassy, Madrid, to Ministry of Foreign Affairs, Spain, 20 Feb. 1946, FO 371/60434, NA.

75. Bercomb to TROOPERS, 15 Feb. 1946 (copy to Foreign Office), FO 371/55345, NA.

76. Vyvyan to Lt. Col. V. M. Hammer, War Office, 22 Feb. 1946, FO 371/55347, NA.

77. Mallett to Bevin, 5 Mar. 1946, FO 371/60434, NA.

78. Mallet to British consuls general in Spain, 1 Apr. 1946, FO 371/60434, NA.

79. Mallett to Bevin, 5 Mar. 1946, FO 371/60434, NA.

80. Note, Ministry of Foreign Affairs, Spain, to British Embassy, Madrid, 26 Feb. 1946, FO 371/60434, NA.

81. Mallett to Bevin, 5 Mar. 1946, FO 371/60434, NA.

82. Douglas Howard to Bevin, 15 Mar. 1946, FO 371/60435, NA.

83. Ibid.

84. Report of British-American Repatriation Centre, 11 Mar. 1946, enclosed in Howard to Bevin, 15 Mar. 1946, FO 371/60435, NA.

85. Memo, Dirección General Política Exterior, Ministry of Foreign Affairs, Spain, 4 Apr. 1946, R 2159/6, MAE.

86. Minute by Garran, 6 Apr. 1946, FO 371/60434, NA.

87. Ibid.

88. Mallet to British consuls general in Spain, 1 Apr. 1946, FO 371/60434, NA.

89. James Byrnes to U.S. Embassy, Madrid, 20 Apr. 1946, copy in Shuman to Garran, Western Department, Foreign Office, 23 Apr. 1946, FO 371/60434, NA.

90. Bonsal to State Department, 4 Apr. 1946, RG 226, Entry 210, Box 35, NARA.

91. U.S. Embassy, Madrid, to U.S. Embassy, London, 21 Mar. 1946 (copy to Foreign Office), FO 371/55349, NA.

92. Mallet to British consuls general in Spain, 22 Mar. 1946, FO 371/60434, NA.

93. *ABC* (Madrid and Seville), 18 May 1946.

94. Minutes of conversation between Lequerica and von Bibra, 14 Nov. 1945, R 5161/19, MAE; Bonsal to State Department, 10 Dec. 1945, RG 84, Entry 3162, Box 76, NARA.

95. Messenger, *L'Espagne Republicaine*, 98–108.

96. Department of State, *Bulletin*, 17 Mar. 1946, 412–27.

97. Preston, *Franco*, 554–55; Liedtke, *Embracing a Dictatorship*, 1.

98. Messenger, *L'Espagne Republicaine*, 123–31.

99. Hoyer-Millar to Sir Orme Sargent, 9 May 1946, FO 371/60435, NA.

100. This speech was referred to by British officials in Madrid and by Sir Orme Sargent, of the Foreign Office, in a meeting with Spanish ambassador to the United Kingdom on 9 May 1946. Hoyer-Millar to Mallet, 11 May 1946, FO 371/60435, NA.

101. Sargent, Foreign Office, in meeting with Spanish ambassador to the United Kingdom, on 9 May 1946. Hoyer-Millar to Mallet, 11 May 1946, FO 371/60435, NA.

102. British Embassy, Madrid, to German Department, Foreign Office, 26 Apr. 1946, FO 371/60434, NA.

103. Ibid.

104. State Department to Office of the Political Advisor, OMGUS, 3 May 1946, RG 260, NARA.

105. Memo, Dirección General Política Exterior, Ministry of Foreign Affairs, Spain, 4 Apr. 1946, R 2159/6, MAE.

106. British Embassy, Madrid, to Ministry of Foreign Affairs, Spain, 21 May 1946, FO 371/60435, NA.

107. Mallet, note on meeting with Artajo, 8 June 1946, FO 371/60436, NA.

108. Bonsal to U.S. Embassy, London, 10 June 1946 (copy to Foreign Office), FO 371/60436, NA.

109. Harry Hawley to Bonsal, 6 July 1946, RG 84, Entry 3175, Box 18, NARA.

110. Bonsal, memo of conversation with Howard and Artajo, 9 July 1946, RG 226, Entry 190A, Box 24, NARA.

111. British Passport Control Officer to British Chancery, 27 June 1946 (copy to U.S. Embassy, Madrid), RG 226, Entry 210, Box 35, NARA.

112. See note, U.S. and British embassies, Madrid, to Ministry of Foreign Affairs, Spain, 10 Aug. 1946, RG 226, Entry 210, Box 35, NARA. This protest was in addition to notes of 6 May and 8 July 1946 from both embassies to the ministry and a note of 30 May 1946 from the U.S. embassy to the ministry containing the names of eleven such Germans.

113. Memo by Artajo, 8 Aug. 1946, R 5161/3, MAE.

114. Phillip Crosthwaite to Foreign Office, 23 Aug. 1946, FO 371/6043, NA.

115. Ministry of Foreign Affairs to U.S. Embassy, Madrid, 21 Aug. 1946, RG 226, Entry 190A, Box 24, NARA.

116. U.S. Embassy, Madrid, to Ministry of Foreign Affairs, Spain, 28 Aug. 1946, R 2161/2, MAE.

117. Crosthwaite to José Sebastian de Erice, R 2161/2, MAE.

118. Memo, U.S. Embassy, Madrid, 6 Sept. 1946, RG 226, Entry 190A, Box 24, NARA.

119. Crosthwaite to Foreign Office, 2 Sept. 1946, FO 371/60438, NA.

120. Crosthwaite to Satorres, 30 Oct. 1946, R 2161/3, MAE.

121. Crosthwaite to Foreign Office, 2 Sept. 1946, FO 371/60438, NA.

122. Mallet to Bevin, 12 Aug. 1946, FO 371/60437, NA.

123. Mallet to Foreign Office, 16 Sept. 1946, FO 371/60438, NA.

124. Foreign Office to Mallet, 18 Sept. 1946, and Mallet to Foreign Office, 18 Sept. 1946, FO 371/60438, NA.

125. Titus to Bonsal, 11 Dec. 1946, RG 226, Entry 127, Box 4, NARA.

126. Memo by Satorres, 8 Aug. 1946, R 2161/2, MAE.

127. Mallet to Foreign Office, 20 Oct. 1946, FO 371/60439, NA.

128. Hoyer-Millar to Oliver Harvey, 3 Oct. 1946, FO 371/60439, NA.

129. U.S. Embassy, Madrid, to State Department, 18 Nov. 1946, copy in Harold Macmillan to Hogg, 20 Nov. 1946, FO 371/60439, NA.

130. Memo, Sept. 1946, RG 226, Entry 210, Box 35, NARA.

131. Minutes of the seventy-ninth meeting of the Security Council, 4 Nov. 1946, U.N. Security Council, *Official Records*, 1st year, 2nd ser., no. 1.

CHAPTER 4

1. Puig, "La conexión alemana," 9.

2. For more on Ziegra's prewar activities, see Norman J. W. Goda, "Banking on Hitler: Chase National Bank and the Ruckwanderer Mark Scheme, 1936–1941," in *U.S. Intelligence and the Nazis,* by Richard Breitman, Norman J. W. Goda, Timothy Naftali, and Robert Wolfe (Cambridge: Cambridge University Press, 2005), 174, 176–81, 184.

3. Blacklow to Audits & Investigations, Financial Division, OMGUS, 29 Jan. 1947, RG 260, Entry 421(A1), Box 586, NARA.

4. Titus to Butterworth, 19 Feb. 1945, RG 226, Entry 190A, Box 24, NARA.

5. Memo, 24 Aug. 1945, RG 226, Entry 190A, Box 24, NARA.

6. Junior to SAINT, 15 Nov. 1945, RG 226, Entry 127, Box 28, NARA.

7. Transcript, interrogation of W. Minameyer, 26 June 1946, RG 260, Entry 421(A1), Box 586, NARA.

8. Transcript, interrogation of Berndotto Freiherr von Heyden-Rynsch, 19 June 1945, RG 226, Entry 183, Box 7, NARA; see also Werner Michael Schultz, interview by Titus, 2 Feb. 1946, RG 226, Entry 190A, Box 24, NARA.

9. Miles Bond to Chargé d'Affaires, 8 Aug. 1946, RG 226, Entry 190A, Box 24, NARA.

10. Note for SAINT/HQ, 27 Dec. 1945, RG 226, Entry 127, Box 28, NARA.

11. Memo, 17 June 1946, RG 226, Entry 210, Box 34, NARA.

12. Parks to Bond, "Eva Reports," 12 July 1946, RG 226, Entry 210, Box 38, NARA.

13. By the 1970s Tur was the French consul in Zaragoza. He was murdered there by the leftist revolutionary group Frente Revolucionario Antifascista y Patriota (FRAP) in November 1972, and Franco granted him the Order of Isabel, a Catholic medal, posthumously. See Alberto Sabio Alcutén, *Peligrosos demócratas: Antifranquistas vistos por la policía política (1958–1977)* (Madrid: Cátedra, 2011), 158–59.

14. Note, U.S. Embassy, Madrid, 11 Dec. 1945, RG 84, Entry 3163, Box 2, NARA.

15. U.S. Embassy, Madrid, to State Department, 9 Nov. 1945, RG 84, Entry 3162, Box 75, NARA.

16. U.S. Embassy, Madrid, to State Department, 19 Jan. 1946, RG 84, Entry 3162, Box 97, NARA.

17. U.S. Embassy, Madrid, to State Department, 7 Mar. 1946, RG 84, Entry 3162, Box 97, NARA.

18. Memo by Howell, "Germans for repatriation," 27 Feb. 1946, RG 226, Entry 190A, Box 23, NARA.

19. U.S. Embassy, Madrid, to State Department, 26 June 1945, RG 84, Entry 3162, Box 73, NARA.

20. Marelius to Bonsal, 12 Apr. 1946, RG 84, Entry 3162, Box 99, NARA.

21. Artajo to Perez Gonzalez, 15 July 1945, R 5161/19, MAE.

22. Hawley to Butterworth, 14 Feb. 1946, RG 84, Entry 3175, Box 18, NARA.

23. Hawley to Bonsal, 12 June 1946, RG 84, Entry 3175, Box 18, NARA.

24. U.S. Embassy, Madrid, to Ministry of Foreign Affairs, Spain, 16 Aug. 1946, R 2161/2, MAE.

25. U.S. and British embassies, Madrid, to Ministry of Foreign Affairs, Spain, 3 July 1946, RG 84, Entry 3162, Box 98, NARA.

26. Marelius to Bonsal, 27 May 1946, RG 84, Entry 3162, Box 101, NARA.

27. British Embassy, Madrid, to Ministry of Foreign Affairs, Spain, 23 Aug. 1946, R 2161/2, MAE.

28. Harold B. Quarton to Bonsal, 16 Aug. 1946, RG 226, Entry 190A, Box 24, NARA.

29. Bowen, *Spaniards and Nazi Germany,* 29.

30. Stanley G. Payne, *Franco and Hitler: Spain, Germany and World War II* (New Haven, CT: Yale University Press, 2008), 29–30, 118.

31. Ros Agudo, *La guerra secreta,* 76.

32. Ibid., 133, 200, 321.

33. Safe Haven Report No. 143, 2 July 1945, RG 226, Entry 183, Box 8, NARA.

34. Joint memo, British and U.S. embassies, Madrid, to Director General of Political Economy, Ministry of Foreign Affairs, Spain, 2 July 1945, RG 226, Entry 183, Box 8, NARA.

35. See, for example, transcripts, interrogations of H. Bethke, 31 May and 6 July 1945, RG 226, Entry 183, Box 8, NARA.

36. Memo of conversation, Col. Ebright, Horwin, and Milton with Walter Becker, 20 July 1945, RG 226, Entry 183, Box 8, NARA.

37. Report XX-7785, 28 June 1945, RG 226, Entry 183, Box 8, NARA.

38. Earl, *Nuremberg SS-Einzagruppen Trial,* 49.

39. Memo of conversation, Logie, Copeland, Milton, Bennett, and Horwin with Johannes Bernhardt, 26 July 1945, RG 226, Entry 183, Box 8, NARA.

40. Seyla Benhabib, *The Rights of Others: Aliens, Residents and Citizens* (Cambridge: Cambridge University Press, 2004), 55.

41. Bloxham, "Genocidal Past," 307.

42. Herf, *Divided Memory*, 202.

43. Ibid., 225.

44. U.S. Embassy, Madrid, to State Department, 10 Sept. 1946, RG 226, Entry 127, Box 3, NARA.

45. Paloma Aguilar, *Memory and Amnesia: The Role of the Spanish Civil War in the Transition to Democracy*, trans. Mark Oakley (New York: Berghahn Books, 2002), 30.

46. Ibid., 46, 61.

47. Javier Rodrigo, *Cautivos: Campos de concentración en la España franquista, 1936–1947* (Barcelona: Crítica, 2005), 127.

48. Ibid., 128.

49. Michael Richards, "From War Culture to Civil Society: Francoism, Social Change and Memories of the Spanish Civil War," *History & Memory* 14, nos. 1/2 (2002): 99.

50. Antonio Cazorla-Sánchez, *Fear and Progress: Ordinary Lives in Franco's Spain, 1939–1975* (Oxford: Wiley-Blackwell, 2010), 25.

51. Max Nutz to Ministry of Foreign Affairs, Spain, 22 Jan. 1946, R 2159/6, MAE.

52. Giese to Ministry of Foreign Affairs, Spain, 31 July 1945, R 2159/3, MAE.

53. British Passport Control Officer to British Chancery, 27 June 1946 (copy to U.S. Embassy, Madrid), RG 226, Entry 210, Box 35, NARA.

54. Lequerica to Luis Carrero Blanco, 22 Nov. 1944, R 21690/4, MAE.

55. Meino von Eitzen to Ministry of Foreign Affairs, Spain, 11 Aug. 1945, R 2159/4, and 18 Jan. 1946, R 2159/6, both in MAE; Casa Civil de El Jefe del Estado y Generalisimo de los Ejercitos to Artajo, 20 Feb. 1946, R 2159/6, MAE.

56. Moreno to Lequerica, 15 Nov. 1944, R 2160/4, MAE.

57. SAINT BC 012 to SAINT BC 001, 19 May 1945, RG 226, Entry 127, Box 1, NARA.

58. British Embassy, Madrid, to Ministry of Foreign Affairs, Spain, 16 Mar. 1944, R 2159/1, MAE.

59. SAINT BC 012 to SAINT BC 001, 31 May and 31 Aug. 1945, RG 226, Entry 127, Box 1, NARA.

60. Genserowsky to Foreign Minister, 28 May 1945, R 2159/3, MAE.

61. Gen. Martinez de Campos to Lequerica, 16 June 1945, R 2160/4, MAE.

62. Memo by Dirección General Seguridad, 7 May 1948, R 5161/7, MAE.

63. Dirección General Seguridad to Dirección General Política Exterior, Ministry of Foreign Affairs, Spain, 8 Aug. 1944, R 2159/1, MAE.

64. Memo, Ministry of Foreign Affairs, Spain, n.d., R 2160/4, MAE.

65. Irujo, *La lista negra*, 140–43.

66. Yturralde y Orbegosos to Demetrio Carceller, 4 Mar. 1948, R 5161/15, MAE.

67. Florentino Portero, *Franco aislado: La cuestión española, 1945–1950* (Madrid: Aguilar, 1989), 72–76.

68. Armour to Secretary of State, 24 Mar. 1945, in *FRUS, 1945*, 5:668.

69. Joan Maria Thomàs, *Roosevelt, Franco and the End of the Second World War* (New York: Palgrave Macmillan, 2011), 177.

70. Rodrigo, *Cautivos*, 138.

71. Burbach to Francisco Franco, 12 Apr. 1946, R 2159/6, MAE.

72. Ibid.

73. Burbach to Hawley, 27 Apr. 1946 (copy to Ministry of Foreign Affairs, Spain), R 2159/6, MAE.

74. Kurt Meyer-Doehner to Artajo, 24 Apr. 1946, R2159/6, MAE.

75. Richards, "From War Culture to Civil Society," 98.

76. Richard Enge to Ministry of Foreign Affairs, Spain, 17 Apr. 1946, R 2160/4, MAE.

77. Sasha D. Pack, *Tourism and Dictatorship: Europe's Peaceful Invasion of Franco's Spain* (New York: Palgrave Macmillan, 2006), 40.

78. Alfred Menzell to Artajo, 24 Apr. 1946, R 2159/6, MAE.

79. Walter Leutner to Ministry of Foreign Affairs, Spain, 9 Dec. 1944 and 2 Jan. 1946, R 2159/2, MAE.

80. Leutner to Artajo, 11 Jan. 1946, R 2159/6, MAE.

81. Ibid.

82. Leutner to Ministry of Foreign Affairs, Spain, 2 Jan. 1946, R 2159/2, MAE.

83. Cardinal Enrique Pla y Daniel to Artajo, 8 June 1946, R 5161/19, MAE.

84. Gottfried von Waldheim to Baldwin, U.S. Embassy, Madrid, 27 June 1946, R 2160/4, MAE.

85. Richards, "From War Culture to Civil Society," 102.

86. Rodrigo, *Cautivos*, 133, 137.

87. José Lipperheide Henke to Ministry of Foreign Affairs, Spain, 20 Apr. 1946, R 2159/6, MAE.

88. Cardinal Enrique Pla y Daniel to Artajo, 18 June 1946, R 5161/19, MAE.

89. Agent 23715/C to agent 23700, Folder "Incoming British," RG 226, Entry 127, Box 28, NARA.

90. Federico Lipperheide to U.S. Embassy, Madrid, 4 Feb. 1946 (copy to Ministry of Foreign Affairs, Spain), R 2159/1, MAE.

91. Father José María Huber to Ministry of Foreign Affairs, Spain, 30 May 1946, R 2160/1, MAE.

92. Transcript, interrogation of Georg Wolfgang Scuebel, Hohenasperg, Germany, 28–29 June and 1 July 1946, RG 260, Entry 421(A), Box 585, NARA.

93. Antonio Oboril to Ministry of Foreign Affairs, 23 Feb. 1946, R 2159/6, MAE.

94. U.S. Embassy to State Department, 19 Jan. 1946, RG 84, Entry 3162, Box 97, NARA.

95. "Note from Recent Haig Reports" Haig Files (Incoming British), RG 226, Entry 127, Box 2, NARA.

96. Memo by Titus, U.S. Embassy, 22 Jan. 1946, RG 226, Entry 190A, Box 27, NARA.

97. Father José Boos to Ministry of Foreign Affairs, Spain, 1 June 1946, R 2161/1, MAE.

98. Cardinal Enrique Pla y Daniel to Artajo, 8 June 1946, R 5161/9, MAE.

99. Cardinal Enrique Pla y Daniel to Artajo, 13 May 1946, R 5161/9, MAE.

100. Memo, Dirección General Política Exterior, Ministry of Foreign Affairs, Spain, to Dirección General Seguridad, 5 June 1946, R 2160/2, MAE.

101. Boos to Artajo, 1 June 1946, R 2160/1, MAE.

102. Safe Haven Report No. 172, 18 June 1945, RG 226, Entry 183, NARA.

103. Memo by Howell, "Germans for repatriation," 26 Feb. 1946, RG 226, Entry 190A, Box 23, NARA.

104. Titus to Parks, 18 Nov. 1946, RG 84, Entry 3162, Box 98, NARA.

105. Rhodes to Ford, 21 Jan. 1946, RG 84, Entry 3162, Box 97, NARA.

106. Memo by Titus, 14 July 1948, RG 226, Entry 190A, Box 26, NARA.

107. Hans Rothe, report, 16 Jan. 1946, RG 226, Entry 210, Box 35, NARA.

108. U.S. Embassy, report, 10 Feb. 1947 (copy to FBI, Washington, DC), RG 65, Box 152, NARA.

109. Memo by Titus, 2 Dec. 1945, RG 226, Entry 190A, Box 27, NARA.

110. Father Conrad Simonsen to Titus, 12 Jan. 1946, RG 226, Entry 210, Box 35, NARA.

111. Simonsen to Ministry of Foreign Affairs, Spain, 26 Jan. 1946, R 5161/19, MAE.

112. Memo by Titus, 2 Dec. 1945, RG 226, Entry 190A, Box 27, NARA.

113. Gerald Steinacher, *Nazis on the Run: How Hitler's Henchmen Fled Justice* (Oxford: Oxford University Press, 2011), 154.

114. Ibid., 101–58.

115. Simonsen to José María Doussinague, 22 July 1945, copied in Doussinague to Artajo, 16 Nov. 1945, R 2160/4, MAE.

116. Carrero Blanco to Doussinague, 19 Feb. 1946, R 2160/4, MAE.

117. Herbert Hahn to Ministry of Foreign Affairs, Spain, 1 Mar. 1946, R 2159/6, MAE.

118. Ros Agudo, *La guerra secreta,* 217.

119. Friedrich Burkhardt to Ministry of Foreign Affairs, Spain, R 2160/1, MAE.

120. "Consolidated List of Persons who Worked for the German Intelligence Services in Spain, Compiled from Sources Within Germany," 26 Sept. 1946, RG 226, Entry 127, Box 3, NARA.

121. Wilhelm Meyer to Minister of Foreign Affairs, Spain, 26 May 1945, R 2159/3, MAE.

122. Max Ludwig Muller-Bohm to Ministry of Foreign Affairs, Spain, 29 Mar. 1946, R 2159/6, MAE.

123. Carrero Blanco to Artajo, 4 Sept. 1946, R 2160/4, MAE.

124. Titus to Bonsal, 29 Nov. 1946, RG 226, Entry 210, Box 35, NARA.

125. Ministry of Foreign Affairs to Franco, 14 May 1946, R 2160/4, MAE.

126. Dirección General Política Exterior, Ministry of Foreign Affairs, Spain, to Registry Office, Ministry of Justice, Spain, 10 Oct. 1945, R 2159/4, MAE.>

127. "Revised First and Second Priority List of German Agents and Officials for Expulsion," 17 July 1946, RG 226, Entry 127, Box 4, NARA.

128. Dirección General Política Exterior, Ministry of Foreign Affairs, Spain, to Registry Office, Ministry of Justice, Spain, 10 Oct. 1945, R 2159/4, MAE.

129. Baldwin to Armour, 9 July 1945, RG 226, Entry 127, Box 5, NARA.

130. Ibid.

131. See, for example, U.S. Embassy to Ministry of Foreign Affairs, Spain, 30 May 1945, in the cases of Francisco Liseu, Willi Lang, and Federico Lipperheide, RG 226, Entry 210, Box 35, NARA.

132. U.S. and British embassies, Madrid, to Ministry of Foreign Affairs, Spain, 15 Apr. 1946, R 2159/6, MAE.

133. Lipperheide Henke to Ministry of Foreign Affairs, 20 Apr. 1946, R 2160/4, MAE.

134. Memo, summary of meeting with Ministry of Foreign Affairs, Spain, in British Embassy, Madrid, to Western Department, Foreign Office, 1 July 1948, FO 371/72086A, NA.

135. Collado Seidel, *España: Refugio nazi*, 25–140.

CHAPTER 5

1. Control Office for Germany and Austria to Bercomb, ACC, Directorate of Prisoners of War and Displaced Persons, 17 July 1946, FO 371/55353, NA.

2. State Department to U.S. Embassy, Madrid, 29 May 1946, RG 260, Combined Repatriation Executive, NARA.

3. Central Secretariat, British Zone, to Foreign Office, 8 July 1947, FO 945/642, NA.

4. Memo, ACC (British Element), 31 July 1946, FO 945/642, NA.

5. Audit & Investigations Department, ACC (British Element), to R. C. Fenton, Economic Warfare Division, Foreign Office, 28 Aug. 1946, FO 1013/2497, NA.

6. Interrogation of Hans Heinrich Dieckhoff by Poole, 15 Nov. 1945, RG 84, Entry 2531B, Box 32, NARA.

7. Rodríguez González, "El espionaje nazi," 235.

8. Transcript, interrogation of Walter Giese, 11 Oct. 1945, RG 84, Entry 2531B, Box 28, NARA.

9. Morris, Office of the Political Advisor, Germany, to Morse, OSS, 21 May 1945, RG 84, Entry 2531B, Box 27, NARA.

10. Memo by Poole of Ernst Kaltenbrunner, Wilhelm Hoettl, and Walter Schellenberg interrogations, 12 Oct. 1945, RG 84, Entry 2531B, Box 27, NARA.

11. Arthur D. Jacobs, *The Prison Called Hohenasperg: An American Boy Betrayed by his Government during World War II* (New York: Universal, 1999), 60.

12. Romani Rose, *Roma and Sinti: Human Rights for Europe's Largest Minority* (Heidelberg: Documentation and Cultural Centre of German Sinti and Roma, 2007), 36.

13. Weekly G-2 Report, Third Army, 27 July 1946, RG 498, Entry UD 910, Box 4485, NARA.

14. Monthly G-2 Report, Third Army, 10 Sept. 1946, RG 498, Entry UD 910, Box 4485, NARA.

15. G-2 Weekly Journal, Third Army, 21 Sept. 1946, RG 498, Entry UD 910, Box 4485, NARA.

16. Monthly G-2 Reports, Third Army, 13 Nov. and 14 Dec. 1946, RG 498, Entry UD 910, Box 4486, NARA.

17. Daily G-2 Report, Third Army, 9 Dec. 1946, RG 498, Entry UD 910, Box 4486, NARA.

18. Daily G-2 Reports, Third Army, 30 Nov. and 12 Dec. 1946, RG 498, Entry UD 910, Box 4486, NARA.

19. The archives for the Hohenasperg *Spruchkammern* are located at EL 903/4 Spruchkammer der Interniertenlager: Verfahrensakten des Lagers 76 Hohenasperg, 1945–50, Landesarchiv Baden-Württemberg, Staatsarchiv Ludwigsburg, Ludwigsburg, Germany.

20. Paul Gernert, Chief of Prisons, U.S. High Commission for Germany, to Jorg, Director of Prisons, Baden-Württemberg, 17 Feb. and 20 Sept. 1948, RG 466, Prisons Division, Inspection Reports, NARA.

21. Titus to Privy Council Office, London, 29 Jan. 1947, RG 226, Entry 127, Box 4, NARA.

22. Medalie to Baldwin, 20 Feb. 1946, RG 84, Entry 3162, Box 106, NARA.

23. Note, Rothe, 15 Jan. 1946, RG 84, Entry 3162, Box 106, NARA.

24. Ibid.

25. Baldwin to Ford, 12 Feb. 1946, RG 84, Entry 3162, Box 106, NARA.

26. Memo by Baldwin, 16 May 1946, RG 84, Entry 3162, Box 106, NARA.

27. Transcript, interrogation of Alfred Muller-Thyssen, RG 84, Entry 3162, Box 106, NARA.

28. Wardlaw to Paul Culbertson, 27 Oct. 1947, RG 84, Entry 3175, Box 22, NARA.

29. Transcript, interrogation of Wilhelm Lampe, 25 July 1946, RG 84, Entry 2531B, Box 87, NARA.

30. Transcript, interrogation of Ernst Schultze, 9, 12, 13 Sept. 1946, RG 84, Entry 2531B, Box 88.

31. Bonsal to State Department, 8 Apr. 1946, RG 226, Entry 190A, Box 24, NARA.

32. Transcript, interrogation of Col. German von Wenckstern, 13 Jan. 1947, RG 84, Entry 2531B, Box 167, NARA.

33. Blancke to U.S. Embassy, Madrid, 29 Nov. 1946, RG 226, Entry 2531B, Box 88, NARA.

34. Statement, Hans Loetsch, 22 Sept. 1946, enclosed in Samuel M. Rose to Haraldson, 8 Oct. 1946, RG 226, Entry 2531B, Box 87, NARA.

35. Transcript, interrogation of Herbert Richter by Blancke, 11 July 1946, RG 226, Entry 2531B, Box 88, NARA.

36. Blankinship to Bonsal, 18 Aug. 1946, RG 84, Entry 3162, Box 107, NARA.

37. Titus to Horwin, 23 Jan. 1947, RG 226, Entry 210, Box 35, NARA.

38. Adolf Langenheim to British-U.S. Trusteeship, Madrid, 6 Feb. 1946, enclosed in Quarton to Butterworth, 7 Feb. 1946, RG 84, Entry 3162, Box 104, NARA.

39. Quarton to Bonsal, 19 Sept. 1946, RG 84, Entry 3162, Box 104, NARA.

40. British Embassy, Madrid, to Foreign Office, 30 Aug. 1946, FO 371/55354, NA.

41. Memo by Titus, 17 Mar. 1947, RG 226, Entry 127, Box 4, NARA.

42. Titus to Privy Council Office, London, 29 Jan. 1947, RG 226, Entry 127, Box 4, NARA.

43. Minute by D.W., 3 Dec. 1946, FO 371/55359, NA.

44. Titus to Culbertson, 18 Mar. 1948, RG 226, Entry 127, Box 8, NARA.

45. Minute by Burroughs, 27 Aug. 1946, FO 371/60438, NA.

46. Minutes by Crosthwaite, 11 and 28 Nov. 1947, FO 371/67902B, NA.

47. Howard to Attlee, 15 Jan. 1948, FO 371/73357, NA.

48. Memo by Titus, 24 Apr. 1948, RG 226, Entry 190A, Box 24, NARA.

49. Ibid.

50. Transcript, interrogation of Walter Eugen Mosig by Wendell Blancke, 1 Oct. 1946, RG 226, Entry 2531B, Box 167, NARA; see also Goñi, *Real Odessa*, 74.

51. Transcript, interrogation of Walter Eugen Mosig by Arnold M. Silver, 27 Aug. 1947, RG 65, Box 215, NARA.

52. Ibid.

53. Memo by Howell, "Germans for repatriation," 27 Feb. 1946, RG 226, Entry 190A, Box 23, NARA.

54. Ibid.

55. Memo by Titus, 11 Mar. 1947, RG 226, Entry 190A, Box 24, NARA.

56. Memo by Titus, 15 May 1947, RG 226, Entry 190A, Box 24, NARA.

57. Memo by Titus, 1 May 1947, RG 226, Entry 190A, Box 24, NARA.

58. "Intelligence Report Madrid," 17 July 1947, RG 226, Entry 210, Box 35, NARA.

59. Cox to Titus, 2 Feb. 1947, RG 226, Entry 210, Box 35, NARA.

60. Memos by Titus, 17 and 21 Mar. 1947, RG 226, Entry 127, Box 4, NARA.

61. Memo by Titus, 11 Mar. 1947, RG 226, Entry 190A, Box 24, NARA.

62. Titus to consuls general of the United States in Spain, 8 Nov. 1946, RG 84, Entry 3175, Box 18, NARA.

63. Howard to Bevin, 19 June 1947, FO 371/67902B, NA.

64. Memo by Titus, 15 May 1947, RG 226, Entry 190A, Box 24, NARA.

65. Memo by Titus, 30 Oct. 1947, RG 226, Entry 190A, Box 24, NARA.

66. Memo by Titus, 12 Jan. 1948, RG 226, Entry 190A, Box 24, NARA.

67. U.S. Embassy, Madrid, to State Department, 14 July 1945, RG 84 Entry 3162, Box 75, NARA.

68. Randall to Wardlaw, 18 Sept. 1947, RG 84, Entry 3175, Box 22, NARA.

69. Memo by Titus, 15 May 1947, RG 226, Entry 190A, Box 24, NARA.

70. Memo by Titus, 18 Nov. 1947, RG 226, Entry 190A, Box 24, NARA.

71. Memo by Titus, 12 Jan. 1948, RG 226, Entry 190A, Box 24, NARA.

72. Goñi, *Real Odessa*, 88–89.

73. Ibid., 89–91.

74. Memo by Howell, "Germans for repatriation," 27 Feb. 1946, RG 226, Entry 190A, Box 23, NARA.

75. Memo by Titus, 11 Mar. 1947, RG 226, Entry 190A, Box 24, NARA.

76. Ibid.

77. Memo by Howell, "Germans for repatriation," 27 Feb. 1946, RG 226, Entry 190A, Box 23, NARA.

78. Ministry of Foreign Affairs, Spain, to ACC, 5 July 1948, R 004209/7, MAE.

79. Memo by Howell, "Germans for repatriation," 27 Feb. 1946, RG 226, Entry 190A, Box 23, NARA.

80. U.S. and British embassies, Madrid, to Ministry of Foreign Affairs, Spain, 9 Apr. 1946, R 2159/6, MAE.

81. Memo by Howell, "Germans for repatriation," 27 Feb. 1946, RG 226, Entry 190A, Box 23, NARA.

82. Ibid.

83. Goñi, *Real Odessa*, 75.

84. Michael Phayer, *Pius XII, the Holocaust and the Cold War* (Bloomington: Indiana University Press, 2008), 183.

85. Goñi, *Real Odessa*, 71–75.

86. Memo by Titus, 22 Oct. 1947, RG 226, Entry 190A, Box 24, NARA.

87. Rolland, *Galicia en guerra*, 159–61.

88. Robert Murphy to State Department, 31 July 1946, RG 84, Entry 3162, Box 98, NARA.

89. Transcript, interrogation of Herbert Senner, enclosed in ibid.

90. Steinacher, *Nazis on the Run*, 212–21.

91. Goñi, *Real Odessa*, 65–70, 74, 77.

92. Ibid., 93.

93. Phayer, *Pius XII*, 178–82.

94. Goñi, *Real Odessa*, 97.

95. Phayer, *Pius XII*, 190.

96. Titus to Culbertson, 2 Feb. 1948, RG 226, Entry 210, Box 35, NARA.

97. Memo by Titus, 24 Apr. 1948, RG 226, Entry 190A, Box 24, NARA.

98. Memo by Dasher, 2 Feb. 1948, RG 226, Entry 210, Box 35, NARA.

99. Memo by Titus, 30 Mar. 1948, RG 226, Entry 190A, Box 24, NARA.

100. U.S. Embassy, Madrid, to U.S. Embassy, Buenos Aires, 30 Jan. 1948, RG 226, Entry 190A, Box 26, NARA.

101. Memo by Titus, 9 Feb. 1948, RG 226, Entry 190A, Box 26, NARA.

102. Titus to Culbertson, 2 Feb. 1948, RG 226, Entry 210, Box 35, NARA.

103. Goñi, *Real Odessa*, 100–101.

104. Titus to Culbertson, 2 Feb. 1948; memo by Titus, 9 Feb. 1947; and Presley to Titus, 14 Apr. 1948, all in RG 226, Entry 210, Box 35, NARA.

105. Reports to Titus, 4 and 24 Mar. 1948, RG 226, Entry 190A, Box 24, NARA.

106. Memo by Titus, 4 Mar. 1948, RG 226, Entry 190A, Box 24, NARA.

107. Memo by Titus, 16 June 1948, RG 226, Entry 190A, Box 24, NARA.

108. Goñi, *Real Odessa*, 323.

109. Titus to Culbertson, 2 Feb. 1948, RG 226, Entry 210, Box 35, NARA.

110. Howard to Bevin, 19 July 1947, FO 371/67902B, NA.

111. Minute by Crosthwaite, 28 Nov. 1947, FO 371/67902B, NA.

112. Acheson to U.S. Embassy, Madrid, 19 Aug. 1946, RG 84, Entry 3162, Box 107, NARA.

113. Minute by Garran, 27 June 1946, FO 371/60436, NA.

114. Mallet to Foreign Office, 24 June 1946, FO 371/60346, NA.

115. Memo, 8 Aug. 1946, R 5161/3, MAE. See also Bond, memo of conversation, 8 Aug. 1946, RG 84, Entry 3162, Box 107, NARA.

116. Memo by Bonsal, 9 Aug. 1946, RG 84, Entry 3162, Box 107, NARA.

117. Bonsal to Secretary of State, 11 Aug. 1946, RG 84, Entry 3162, Box 107, NARA.

118. Bonsal to State Department, 14 Sept. 1946, RG 84, Entry 3162, Box 107, NARA.

119. Ibid.

120. U.S. Embassy, Madrid, to State Department, 2 Aug. 1946, copy in Macmillan to Hogg, 6 Aug. 1946, FO 371/60437, NA. The beginning of the list revision is outlined in Bonsal to State Department, 22 Sept. 1946, RG 84, Entry 3162, Box 107, NARA.

121. Bonsal to State Department, 14 Sept. 1946, RG 84, Entry 3162, Box 107, NARA.

122. Bonsal to Secretary of State, 15 Nov. 1946, RG 84, Entry 3162, Box 107, NARA.

123. Bonsal to Secretary of State, 18 Nov. 1946, RG 84, Entry 3162, Box 107, NARA.

124. British Embassy, Madrid, to British delegation to the United Nations, 23 Nov. 1946, FO 371/60439, NA.

125. Memo, British Embassy, Madrid, 23 Jan. 1947, FO 371/67878A, NA.

126. Minute by Sloan, 30 Jan. 1947, FO 371/67878A, NA.

127. Macmillan to Hogg, 20 Nov. 1946, FO 371/60439, NA.

128. Foreign Office to British Embassy, Madrid, 22 Aug. 1946, FO 371/60437, NA.

129. British Embassy, Madrid, to Foreign Office, 10 May 1947, FO 371/67878A, NA.

130. Culbertson to Secretary of State, 10 July 1947, RG 226, Entry 12, Box 8, NARA.

131. Cox to Titus, 2 Feb. 1947, RG 226, Entry 210, Box 35, NARA.

132. Satorres to John Galsworthy, 8 July 1947, FO 371/67878A, NA.

133. Satorres to Galsworthy, 10 July 1947 (copy to U.S. Embassy, Madrid), RG 226, Entry 127, Box 8, NARA.

134. Culbertson to Secretary of State, 10 July 1947, RG 226, Entry 12, Box 8, NARA.

135. Foreign Office to British Embassy, Madrid, 25 Aug. 1947, FO 371/67878A, NA.

136. British and U.S. embassies, Madrid, to Ministry of Foreign Affairs, Spain, 22 Oct. 1947, R 5161/15, MAE; also in RG 226, Entry 127, Box 8, NARA, and FO 1049/1046, NA.

137. Ibid.

138. U.S. Embassy, Madrid, to Ministry of Foreign Affairs, Spain, 23 Oct. 1947, R 5161/15, MAE.

139. Culbertson to Secretary of State, 14 Apr. 1948, RG 226, Entry 127, Box 8, NARA.

140. Minute by Walter Randolph-Rose, 20 Apr. 1948, FO 371/72086A, NA.

141. Howard to Foreign Office, 4 May 1948, FO 371/72086A, NA.

142. Titus to State Department, 24 June 1948, RG 226, Entry 127, Box 8, NARA.

143. Howard to Foreign Office, 5 June 1948, FO 371/72086A, NA.

144. Memo, summary of meeting with Spanish Foreign Ministry, in British Embassy, Madrid, to Western Department, Foreign Office, 1 July 1948, FO 371/72086A, NA.

145. Dirección General Política Exterior, Ministry of Foreign Affairs, Spain, to Dirección General Seguridad, 11 Feb. 1948, R 5161/17, MAE.

146. See Kurt Bormann to Artajo, 18 May 1948, R 5161/17, MAE.

147. "List of 104," 22 Oct. 1947, FO 1049/1046, NA.

148. Eduardo Gallarza to Artajo, 31 Mar. 1948, R 5161/15, MAE.

149. Memo by Culbertson on letter from Satorres to Galsworthy, 10 July 1947, RG 226, Entry 127, Box 8, NARA.

150. Culbertson to Secretary of State, 10 July 1947, RG 226, Entry 127, Box 8, NARA.

151. Ibid.

152. Culbertson to Secretary of State, 14 Apr. 1948, RG 226, Entry 127, Box 8, NARA.

153. Titus to Culbertson, 18 Mar. 1948, RG 226, Entry 127, Box 8, NARA.

154. Memo by Culbertson attached to U.S. Embassy, Madrid, to Office of the Political Advisor, Germany, 11 May 1948, RG 226, Entry 190A, Box 27, NARA.

155. J. Y. Millar to Culbertson, 30 Sept. 1948, RG 226, Entry 127, Box 8, NARA.

156. Memo, "ACC Directives," 6 Dec. 1948, RG 226, Entry 127, Box 8, NARA.

157. Titus to Culbertson, 2 Feb. 1948, Entry 210, Box 35, NARA.

158. Titus to Culbertson, 29 Apr. 1948, RG 226, Entry 210, Box 35, NARA.

159. Ibid.

160. Refugee Department, Foreign Office, to British Embassy, Madrid, 9 Oct. 1948, FO 371/72086A, NA.

161. Minute by Crosthwaite, 13 Sept. 1948, FO 371/72086A, NA.

162. Minute by John Russell, 30 Sept. 1948, FO 371/72086A, NA.

163. Minute by Basil Boothny, 27 Oct. 1948, FO 371/72086A, NA.

164. British Embassy, Madrid, to Refugee Department, Foreign Office, 9 Nov. 1948, FO 371/72086A, NA.

CONCLUSION

1. Byrnes, "Unfinished Business," 142, 147.

2. Ibid., 153–54.

3. Policy Planning Staff, PPS/12, "US Policy Toward Spain," 24 Oct. 1947, in U.S. Department of State, *Foreign Relations of the United States, 1947* (Washington, DC: U.S. Government Printing Office, 1969), 3:1092–95.

4. Angel Viñas, *En las garras del águila: Los pactos con Estados Unidos, de Francisco Franco a Felipe González (1945–1995)* (Barcelona: Crítica, 2003), 51.

5. Ibid., 23.

6. Steinacher, *Nazis on the Run*, 159.

7. Ibid., 222.

8. U.S. and British embassies, Madrid, to Ministry of Foreign Affairs, Spain, 22 Oct. 1947, R 5161/15, MAE.

9. Irujo, *La lista negra*, 88, 89.

10. Ibid., 151.

11. Memo by Howell, "Germans for repatriation," 27 Feb. 1946, RG 226, Entry 190A, Box 23, NARA.

12. Dirección General Seguridad to Ministry of Foreign Affairs, Spain, 30 May 1945, R 2159/3, MAE.

13. Josef Boogen to U.S. Embassy, Madrid, 11 Dec. 1945, RG 84, Entry 3162, Box 76.

14. Boogen to Ministry of Foreign Affairs, Spain, 17 May, 10 Oct., and 22 Dec. 1945, R 2160/4, MAE.

15. Artajo to Satorres, 25 Jan. 1946, R 2160/4, MAE.

16. Rodriguez Martínez to Perez Gonzalez, 25 Sept. 1946, R 5161/19, MAE.

17. U.S. Embassy, Madrid, to Ministry of Foreign Affairs, Spain, 28 Aug. 1946, R 2161/2, MAE.

18. U.S. and British embassies, Madrid, to Ministry of Foreign Affairs, Spain, 22 Oct. 1947, R 5161/15, MAE.

19. Dirección General Política Económica, Ministry of Foreign Affairs, Spain, to Ministry of Industry and Commerce, Spain, 4 Mar. 1948, R 5161/15, MAE.

20. Randall to Wardlaw, 9 Apr. 1947, RG 84, Entry 3175, Box 22, NARA.

21. Boogen to José de Erice O'Shea, 6 Apr. 1949, and de Erice O'Shea to Boogen, 16 July 1949, R 5161/17, MAE.

22. *El País*, 30 Mar. 1997.

23. See www.spanien.diplo.de/Vertretung/spanien/es/02-madrid/hk/bilbao/seite -hk-bilbao.html.

24. "Los Lipperheide y la industria petroquímica vasca," CyberEuscadi, 5 Jan. 2009, cybereuscadi.com/lipperheide.

25. Puig, "La conexión alemana," 7.

26. Agent 23715/C to agent 23700, 4 Dec. 1945, RG 226, Entry 127, Box 2, NARA.

27. Lipperheide to Hawley, 4 Feb. 1946, and Hawley, memo of conversation with Lipperheide, 29 Jan. 1946, RG 84, Entry 3175, Box 18, NARA.

28. Núria Puig Raposo and Adoración Alvaro Moya, "Misión Imposible? La expropiación de las empresas alemanas en España (1945–1975)," *Investigaciones de Historia Económica* 7 (2007).

29. *El País*, 30 Mar. 1997.

30. Puig, "La conexión alemana," 10.

31. Joan Cantarero, *La huella de la bota: De los Nazis del franquismo a la nueva ultraderecha* (Madrid: Temas de Hoy, 2010), 23, 25–26, 47.

32. Steinacher, *Nazis on the Run*, 266.

33. Obituary for Hans Juretschke, *El Mundo*, 22 June 2004.

34. Memo to SAINT/HQ, 27 Dec. 1945, RG 226, Entry 127, Box 28, NARA.

35. Bond to Bonsal, 8 Aug. 1946, RG 226, Entry 190A, Box 24, NARA.

36. Memo, 26 Jan. 1946, RG 226, Entry 210, Box 35, NARA.

37. U.S. Embassy, Madrid, to FBI, 10 Feb. 1947, RG 65, Box 152, NARA.

38. Titus to Culbertson, 2 Feb. 1948, RG 226, Entry 210, Box 35, NARA.

39. Memo by Titus, 9 Feb. 1948, RG 226, Entry 190A, Box 26, NARA.

BIBLIOGRAPHY

PRIMARY SOURCES

Archives

France. Archives de la Ministère des Affaires Etrangères, Paris.
    Série Z/Europe 1944–1949/Espagne
Spain. Archivo General del Ministerio de Asuntos Exteriores, Madrid.
    R Series, Archivo Renovado
United Kingdom. National Archives of the United Kingdom, Kew.
    FO 371, Foreign Office, General Correspondence
    FO 425/423, Foreign Office, Confidential Print, Western Europe
    FO 939, FO 945, FO 1013, FO 1014, FO 1032, FO 1049, FO 1051–52, FO
        1060, Foreign Office, Control Office for Germany and Austria
    HS 6, Special Operations Executive—Iberia
    KV 2–3, Security Service
United States. National Archives and Records Administration II, College
    Park, MD.
    RG 59, State Department Decimal Files
    RG 65, Federal Bureau of Investigation
    RG 84, State Department Consular Records
        Office of the Political Advisor, Germany
        Madrid
        Barcelona
        Bilbao
        Vigo
    RG 163, Foreign Economic Administration
    RG 226, Office of Strategic Services
    RG 260, Office of the Military Government, United States (OMGUS)
        Combined Repatriation Executive
        Property Control, Finance Division, External Assets Branch

RG 263, Central Intelligence Agency
    Name Files released by IWG Nazi War Crimes Act
RG 457, National Security Agency/Central Security Service
RG 466, Office of the U.S. High Commissioner for Germany
RG 498, U.S. Army, U.S. Forces in Europe

Official Publications

Fundacion Nacional Francisco Franco. *Documentos inéditos para la historia del Generalissimo Franco.* Vol. 2, pt. 2. Madrid, 1992.

Slany, William Z. *U.S. and Allied Efforts to Recover and Restore Gold and Other Assets Stolen or Hidden by Germany During World War II.* Washington, DC: Department of State, 1997.

———. *U.S. and Allied Wartime and Postwar Relations and Negotiations with Argentina, Portugal, Spain, Sweden, and Turkey on Looted Gold and German External Assets and U.S. Concerns about the Fate of the Wartime Ustasha Treasury; A Supplement to Preliminary Study on U.S. and Allied Efforts to Recover and Restore Gold and Other Assets Stolen or Hidden by Germany During World War II.* Washington, DC: Department of State, 1998.

United Kingdom. Cabinet Office. *Cabinet Papers: Series Three, CAB 128/129, Parts I and II.* London, 1996.

United Nations. Security Council. *Official Records.* 1st year, 2nd ser. New York, 1946.

United States. Department of State. *Foreign Relations of the United States, 1944.* Vol. 2. Washington, DC: U.S. Government Printing Office, 1967.

———. *Foreign Relations of the United States, 1945.* Vols. 3, 5. Washington, DC: U.S. Government Printing Office, 1967.

———. *Foreign Relations of the United States, 1947.* Vol. 3. Washington, DC: U.S. Government Printing Office, 1969.

Newspapers

ABC (Madrid, Seville)
El Mundo (Madrid)
El País (Madrid)
Guardian (Manchester, London)
New York Times
La Vanguardia (Barcelona)

SECONDARY SOURCES

Aguilar, Paloma. *Memory and Amnesia: The Role of the Spanish Civil War in the Transition to Democracy.* Translated by Mark Oakley. New York: Berghahn Books, 2002.

Alcuten, Alberto Sabio. *Peligrosos demócratas: Antifranquistas vistos por la policía política (1958–1977).* Madrid: Cátedra, 2011.

Alpert, Michael. "Operaciones secretas inglesas en España durante la Segunda Guerra Mundial." *Espacio, Tiempo y Forma, Serie V* 15 (2002).

Benhabib, Seyla. *The Rights of Others: Aliens, Residents and Citizens.* Cambridge: Cambridge University Press, 2004.

Biddiscombe, Perry. *The Denazification of Germany: A History, 1945–1950.* Stroud, UK: Tempus, 2007.

———. *WERWOLF! The History of the National Socialist Guerilla Movement, 1944–1946.* Toronto: University of Toronto Press, 1998.

Bloxham, Donald. "The Genocidal Past in Western Germany and the Experience of Occupation, 1945–6." *European History Quarterly* 34, no. 3 (2004): 305–35.

Bowen, Wayne H. *Spaniards and Nazi Germany: Collaboration in the New Order.* Columbia: University of Missouri Press, 2000.

Bower, Tom. *The Pledge Betrayed: America and Britain and the Denazification of Postwar Germany.* New York: Doubleday, 1982.

Breitman, Richard, Norman J. W. Goda, Timothy Naftali, and Robert Wolfe. *U.S. Intelligence and the Nazis.* Cambridge: Cambridge University Press, 2005.

Brown, Anthony Cave. *"C": The Secret Life of Sir Stewart Graham Menzies, Spymaster to Winston Churchill.* New York: Macmillan, 1987.

Buchanan, Andrew. "Washington's 'Silent Ally' in World War II? United States Policy towards Spain, 1939–1945." *Journal of Transatlantic Studies* 7, no. 2 (2009).

Buscher, Frank M. *The U.S. War Crimes Trial Program in Germany, 1946–1955.* New York: Greenwood, 1989.

Byrnes, Mark. "Unfinished Business: The United States and Franco's Spain, 1944–1947." *Diplomacy & Statecraft* 11, no. 1 (2000).

Calvo-Gonzalez, Oscar. "Neither a Carrot nor a Stick: American Foreign Aid and Economic Policymaking in Spain during the 1950s." *Diplomatic History* 30, no. 3 (2006).

Cantarero, Joan. *La huella de la bota: De los Nazis del franquismo a la nueva ultraderecho.* Madrid: Temas de Hoy, 2010.

Cazorla-Sánchez, Antonio. *Fear and Progress: Ordinary Lives in Franco's Spain, 1939–1975.* Oxford: Wiley-Blackwell, 2010.

Cochrane, Feargal. *Ending Wars.* Cambridge: Polity, 2008.

Collado Seidel, Carlos. *España: Refugio nazi.* Madrid: Temas de Hoy, 2005.

———. "España y los agentes alemanes 1944–1947: Intransigencia y pragmatism politico." *Espacio, Tiempo y Forma, Serie V* 5 (1992).

Conway, Martin. *Collaboration in Belgium: Léon Degrelle and the Rexist Movement, 1940–1944.* New Haven, CT: Yale University Press, 1993.

Cortada, James W. *United States–Spanish Relations, Wolfram and World War II.* Barcelona: Manuel Pareja, 1971.

Dunthorn, David J. *Britain and the Spanish Anti-Franco Opposition, 1940–1950.* London: Palgrave Macmillan, 2000.

Earl, Hilary. *The Nuremberg SS-Einsatzgruppen Trial, 1945–1958: Atrocity, Law and History.* Cambridge: Cambridge University Press, 2009.

Edwards, Jill. *Anglo-American Relations and the Franco Question, 1945–1955.* Oxford: Clarendon, 1999.

Eizenstat, Stuart. *Imperfect Justice: Looted Assets, Slave Labor and the Unfinished Business of World War II.* New York: Public Affairs, 2003.

Erskine, Ralph. "Eavesdropping on 'Bodden': ISOS v. the Abwehr in the Straits of Gibraltar." *Intelligence and National Security* 12, no. 3 (1997): 110–29.

Foot, M. R. D. *SOE in France: An Account of the Work of the British Special Operations Executive in France, 1940–1944.* London: HMSO, 1966.

Frei, Norbert. *Adenauer's Germany and the Nazi Past: The Politics of Amnesty and Integration.* Translated by Joel Golb. New York: Columbia University Press, 2002.

Gimbel, John. *The American Occupation of Germany: Politics and the Military, 1945–1949.* Stanford, CA: Stanford University Press, 1968.

Goda, Norman J. W. "Banking on Hitler: Chase National Bank and the Ruckwanderer Mark Scheme, 1936–1941." In Breitman et al., *U.S. Intelligence and the Nazis.*

Goñi, Uki. *The Real Odessa: How Perón Brought the Nazi War Criminals to Argentina.* Rev. ed. London: Granta Books, 2003.

Green, Nancy L. "Americans Abroad and the Uses of Citizenship: Paris, 1914–1940." *Journal of American Ethnic History* 31, no. 3 (2012).

Guirao, Fernando. *Spain and the Reconstruction of Western Europe, 1945–57: Challenge and Response.* New York: St. Martin's, 1998.

Guttman, Egon. "The Concept of Neutrality since the Adoption and Ratification of the Hague Neutrality Convention of 1907." *American University International Law Review* 14, no. 1 (1998).

Hébert, Valerie Geneviève. *Hitler's Generals on Trial: The Last War Crimes Tribunal at Nuremberg.* Lawrence: University Press of Kansas, 2010.

Herf, Jeffrey. *Divided Memory: The Nazi Past in the Two Germanies.* Cambridge, MA: Harvard University Press, 1997.

Hernández-Sandoica, Elena, and Enrique Moradiellos. "Spain and the Second World War, 1939–1945." In Wylie, *European Neutrals and Non-Belligerents.*

Hinsley, F. H., and C. A. G. Simkins. *British Intelligence in the Second World War.* Vol. 4, *Security and Counter-Intelligence.* New York: Cambridge University Press, 1990.

Hitchcock, William I. *The Bitter Road to Freedom: A New History of the Liberation of Europe.* New York: Free Press, 2008.

Irujo, José María. *La lista negra: Los espías nazis protegidos por Franco y la Iglesia.* Madrid: Aguilar, 2003.

Jacobs, Arthur D. *The Prison Called Hohenasperg: An American Boy Betrayed by his Government during World War II.* New York: Universal, 1999.

Jarausch, Konrad H. *After Hitler: Recivilizing Germans, 1945–1995.* Oxford: Oxford University Press, 2006.

Jones, Jill. "Eradicating Nazism from the British Zone of Germany: Early Policy and Practice." *German History* 8, no. 2 (1990).

Judt, Tony. *Postwar: A History of Europe since 1945.* New York: Penguin, 2005.

Kahn, David. *Hitler's Spies: German Military Intelligence in World War II.* New York: Da Capo, 2000. First published 1978 by Macmillan.

LaPlante, Lisa J. "Transitional Justice and Peace Building: Diagnosing and Addressing the Socioeconomic Roots of Violence through a Human Rights Framework." *International Journal of Transitional Justice* 2 (2008).

Leitz, Christian. *Economic Relations between Nazi Germany and Franco's Spain, 1936–1945.* Oxford: Oxford University Press, 1996.

———. *Nazi Germany and Neutral Europe during the Second World War.* Manchester: Manchester University Press, 2000.

———. "Nazi Germany and the Luso-Hispanic World." *Contemporary European History* 12, no. 2 (2003): 183–96.

———. "Nazi Germany's Struggle for Spanish Wolfram during the Second World War." *European History Quarterly* 25, no. 1 (1995): 71–92.

Liedtke, Boris N. *Embracing a Dictatorship: US Relations with Spain, 1945–53.* New York: St. Martin's, 1998.

Locksley, Christopher C. "Condor over Spain: The Civil War, Combat Experience and the Development of Luftwaffe Airpower Doctrine." *Civil Wars* 2, no. 1 (1999).

Lorenz-Meyer, Martin. *Safehaven: The Allied Pursuit of Nazi Assets Abroad.* Columbia: University of Missouri Press, 2007.

Mackenzie, W. J. M. *The Secret History of SOE: The Special Operations Executive, 1940–1945.* London: St Ermin's, 2000.

Marquina, Antonio. "The Spanish Neutrality during the Second World War." *American University International Law Review* 14, no. 1 (1998).

Marrus, Michael, ed. *The Nuremberg War Crimes Trial, 1945–46: A Documentary History.* Boston: Longman, 1997.

Medlicott, W. N. *The Economic Blockade.* Vol. 2. London: HMSO, 1959.

Messenger, David A. "Against the Grain: Special Operations Executive in Spain, 1941–1945." In *The Politics and Strategy of Clandestine War: Special Operations Executive, 1940–1946,* edited by Neville Wylie, 177–92. London: Routledge, 2007.

———. "La colònia alemanya, els consulats nord-americans i la desnazifició a Vigo I Bilbao després de la Segona Guerra Mundial." *Segle XX: Revista Catalana d'Història* 5 (2012).

———. *L'Espagne Républicaine: French Policy and Spanish Republicanism in Liberated France.* Brighton, UK: Sussex Academic, 2008.

———. "Fighting for Relevance: Economic Intelligence and Special Operations Executive in Spain, 1943–1945." *Intelligence and National Security* 15, no. 3 (2000).

———. "'Our Spanish Brothers' or 'As at Plombières': France and the Spanish Opposition to Franco, 1945–1948." *French History* 20, no. 1 (2006).

Moradiellos, Enrique. "The Potsdam Conference and the Spanish Problem." *Contemporary European History* 10, no. 1 (2001).

Newton, Ronald C. *The "Nazi Menace" in Argentina, 1931–1947.* Stanford, CA: Stanford University Press, 1992.

———. "The United States, the German-Argentines, and the Myth of the Fourth Reich, 1943–47." *Hispanic American Historical Review* 64, no. 1 (1984): 81–103.

Niethammer, Lutz. *Entnazifizierung in Bayern: Sauberung und Rehabilitierung unter amerikanischer Besatzung.* Frankfurt am Main: S. Fischer, 1972.

Olivier, Egon. *Mémoire sur l'impossible extradition de Léon Degrelle.* Brussels: privately printed, 2010.

Pack, Sasha D. *Tourism and Dictatorship: Europe's Peaceful Invasion of Franco's Spain.* New York: Palgrave Macmillan, 2006.

Paehler, Katrin. "Foreign Intelligence in a New Paradigm: Amt VI of the Reich Main Security Office (RSHA)." In *Secret Intelligence and the Holocaust,* edited by David Bankier. Jerusalem: Yad Vashem, 2006.

Payne, Stanley G. *Franco and Hitler: Spain, Germany and World War II.* New Haven, CT: Yale University Press, 2008.

Pendas, Devin O. "Seeking Justice, Finding Law: Nazi Trials in Postwar Europe." *Journal of Modern History* 81 (June 2009): 347–68.

Peterson, Edward N. *The American Occupation of Germany: Retreat to Victory.* Detroit: Wayne State University Press, 1977.

Phayer, Michael. *Pius XII, the Holocaust and the Cold War.* Bloomington: Indiana University Press, 2008.

Philby, Kim. *My Silent War.* Introduction by Phillip Knightly, foreword by Graham Greene. New York: Modern Library, 2002.

Portero, Florentino. *Franco aislado: La cuéstion española, 1945–1950.* Madrid: Aguilar, 1989.

———. "Spain, Britain and the Cold War." In Preston and Balfour, *Spain and the Great Powers.*

Preston, Paul, *Franco: A Biography.* London: Fontana, 1994.

———. *The Spanish Holocaust: Inquisition and Extermination in Twentieth Century Spain.* New York: Norton, 2012.

Preston, Paul, and Sebastian Balfour, eds. *Spain and the Great Powers in the Twentieth Century.* London: Routledge, 1999.

Puig, Núria. "La conexión alemana: Redes empresariales hispano-alemanas en la Espana del Siglo XX." *VIII Congreso de la Asociación Espanola de Historia Económica* (2005). www.usc.es/estaticos/congresos/histeco5/b12_puig.pdf.

Puig Raposo, Núria, and Adoración Alvaro Moya. "Misión Imposible? La expropiación de las empresas alemanas en España (1945–1975)." *Investigaciones de Historia Económica* 7 (2007).

Richards, Michael. "From War Culture to Civil Society: Francoism, Social Change and Memories of the Spanish Civil War." *History & Memory* 14, nos. 1/2 (2002).

Rodrigo, Javier. *Cautivos: Campos de concentración en la Espana franquista, 1936–1947.* Barcelona: Crítica, 2005.

Rodríguez González, Javier. "El espionaje nazi." In Seone and Rodríguez González, *War Zone.*

Rolland, Eduardo. *Galicia en guerra: Espías, batallas, submarinos e volframio; do desfile da Wehrmacht en Vigo á fuxida dos criminais nazis.* Vigo: Edicións Xerais, 2006.

Ros Agudo, Manuel. *La guerra secreta de Franco (1939–1945).* Barcelona: Crítica, 2002.

Rose, Romani. *Roma and Sinti: Human Rights for Europe's Largest Minority.*

Heidelberg: Documentation and Cultural Centre of German Sinti and Roma, 2007.

Rubin, Seymour J. "The Washington Accord Fifty Years Later: Neutrality, Morality and International Law." *American University International Law Review* 14, no. 1 (1998).

Ruhl, Klaus-Jorg. "L'alliance à distance: Les relations economiques germano-espagnoles de 1936 à 1945." *Revue d'Histoire de la Deuxieme Guerre Mondiale* 118 (1980): 69–102.

Sá, Magali Romero, and André Felipe Candido da Silva. "La *Revista Médica de Hamburgo* y la *Revista Médica Germano-Ibero-Americana:* Diseminación de la medicina germánica en Espana y América Latina (1920–1933)." *Asclepio: Revista de Historia de la Medicina y de la Ciencia* 42, no. 1 (2010).

Sabio Alcutén, Alberto. *Peligrosos demócratas: Antifranquistas vistos por la policía política (1958–1977).* Madrid: Cátedra, 2011.

Salter, Michael. *Nazi War Crimes, US Intelligence and Selective Prosecution at Nuremberg: Controversies Regarding the Role of the Office of Strategic Services.* New York: Routledge, 2007.

Schüler-Springorum, Stefanie. *Krieg und Fliegen: Die Legion Condor im Spanische Bürgerkrieg.* Paderborn: Ferdinand Schöningh, 2010.

Seone, Emilio Grandío, and Javier Rodríguez González, eds. *War Zone: La Segunda Guerra Mundial en el noroeste de la península ibérica.* Madrid: Eneida, 2012.

Singer, Brian C. J. "Cultural versus Contractual Nations: Rethinking their Opposition." *History and Theory* 35, no. 3 (1996).

Smyth, Denis. "Les chevaliers de Saint-George: La Grande-Bretagne et la corruption des généraux espagnols (1940–1942)." *Guerres Mondiales et Conflits Contemporains* 162 (1991): 29–54.

———. *Deathly Deception: The Real Story of Operation Mincemeat.* Oxford: Oxford University Press, 2010.

———. *Diplomacy and Strategy of Survival: British Policy and Franco's Spain, 1940–41.* Cambridge: Cambridge University Press, 1986.

———. "Franco and the Allies." In Preston and Balfour, *Spain and the Great Powers.*

———. "Screening 'Torch': Allied Counter-Intelligence and the Spanish Threat to the Secrecy of the Allied Invasion of French North Africa in November, 1942." *Intelligence and National Security* 4, no. 2 (1989).

Stafford, David. *Britain and European Resistance, 1940–1945: A Survey of Special Operations Executive, with Documents.* Toronto: University of Toronto Press, 1980.

———. "Secret Operations versus Secret Intelligence in World War II: The British Experience." In *Men at War: Politics, Technology and Innovation in the Twentieth Century,* edited by T. Travers and C. Archer. Chicago: University of Chicago Press, 1982.

Stedman, Stephen. "Spoiler Problems in Peace Processes." *International Security* 22, no. 2 (1997).

Steinacher, Gerald. *Nazis on the Run: How Hitler's Henchmen Fled Justice.* Oxford: Oxford University Press, 2011.

Steury, Donald P. "The OSS and Project SAFE HAVEN." *Studies in Intelligence* 9 (Summer 2000).

Tent, James. *Mission on the Rhine: Reeducation and Denazification in American-Occupied Germany.* Chicago: University of Chicago Press, 1982.

Thacker, Toby. *The End of the Third Reich: Defeat, Denazification and Nuremberg January 1944–November 1946.* Stroud, UK: Tempus, 2006.

Thomàs, Joan Maria. *Roosevelt, Franco and the End of the Second World War.* New York: Palgrave Macmillan, 2011.

Tussell, Javier. *Franco, España y la II Guerra Mundial: Entre el eje y la neutralidad.* Madrid: Temas de Hoy, 1995.

Viñas, Angel. *En las garras del águila: Los pactos con Estados Unidos, de Francisco Franco a Felipe González (1945–1995).* Barcelona: Crítica, 2003.

———. *Franco, Hitler y el estallido de la guerra civil: Antecedentes y consequencias.* Madrid: Alianza, 2001.

Wallerstein, Immanuel. "Citizens All? Citizens Some! The Making of the Citizen." *Comparative Studies in Society and History* 45, no. 4 (2003).

Whealey, Robert H. *Hitler and Spain: The Nazi Role in the Spanish Civil War.* Lexington: University Press of Kentucky, 1989.

Wylie, Neville. "An Amateur Learns his Job? Special Operations Executive in Portugal, 1940–2." *Journal of Contemporary History* 36, no. 3 (2001).

———, ed. *European Neutrals and Non-Belligerents during the Second World War.* Cambridge: Cambridge University Press, 2002.

Yavnai, Lisa. "U.S. Army War Crimes Trials in Germany, 1945–1947." In *Atrocities on Trial: Historical Perspectives on the Politics of Prosecuting War Crimes,* edited by Patricia Heberer and Jurgen Matthaus. Lincoln: University of Nebraska Press, 2008.

INDEX

Abwehr, 40–42, 49, 65, 83–84, 127
Adenauer, Konrad, 110
agent 23793, 66
Aguilar, Paloma, 111–12
Albrecht, Karl, 124, 150, 153
Allied Control Council (ACC): Combined
    Repatriation Executive, 20; debate over
    pressuring neutral states, 85; directives
    and laws of, 15, 18, 19; German as-
    sets and, 75–76; Prisoners of War and
    Displaced Persons Directorate, 11, 33;
    repatriation resolution, 11, 21; Spanish
    rejection of legitimacy of, 77–78. *See
    also* denazification policy; Germany,
    occupied; repatriation policy
Andress, Karl Moser, 64, 116, 143
anti-Nazi Germans: Catholicism and, 121,
    125; as intelligence sources, 62–63, 105;
    intimidation of, 62, 103, 147, 169; in
    Portugal, 28
Argentina, 25, 28, 151–54
Armbruster, Eugen, 147
Armour, Norman, 29, 53, 55, 56, 74, 86,
    116, 162
Arnold, Karl, 42, 87, 102, 135, 155–56
Artajo, Martín, 50, 56, 72–73, 80, 86, 88,
    92–97, 105, 123, 148, 155, 156, 159
assets, hidden, 22–25, 34, 51–56, 60,
    75–76
Association of German Catholics, 121
Attlee, Clement, 31
Auslandorganization, 107

Baalk, Robert, 150
Baldwin, LaVerne, 56, 58–59, 66, 78, 84,
    129–30, 137
Bar Germania, Bilbao, 63
Basque country, 60, 64
Becker, Walter, 108
Berlin Interrogation Center, 135
Bernhardt, Johannes, 1, 39, 40, 66,
    107–11, 116, 117, 129, 149, 166
Bevin, Ernst, 31
Bey, Franz, 159
Bibra, Sigismund von, 43, 60–61, 72–73,
    87, 91
Bilbao, 59–64, 65, 67, 105–6, 122, 139, 144,
    146, 147, 164–66
Blancke, Wendell, 133, 135, 136, 138, 142
Blankinship, Byron, 53–54, 56, 139
Bock, Karl, 81
Bodden (infrared surveillance system),
    44
Bond, Miles, 155
Bonsal, Phillip, 94, 155–56, 159, 162
Boogen, Josef (José), 41, 59, 60, 144,
    164–66
Boogen Heudorf, Horst-José, 166
Boos, José, 122–24, 145, 147–49, 152–54
Bormann, Kurt, 159
Bowker, James, 56
Bramwell, Christopher, 78, 81
Braun, Wernher von, 163
Bretton Woods Resolution VI, 23–25,
    75–76

Britain (U.K.): economic warfare and, 33, 34, 45–47; foreign-policy toward Franco, 31–32; wartime counterespionage by, 43–47. *See also specific topics, such as* repatriation policy

British-American Repatriation Centre for Germans, Madrid, 88–89, 91, 110–11, 128

British-American Trusteeship, 147

British Foreign Office: Economic Warfare Department, 34; intelligence activities and, 44–45, 46, 48; nonintervention and, 31; on "obnoxious Germans," 8, 29, 32; repatriation and, 82, 83, 89, 96–97; SIS and, 54; Soviet Union and, 85, 86

British intelligence. *See* intelligence activities

Brohmann, Major, 151

Bunge, Edward, 63, 130, 144

Burbach, Friedhelm, 61, 63, 64, 94, 117–18

Burkhardt, Friedrich, 127–28

Burroughs, R. A., 141–42

Butterworth, Walton, 53, 58, 86

Byrnes, James, 32, 89

Cadogan, Sir Alexander, 92

Caggiano, Antonio, 152

Caldas de Malavella internment facility, 71–72, 94, 114, 123, 128, 129

Canaris, Wilhelm, 42

Carrero Blanco, Luis, 126, 128–29, 144–45

Catholicism, 120–27

Cazorla-Sánchez, Antonio, 113

Central Intelligence Agency (CIA), 55

Churchill, Winston, 26, 45, 116–17

Círculo Español de Amigos de Europa (CEDADE), 168

citizenship, 79–80, 100, 113, 129–30

Civil War, Spanish, 3, 39, 111–16, 120–21

Clay, Lucius D., 17

Cold War, 86, 116, 162–64

collective guilt theory, 14–15

Combined Repatriation Executive, 11

Commission for the Clarification of Nazi Activities in Argentina (CENEA), 154

Communism and anti-Communism, 116–20

concentration camps, Francoist, 112

Condor Legion (Luftwaffe), 39, 40, 41, 59, 113, 116, 119–20

consulates, Allied, 105–6, 166

Correa Fund, 124

Crosthwaite, Phillip, 95, 142, 161

CROWCASS (Central Registry of War Criminals and Security Suspects), 13

Culbertson, Paul, 157–61, 162, 170

Dachau internment camp, 140

Daye, Pierre, 148

Dede, Hans, 168

Degrelle, Léon, 67, 168, 169

Demel, Georg, 63

denazification policy: automatic arrest and internment in Germany, 13–14, 18; in British zone, 19; Cold War and, 163; definitions of, 11–12, 15–16; early breadth of the concept, 17–19; FEA report and, 73; German responses to, 110; implementation vs. ambitions of, 16–17; internment and releases in Germany, 135–43; interrogation and investigation of repatriates, 132–35, 136–37; OSS and, 54–55; outside Germany, need for, 55; punishment, debate over role of, 12; purpose and impetus of, 5–8; registry of war criminals and, 13; repatriates returning to Spain, 140–42; *Spruchkammern* panels, 17, 136, 141; theories of military occupation and, 14–15, 16; in U.S. zone, 16–18; war-crimes trials and, 12, 15, 18. *See also* repatriation policy

Dieckhoff, Hans Heinrich, 134

diplomacy: intelligence operations and, 44–45; neutrality and need for, 70; revision and reduction of repatriation lists and, 81–85; Spanish response to repatriation and Safe Haven, 70–81; UN and international debates on repatriation, 85–86, 91–93, 97

Dirección General de Seguridad, 66, 115, 129, 149

"Directive for Military Government in Germany" (SHAEF), 14

Donovan, William, 53, 55

Draeger, Gustav, 61

economic intelligence, 27, 47–48, 52–53

economic security, 34

economic ties between Spain and Germany, 21, 39–40, 101

economic warfare: enemy assets and, 22–25; German firms in Spain and, 50–51, 100–101; Spain and, 21; spoiler activities and, 33–34; wolfram (tungsten) and, 25–27, 41, 45–49

Edelweiss 88 group, 103

Eden, Anthony, 51, 54

Ehlert, Fritz, 150

Eisenhower, Dwight D., 13, 14–15

Eitzen, Meino von, 114

Ellis-Rees, Hugh, 46–47, 52, 54

Enge, Richard, 119

Erhardt, Eugene, 59

Erice, José Sebastian de, 95, 158

escapes from Spain, 151–54

"Eva," 103

Falange, 39, 57, 66–68, 106, 146

Falange Femenina, 148–49

FBI (Federal Bureau of Investigation), 56

Flight X, 156

Foreign Affairs Ministry, Spanish. *See* petitions by Germans to Franco and Foreign Ministry; repatriation policy

Foreign Economic Administration (U.S.), 53–54, 73–74

France, 27, 46, 60, 64–65, 85, 91–92, 152–53

Franco, Francisco, 3, 29–32, 37, 39–40,

111–12, 116–17. *See also* petitions by Germans to Franco and Foreign Ministry; Spain, Francoist

Frohberg, W. O., 62

Fuldner, Horst Carlos, 152

fund-raising activities, German, 124, 145–46

Gabelt, Erich, 116

Galicia, 60, 65, 81–82, 106

Galindez, Pedro, 121

Gallarza, Eduardo, 159

Galsworthy, John, 155

Garran, Peter, 82, 89, 155

Genserowsky, Alfred, 49–50, 72, 114–15

German colony in Spain: economic significance of, 100–101; intelligence meetings with contacts in, 60–62; Nazi presence in, 103; Nazi revival in, 145–47; Nazis viewed as group members, 6; number of Germans, 24, 43; persistence of, 166–68; prominent institutions, Germans in, 104–5; repatriates returning to Spain, 140–42; underground and escape activity, 148–54; wanted Germans remaining in Spain (1946–47), 143–47. *See also* petitions by Germans to Franco and Foreign Ministry; repatriation policy; "werewolf" groups and "stay-behind" networks

German-Italian Pact of Steel, 3

Germany, Nazi: economic plans for Iberia, 107; Spain's linkages to, 3–4, 21–22; wartime intelligence operations, 38–43. *See also* economic warfare; German colony in Spain; Nazi Party (NSDAP)

Germany, occupied: interrogation and investigation of repatriates in, 132–35; legitimacy, Spanish rejection of, 77–78; Public Safety Branch and denazification panels, 16–17; resistance in, 110; zones in, 16–20, 118–19, 132–33. *See also* denazification policy

Germany Country Unit, U.S.-British (GCIU), 13

Gestapo, 13, 39, 42, 65, 101–3

Giese, Alfred, 113–14

Giese, Walther, 41, 81, 134–35

Göring, Hermann, 40, 107

Green, Nancy, 79, 100

Griffis, Stanton, 162

Habnicht, Otto, 61–62

Hafner, Paul (Pablo), 168

Hahn, Herbert, 67–68, 72, 127

Hammes, Ernst, 42

Handbook for Military Government in Germany (SHAEF), 13, 19

Hardion, Bernard, 31

Hawley, Harry, 61, 105–6, 118

Hayes, Carlton, 53

Head, R. G., 51–52

Heim, Herbert, 168

Heinemann, Hans, 64–65

Hellman, Herbert, 145, 148–49

Herberg, Ricard, 115

Heuss, Wilhelm Beisel, 143–44

Heydt, Herman, 66–67

Highland Monarch (ship), 88–89, 132

Hilfsverein groups, 145–46, 148–49, 151

Hillgarth, Alan, 44

HIMSA (Hispano-Marroquí de Transportes), 107

Hinrichsen, Otto, 41, 59, 60, 63, 115

Hitler, Adolf, 37, 39, 42, 51

Hoare, Sir Samuel, 44–45, 47, 51, 52

Hoettl, Wilhelm, 135

Hoffman, Hans, 168

Hohenasperg internment camp, 135–36, 137, 142

Horcher, Otto, 151

Horwin, Leonard, 56

Howard, Douglas, 31, 89, 94, 154, 158

Howell, Gillie, 139, 143

Hoyer-Millar, Derrick, 32, 85, 97

H Section (SOE), 45–48, 51–52

Huber, José María, 121–24, 146

IG Farben, 41

"incorporation into Spanish life" principle, 78–80, 128

intelligence activities: Allied wartime counterespionage, 43–49; in Barcelona, 62, 64–65; in Bilbao, Basque country, and Galicia, 59–64, 65; contacts within the German colony, 60–63; denazification policy and, 69; economic, 27, 47–48, 52–53; former Nazi agents employed by U.S., 163–64; hiding activities and, 150–51; in Madrid, 66–68; Nazi agents, denazification, and Safe Haven program and, 49–55; Nazi wartime operations, 38–43; neutral states' wartime status and, 37–38; postwar objectives, 55–56; stay-behind or "werewolf" groups and, 51, 63, 66–67, 101–2, 103–4; transition from Allied wartime to postwar intelligence, 56–59; in Vigo, 65

International Legal Office of the Spanish Foreign Ministry, 75

International Military Tribunal (IMT), Nuremberg, 15, 16, 18

internment: in Germany, 13–14, 18, 132, 135–43; in Spain, 71–72, 94, 114, 123, 128, 129

interrogation of repatriates, 132–35, 136–37

Ireland, 77

Italy, 3, 24, 91, 126

Jaeger, Ernst, 147

JCS resolution 1067, 15

Jiménez y Mora, José, 50, 114

Joint Intelligence Committee (U.S.), 53–54, 56

Juretschke, Hans, 104, 105, 168

Kampfgemeinschaft Adolf Hitler, 102–3
Kellner, Hans, 115
Kindling, Richard, 61
Kiselev, Kuz'ma Venediktovich, 85
Klaevisch, Alfred, 115
Kleyenstuber, Arno, 40, 87
Knoblach, Joaquim von, 126–27
Koch, Ilse, 133–34
Konnecke, Rolf, 62–63
KO-Spanien, 40. See also Abwehr
Krahmer, Eckhard, 68, 92, 102, 150, 153, 169
Kruckenberg, Gustav, 61
Kuhne, Hermann, 61, 82
Kutschmann, Walter, 151

La Coruña, Galicia, 81–82
Lampe, William, 137–38
Lange, Clemens, 95
Langenheim, Heinrich, 140
Langenheim, Herbert, 87
Langenheim, Oswald, 140
LaPorta, Ramón, 153
Laski, Harold, 31
Lazar, Hans, 68
Leissner, Gustav (aka Gustavo Lenz), 40
Lesca (L'Escat), Charles, 151, 152
Leukering, Johann, 122–23
Leutner, Walter, 119–20
Liesau, Francisco, 54
Lipperheide Henke, Friedrich (Federico), 59, 60, 61, 62, 63, 121, 164, 166
Lipperheide Henke, José, 121–22, 130
Loetsch, Hans, 139
Look, Earl H., 137
Ludwigsburg internment camp, 136, 141, 142
Luftwaffe, 65, 138. See also Condor Legion

Mailly, Alois, 82
Málaga, 106

Mallet, Sir Victor, 32–33, 86–93, 96–97, 155
Mandestan, P., 46
Marelius, Donald, 61, 81–82, 105, 106
Marine Marlin, SS, 94–96, 139
Marine Perch, SS, 93–94, 132, 133
marriage to Spaniards, 127–29
Marshall Plan aid, 163
Medalie, Donn Paul, 56, 143
Menzell, Alfred, 116, 119, 128–29, 144
Merck, 64
Merrello, Eduardo, 80
Mey, Reinhardt, 159
Meyer, Conrad, 65, 81
Meyer, Wilhelm, 128
Meyer-Doehner, Kurt, 102, 118–19
Millar, J. Y., 160
Minerales Españoles, 60
Ministry of Economic Warfare (MEW), 46, 52
Miranda del Ebro internment camp, 71, 105, 140, 146
Mohr, Bruno, 124–25, 137, 147
Molenhauer, Richard, 41
Morgenthau, Henry, Jr., 12
Morris, Harry, 46, 47, 48, 52–54
Moscardó de Ituarte, José, 65
Moscow declaration, 12
Mosig, Walter Eugen, 1–3, 6, 10, 42, 62, 87, 108, 142–43, 155–56, 169
Muendler, Anneliese, 68
Muller-Bohm, Max Ludwig, 128
Muller-Thyssen, Alfred, 136–37, 138, 149
Murphy, Robert, 134
Mussolini, Benito, 3, 30, 37, 39

Navasques, Emilio de, 75
Nazi Party (NSDAP): assets and, 55; Auslandorganization, 107, 134; in Bilbao and Vigo, 63, 65; Catholicism vs., 120–21, 122; denazification and, 12, 15; Falange and, 39; foreign-intelligence

Nazi Party *(continued)*
arm of, 1; German colony and, 25, 100;
members and leaders of, 41, 59, 64,
66–67, 72, 81–84, 87, 113, 137, 144, 150,
164–66; units of, 13, 51; "Winter Aid"
program, 124. *See also* Germany, Nazi
neo-Nazi associations, 168
neutrality, 3, 21–25, 38, 70, 73–75
"New Spain," 100, 112, 131, 167
Newton, Ronald, 38–39
nonbelligerent status, 3, 21–22, 24, 37
Nuremberg tribunal, 15, 16, 18
Nutz, Max, 113

"obnoxious Germans," 4–5, 8, 20, 28, 29,
33–35, 54. *See also* repatriation policy
occupation, theories of, 14–15
Office of Strategic Services (OSS), 5, 20,
47–48, 51, 53–56
Office of the Political Advisor in Germany, 133, 134, 136, 139, 160
Officina Technic Francisco Liesau, 54

Pamplona internment camp, 146
Pasch, William, 72
Paukner, Anton, 129
Perez Gonzalez, Blas, 80
Perón, Juan, 152, 153
petitions by Germans to Franco and
Foreign Ministry: anti-Communist
crusade approach, 116–20; Catholicism
approach, 120–27; Civil War nationalist
approach, 111–16; Germans-as-Span-
iards approach, 127–30
Philby, Kim, 45
Pla y Daniel, Enrique, 120, 123
police, Spanish, 105–6
Poole, DeWitt, 133–36
Portugal, 20, 25, 28, 77, 156–57
Potsdam Conference, 15–16, 30, 162
Prisoners of War and Displaced Persons
Directorate (ACC), 11, 33
punishment, collective, 14

Quarton, Harold B., 106

Radeke, Alfred, 129
Radio Barcelona, 64
Randolph-Rose, Walter, 158
ratlines, 152–53, 163
Reich Main Security Office (RSHA), 1
repatriation policy: ACC decision on, 11,
21; Baldwin memo on, 58–59; economic
warfare and, 25–27; end of, 154–61; foreign policy debates and objectives and,
29–35; Germans in Spain informed of,
91; "incorporation into Spanish life"
and "moral and humanitarian" concerns, 78–80, 128; intelligence operations and, 56–68; internees in Spain,
71–72, 94, 114, 123, 128, 129; internment and releases in Germany, 135–43;
interrogation and investigation of
repatriates in Germany, 132–35, 136–37;
investigation, Spanish insistence on
right of, 77, 78–79; listings, 5, 49, 57–58,
59, 88–91, 115–16, 156–59; list revisions
and suspensions, 81–85; neutrality
and, 21–25, 73–75; number of Germans
in neutral countries, 25, 28; numbers,
failure in, 9, 164; "obnoxious Germans"
and, 4–5; petitions to Allied officials,
107–11; Portugal and, 28; repatriates
returning to Spain, 140–42; Spain's
noncompliance in deportation, 27–28,
49, 88–97; Spain's policy and legal responses to, 70–81; Spanish police and,
105–6; Swiss program, 25; as test of
the Spanish, 90; those still in Spain in
1946–1947, 143–47; transports, 82–83,
87–89, 91, 93–96, 155–56; UN and international debates on, 85–86, 91–93,
97; underground and escape activity,
148–54; voluntary repatriation, 110–11.
See also denazification policy; petitions
by Germans to Franco and Foreign
Ministry

Richter, Herbert, 139
Riesterer, Helmut Waldemar Karl, 83–84
Rodríguez González, Javier, 134
Rodríguez Martínez, Francisco, 66,
80–81, 149
Roosevelt, Franklin D., 26, 29–30, 55
Rothe, Hans, 124–25, 137
ROWAK, 40, 73, 107, 108
Russell, John, 161

sabotage, 45–46
Safe Haven program, 22–25, 34, 51–56,
60, 75–76
Salamanca internment camp, 146
Satorres, Roberto de, 78, 81, 85, 87,
96–97, 155
Schade, Teodore (aka Shubert), 67
Schafer y Reichert, Eduardo, 84
Schellenberg, Walter, 42, 62, 135, 152
schools in Spain, German, 146–47
Schulte-Herbruggen, Heinz Franz Josef,
104–5
Schultze, Ernst, 138
Schulz, Carl, 153–54
Schwarz von Berg, Karl, 62
Scuebel, Georg Wolfgang, 122
SD (Sicherhietsdienst), 1, 13, 42–43, 51,
69, 102, 142
Senner, Herbert, 151–52
Servicio de Bloqueo de Bienes Ex-
trangeros, 75
Silver, Arnold, 143
Simonsen, Conrad, 125, 126
Singer, Heinz, 42
SIS (Secret Intelligence Service), 44–45,
52, 54
Siscoe, Frank, 56
Skorzeny, Otto, 168
Slany, William, 22–23
Sloan, R., 86, 156
Smith, Hudson, 161, 166
smuggling. *See* economic warfare
Sobrón internment camp, 27, 105, 148

SOE (Special Operations Executive),
45–48, 51–52, 54
Sofindus, 1, 40, 73, 107–8
Soviet Union, 30, 82, 85–86, 91, 116–17,
162–63
Spain, Francoist: belligerency offer to
Germany (1940), 37; economic warfare and, 21, 25–27; establishment of
dictatorship, 3; foreign-policy debates
on, 29–33; legitimacy of, 112; Nazi
influence and underground, fear of, 7,
50–51; neutrality and nonbelligerency
status of, 3, 21–22, 24, 37; "New Spain,"
100, 112, 131, 167; renewed civil war,
fear of, 30–32; repatriates returning
to, 140–42; ties to Germany, 39–40;
wanted Germans remaining in Spain
(1946–47), 143–47. *See also* German
colony in Spain; repatriation policy
Spanish High Command (AEM), 64,
114–15
Spanish Military Intelligence (SIM), 2,
114, 169
Spitzy, Reinhard, 4
"spoilers," 7–8, 33–35, 167
Spruchkammern (denazification panels),
17, 136, 141
SS (Schutzstaffel), 5, 13, 51, 66, 108, 109,
168
State Department, U.S.: economic warfare and, 27, 74; interrogation protocol
for obnoxious Germans, 8; normalization of relations, call for, 163; policy debates, 12; repatriation and, 97, 132–33,
158, 160, 161; Safe Haven management
and, 53–54; Special War Problems Division, 20
statelessness, 109
Stauffer, Clarita, 145, 148–49, 153, 161
"stay-behind" networks. *See* "werewolf"
groups and "stay-behind" networks
Strategic Services Unit (SSU), 55
Suñer y Ferrer, Tomas, 2, 80

Supreme Headquarters, Allied Expeditionary Force (SHAEF), 13, 14, 19
Sweden, 25, 28, 77
Switzerland, 25, 28

Taylor, Telford, 18
Thie, Karl, 64
Thomas, H. Gregory, 47, 53, 54
Thomsen, Hans, 66
Titus, Earle, 56, 83–84, 96–97, 122–26, 139–54, 160, 161
Todt Organization, 83–84
Torr, William Wyndham, 6, 66, 84
Transcomar (Compañía Marítima de Transportes), 107–8
Treasury Department, U.S, 12, 53–54, 75
Tripartite Statement (March 4, 1946), 91–92, 162
Tur, Roger ("RIC"), 103–4, 122, 188n13

Única Química y Bluch SA of Barcelona, 41
Unión Nacional Española (UNE), 65
United Nations: repatriation and, 85–86, 91–93, 97
United States: anti-Franco position in, 29–30; foreign-policy debates in, 29–31; intelligence operations, 47–48; relationship with Franco Spain, complexity of, 162–63; repatriation policy and, 5. *See also specific topics, such as* Allied Control Council
university system, Spanish, 104–5

U.S. intelligence. *See* intelligence activities

Vigo, Spain, 65, 81, 82, 105, 106, 114
Vollhardt, Herbert, 68
Vyvyan, J. M. K., 82

Waldheim, Gottfried von, 120
Wallace, Henry, 27
Wallerstein, Immanuel, 79–80
war crimes trials, 12, 15, 16, 19–20
Weinzetl, Harold, 84
"welfare of the governed" theory of occupation, 14, 16
Wenckstern, German von, 138
"werewolf" groups and "stay-behind" networks: fugitives and, 151; Germany colony and, 101–4; intelligence operations and, 51, 63, 66–67, 101, 103–4; spoiler activities and, 33–34
Wiesenthal, Simon, 151
Winzer, Paul, 42
wolfram (tungsten), 25–27, 41, 43, 45–49, 60
World War II: Allied counterespionage during, 43–49; containment policy of Allies, 38; Nazi intelligence operations, 38–43; Spain's position in, 3, 21–22, 37, 43

Zaragoza, 104
Zea, Anton, 2
Ziegra, Hans-David, 61, 101–2
Zimmer, Karl, 81